Hands-On Serverless Computing with Google Cloud

Build, deploy, and containerize apps using Cloud Functions, Cloud Run, and cloud-native technologies

Richard Rose

BIRMINGHAM - MUMBAI

Hands-On Serverless Computing with Google Cloud

Commissioning Editor: Amey Varangaonkar
Acquisition Editor: Rohit Rajkumar
Content Development Editor: Carlton Borges
Senior Editor: Rahul Dsouza
Technical Editor: Prachi Sawant
Copy Editor: Safis Editing
Project Coordinator: Anish Daniel
Proofreader: Safis Editing
Indexer: Priyanka Dhadke
Production Designer: Nilesh Mohite

First published: February 2020

Production reference: 1140220

Published by Packt Publishing Ltd.
Livery Place
35 Livery Street
Birmingham
B3 2PB, UK.

ISBN 978-1-83882-799-1

www.packt.com

`Packt.com`

Subscribe to our online digital library for full access to over 7,000 books and videos, as well as industry leading tools to help you plan your personal development and advance your career. For more information, please visit our website.

Why subscribe?

- Spend less time learning and more time coding with practical eBooks and Videos from over 4,000 industry professionals

- Improve your learning with Skill Plans built especially for you

- Get a free eBook or video every month

- Fully searchable for easy access to vital information

- Copy and paste, print, and bookmark content

Did you know that Packt offers eBook versions of every book published, with PDF and ePub files available? You can upgrade to the eBook version at `www.packt.com` and as a print book customer, you are entitled to a discount on the eBook copy. Get in touch with us at `customercare@packtpub.com` for more details.

At `www.packt.com`, you can also read a collection of free technical articles, sign up for a range of free newsletters, and receive exclusive discounts and offers on Packt books and eBooks.

Contributors

About the author

Richard Rose is a lab architect at Google Cloud and has worked in the IT industry for over 20 years. During this time, he has focused on infrastructure, security, and application development for several global organizations. More recently, he has delivered the ever-popular Google Cloud Professional Cloud Security Engineer course, as well as appearing at major technology events such as Google Next. You can follow him on Twitter: `@coder_rosey`.

First and foremost, I would like to thank my lovely wife for her support and patience, especially for each of the times I've had to spend yet another weekend working on this book. Thanks to my children for keeping the noise levels down during those ever so essential chapters. Thanks to my parents, who still not quite sure what I do for a living, and thanks to my awesome sister for just being awesome.

About the reviewer

Justin Grayston originally programmed and engineered music, but, in the early 2000s, started building web applications. He joined Psycle Interactive, a digital agency in the UK and Spain, and became Technical Director. He started using Google App Engine in 2009 and headed up builds for custom YouTube experiences, including YouTube IPL Cricket, the royal wedding of William and Kate, YT Symphony, YT Spacelab, and YT IOC London Olympics, along with other sites for Google. He has an interest in both backend and frontend technologies, favoring serverless backend services with PWA clients, as well as CI/CD and developer team culture and productivity. Since 2017, Justin has worked at Google as a Google Cloud Customer Engineer working with large enterprise accounts.

I'd like to thank Rich for taking the time and effort to write this book and for the times spent chatting at Google about serverless. I'd also like to thank Google and Psycle for starting me on the serverless journey nearly a decade ago!

Packt is searching for authors like you

If you're interested in becoming an author for Packt, please visit authors.packtpub.com and apply today. We have worked with thousands of developers and tech professionals, just like you, to help them share their insight with the global tech community. You can make a general application, apply for a specific hot topic that we are recruiting an author for, or submit your own idea.

Table of Contents

Preface   1

Section 1: App Engine

Chapter 1: Introducing App Engine   9
  Introducing GAE   10
    Why go serverless with App Engine?   10
    Who is the target audience?   14
  Understanding the App Engine framework   14
    App Engine components   16
      Task queues   16
      Memcache   17
      Data storage   18
        Cloud Datastore   19
        Cloud SQL   20
    Handling auto-scaling on App Engine   20
  Defining App Engine components   21
    Runtime languages supported   22
    App Engine – Standard   22
    App Engine – Flexible   23
  Understanding App Engine features   23
    Application versioning   24
    Traffic splitting   25
    Monitoring, logging, and diagnostics   27
  Summary   28
  Questions   29
  Further reading   29

Chapter 2: Developing with App Engine   31
  Building an application on GAE   32
    Qwiklabs   32
    Getting started   32
    Selecting a region   33
    Selecting a language runtime and environment   34
    Working with the GCloud SDK   35
    Building and deploying a sample application   36
    Wrapping up   40
  Understanding deployment strategies   41
    Creating a new version   41
    Traffic splitting   43
    Migrating traffic   45

Wrapping up   46
Troubleshooting App Engine deployments   46
Building and deploying   47
Basic mode   47
Advanced filter   48
Wrapping up   49
Summary   49
Questions   50
Further reading   50

Section 2: Google Cloud Functions

Chapter 3: Introducing Lightweight Functions   53
Technical requirements   53
Operational management tools   54
Cloud Tasks   55
Cloud Scheduler   56
Introducing Cloud Functions   60
Developing a Cloud Functions-based application   61
App version 1 – introducing Cloud Functions   62
App version 2 – migrating to Cloud Shell   67
App version 3 – adding a view   68
App version 4 – decoupling HTML output   72
App version 5 – extending the RSS reader   75
Summary   76
Questions   77
Further reading   77

Chapter 4: Developing Cloud Functions   79
Technical requirements   79
Introducing Google Cloud Functions   80
Defining the use cases   81
Processing with backend services   81
Processing with real-time data   82
Developing with the Functions Framework   82
Introducing the Functions Framework   83
Deploying an application locally with the Functions Framework   84
Deploying an application to the cloud with the Functions Framework 86
Exploring the Cloud Functions workflow   88
Cloud Function properties   88
Authentication   90
Source control   91
Working with different runtime languages   91
Node.js   91
Python   92
Go   93

Testing the runtime triggering event   94
Stackdriver   95
Understanding the HTTP protocol   96
Defining GET/POST methods   96
Unmasking HTTP response codes   97
Working with Cross-Origin Resource Sharing (CORS)   98
Summary   99
Questions   99
Further reading   100

Chapter 5: Exploring Functions as a Service   101
Technical requirements   102
Developing an HTTP endpoint application   102
Triggering Cloud Pub/Sub   103
Triggering Cloud Storage   106
Exploring Cloud Functions and Google APIs   108
General architecture   108
Frontend service   110
Backend service   111
Exploring Google Cloud Storage events   115
General architecture   116
Frontend service   117
Storage service   117
Building an enhanced signed URL service   118
Frontend service   119
Backend service   120
Summary   123
Questions   124
Further reading   124

Chapter 6: Cloud Functions Labs   125
Technical requirements   125
Building a static website   126
Provisioning the environment   126
Creating a data source   128
Designing a frontend   131
Analyzing a Cloud Function   133
Service account security   136
Economic limits   137
Insecure credential storage   137
Execution flow manipulation   138
FunctionShield   141
Summary   141
Questions   142
Further reading   142

Section 3: Google Cloud Run

Chapter 7: Introducing Cloud Run   145
  Technical requirements   146
  Working with microservices   146
    Asynchronous event processing pattern   148
    Synchronous event processing pattern   149
  Working with containers   149
    Leveraging Docker   151
    Populating Container Registry   157
    Using Cloud Build   160
  Introducing Cloud Run   161
    gVisor   162
    Knative   164
  Cloud Run versus Cloud Run for Anthos   166
  Summary   168
  Questions   168
  Further reading   169

Chapter 8: Developing with Cloud Run   171
  Technical requirements   171
  Exploring the Cloud Run dashboard   172
  Developing with Cloud Run   172
  Building a Representation State Transfer (REST) API   176
    Base URL   178
      Requirements   178
      Implementing a base URL   180
    API consistency   182
      Requirements   182
      Implementing API consistency   182
    Error handling   184
      Requirements   184
      Error handling   184
    API versioning   185
      Requirements   185
      Express versioning with routing   186
  Developer productivity   187
    Cloud Source Repository   188
    Cloud Build   188
    The continuous integration example   189
  Summary   194
  Questions   194
  Further reading   195

Chapter 9: Developing with Cloud Run for Anthos   197
  Technical requirements   198

Identity and policy management   198
  IAM objects   198
  Members   199
  Roles   199
Overview of Google Kubernetes Engine   200
  Differentiating Cloud Run from Cloud Run for Anthos   201
Using Cloud Run for Anthos   201
  Provisioning GKE   202
  Custom networking on GKE   204
    Internal networking   204
    External networking   205
  Deploying Cloud Run for Anthos   205
  Continuous deployment   208
  Applying a domain   211
  Troubleshooting with Stackdriver   213
  Deleting the cluster   216
Summary   217
Questions   217
Further reading   218

Chapter 10: Cloud Run Labs   219
Technical requirements   219
Building a container   220
  Creating a service   220
  Testing the announce service   224
Deploying Cloud Run on GKE   224
  Provisioning a GKE cluster   225
  Testing the GKE service   227
  Applying a custom domain   230
Creating a simple web application   231
CI on GKE   235
Summary   238
Questions   239
Further reading   239

Section 4: Building a Serverless Workload

Chapter 11: Building a PDF Conversion Service   243
Technical requirements   244
Pet Theory case study overview   244
Designing a document service   245
  Storing document information   245
  Handling processing requests   246
  Securing service access   246
  Processing document conversations   247

Developing a document service 249
  Storing document information 249
Developing a Cloud Run service 251
  Developing the service 252
  Deploying the service 254
Securing service access 256
  Creating a service account 256
  Handling processing requests 257
Testing the document service 259
Summary 262
Questions 262
Further reading 262

Chapter 12: Consuming Third-Party Data via a REST API 263
Technical requirements 263
An overview of the Pet Theory case study 264
Designing a lab report solution 264
  Report collation 265
  Message handling 265
  Email communication 265
  SMS communication 266
Developing the lab solution 267
  Linking to Google Docs 267
  Report collation 269
Email/SMS communication 272
  Email 273
  SMS 275
The continuous integration workflow 276
  Configuring Lab Service CI 277
  Triggering Cloud Build 280
  Triggering email and SMS 283
Testing a lab service 286
  Accessing the credentials 288
  Setting up the email Cloud Pub/Sub subscription 288
  Setting up the SMS Cloud Pub/Sub subscription 289
  Testing the service 290
Summary 291
Questions 292
Further reading 292

Assessments 293

Other Books You May Enjoy 299

Index 303

Preface

There has been a significant buzz surrounding the world of serverless and the vast potential it brings to a new generation of developers. In *Hands-On Serverless Computing with Google Cloud*, we focus on the three serverless platforms offered by Google Cloud: App Engine, Cloud Functions, and Cloud Run. Each section will provide a high-level introduction to the product and outline the main attributes of each technology. At the end of the book, two case studies are presented to illustrate the power of serverless. The aim of these case studies is to demonstrate how to manage serverless workloads on Google Cloud.

Who this book is for

The audience for this book is those individuals who are working on Google Cloud and who want to understand how to integrate serverless technologies with their projects. The book content covers the primary products available on Google Cloud for serverless workloads. In addition, there are multiple examples designed to help developers build serverless applications on Google Cloud with confidence.

What this book covers

Chapter 1, *Introducing App Engine*, provides a high-level overview of App Engine, the first serverless platform released by Google back in 2008 (yes, over a decade ago). The chapter provides you with an understanding of what App Engine is, before going into the details of the supporting components.

Chapter 2, *Developing with App Engine*, gives you an overview of what is possible with App Engine. In this chapter, we illustrate the critical elements of the platform to show how easy it is to have even the most basic application effortlessly achieve scale and resilience without requiring additional maintenance.

Chapter 3, *Introducing Lightweight Functions*, discusses the value of moving to functions that have a single purpose. Reducing the size of an application footprint makes it easier to debug and run against a workload. During this chapter, we also introduce the concept of Google Cloud Functions, which take this concept to deliver serverless workloads on Google Cloud.

Chapter 4, *Developing Cloud Functions*, introduces the topic of using Cloud Functions on Google Cloud. In this chapter, we focus on the critical elements of how to build, deploy, and maintain serverless apps. To supplement this chapter, we discuss the Functions Framework, which enables local development to simulate the cloud, and cover the HTTP protocol for new web developers.

Chapter 5, *Exploring Functions as a Service*, works through a series of examples to build a service. In this chapter, we start to utilize Google APIs and various resources to integrate with our Cloud Functions. During this chapter, we see how event processing can minimize the development of code.

Chapter 6, *Cloud Functions Labs*, creates a series of examples to show real-world use cases for Cloud Functions. During this chapter, we will demonstrate how to build web components to respond to events. Also, we'll look into how to secure Cloud Functions through service accounts.

Chapter 7, *Introducing Cloud Run*, moves the discussion on to a new subject – Cloud Run. In this chapter, we cover some critical fundamentals of working with microservices and containers. In addition, we also introduce the topics of Knative, gVisor, and how they relate to Cloud Run.

Chapter 8, *Developing with Cloud Run*, discusses the Cloud Run interface on Google Cloud as well as using it to build sophisticated systems such as a REST API. We also take our first look at increasing developer productivity by automating some tasks using the Google Cloud developer toolset.

Chapter 9, *Developing with Cloud Run for Anthos*, introduces the concept of Cloud Run for Anthos, which means we reference Kubernetes for the first time. This chapter is critically important from the perspective of understanding the platforms of the future and how Cloud Run provides support for multiple environments.

Chapter 10, *Cloud Run Labs*, explains how to use Cloud Run and then how to integrate a serverless workload on Google Kubernetes Engine. Furthermore, we take a look at how to perform CI together with the Cloud Run product.

Chapter 11, *Building a PDF Conversion Service*, introduces the first of two use cases for Cloud Run on Google Cloud. In this example, we learn how to integrate an open source application and deploy it as a container. Also, we utilize event notification for Google Cloud Storage to minimize the development of additional code.

`Chapter 12`, *Consuming Third-Party Data via a REST API*, continues our exploration of Cloud Run on Google Cloud. In this second example, we learn how to build multiple services for a proof of concept application. The application demonstrates several techniques and how to integrate services such as Cloud Pub/Sub, Cloud Build, and Container Registry. By the end of the exercise, you will have experience of how to consume JSON and build a scalable solution around data management and propagation.

To get the most out of this book

It would be best if you have a basic understanding of how to navigate around Google Cloud, including how you navigate to the control panel of products provided, and also how to open Cloud Shell.

While the majority of the activities in this book require a Google Cloud project, an alternative is to use a sandbox environment such as Qwiklabs (`https://qwiklabs.com`). Using a sandbox will ensure that any changes you may make do not impact your regular Google Cloud project.

The majority of the chapters include example code that is available via the following link:

`https://github.com/PacktPublishing/Hands-on-Serverless-Computing-with-Google-Cl`
`oud-Platform`

This repository contains the baseline components required for the sections as well as a solution sub-directory.

Undertake all of the end-of-chapter quizzes, and address any wrong answers before moving on to the next chapter. You must know why something is the answer, rather than just knowing that it is the answer.

The book is split into four parts. To gain an overview of a particular product, I suggest reading the sections on *App Engine* (chapters 1-2), *Cloud Functions* (chapters 3-6), and *Cloud Run* (chapters 7-10). To see a working example of how a serverless workload is deployed on Google Cloud, please refer to the examples provided in chapters 11 and 12.

Download the example code files

You can download the example code files for this book from your account at `www.packt.com`. If you purchased this book elsewhere, you can visit `www.packtpub.com/support` and register to have the files emailed directly to you.

You can download the code files by following these steps:

1. Log in or register at www.packt.com.
2. Select the **Support** tab.
3. Click on **Code Downloads**.
4. Enter the name of the book in the **Search** box and follow the onscreen instructions.

Once the file is downloaded, please make sure that you unzip or extract the folder using the latest version of:

- WinRAR/7-Zip for Windows
- Zipeg/iZip/UnRarX for Mac
- 7-Zip/PeaZip for Linux

The code bundle for the book is also hosted on GitHub at https://github.com/PacktPublishing/Hands-on-Serverless-Computing-with-Google-Cloud. In case there's an update to the code, it will be updated on the existing GitHub repository.

We also have other code bundles from our rich catalog of books and videos available at https://github.com/PacktPublishing/. Check them out!

Download the color images

We also provide a PDF file that has color images of the screenshots/diagrams used in this book. You can download it here: https://static.packt-cdn.com/downloads/9781838827991_ColorImages.pdf.

Conventions used

There are a number of text conventions used throughout this book.

CodeInText: Indicates code words in text, database table names, folder names, filenames, file extensions, pathnames, dummy URLs, user input, and Twitter handles. Here is an example: "In Command Prompt, type hostname and press the *Enter* key."

Bold: Indicates a new term, an important word, or words that you see on screen. For example, words in menus or dialog boxes appear in the text like this. Here is an example: "Select **Properties** from the context menu."

 Warnings or important notes appear like this.

 Tips and tricks appear like this.

Get in touch

Feedback from our readers is always welcome.

General feedback: If you have questions about any aspect of this book, mention the book title in the subject of your message and email us at customercare@packtpub.com.

Errata: Although we have taken every care to ensure the accuracy of our content, mistakes do happen. If you have found a mistake in this book, we would be grateful if you would report this to us. Please visit www.packtpub.com/support/errata, selecting your book, clicking on the Errata Submission Form link, and entering the details.

Piracy: If you come across any illegal copies of our works in any form on the internet, we would be grateful if you would provide us with the location address or website name. Please contact us at copyright@packt.com with a link to the material.

If you are interested in becoming an author: If there is a topic that you have expertise in, and you are interested in either writing or contributing to a book, please visit authors.packtpub.com.

Reviews

Please leave a review. Once you have read and used this book, why not leave a review on the site that you purchased it from? Potential readers can then see and use your unbiased opinion to make purchase decisions, we at Packt can understand what you think about our products, and our authors can see your feedback on their book. Thank you!

For more information about Packt, please visit packt.com.

Section 1: App Engine

In this section, you will learn about App Engine and the features that make it such a compelling product for scalable web applications. The initial discussion will provide an introduction to the product and highlight the key features, for example, the differences between App Engine Standard and App Engine Flex, what actions task queues perform, and how App Engine seamlessly handles application versioning.

This section comprises the following chapters:

- Chapter 1, *Introducing App Engine*
- Chapter 2, *Developing with App Engine*

Introducing App Engine 1

In this first chapter, we will discuss the main properties of **Google App Engine (GAE)** and its **Platform-as-a-Service (PaaS)** approach. Available since 2008, GAE provides a serverless environment in which to deploy HTTP/web-based applications.

Throughout this chapter, we will explore GAE's framework and structure to see how highly scalable applications are made possible on this platform. As part of this, we will consider how to integrate standard web primitives such as traffic splitting and API management on GAE. By the end of this chapter, you should have a solid foundation to help you build web-based applications using GAE quickly.

In a nutshell, we will cover the following topics in this chapter:

- Introducing GAE
- Understanding the GAE framework
- Defining App Engine components
- Understanding GAE's features

Introducing GAE

When it comes to software engineering innovation, it is clear that Google has a rich history. This innovation has been evident across many successful projects, including several billion-user products brought to market, such as Google Search, Android, and YouTube. Google Cloud and its vibrant ecosystem of services provide tools built to serve these critical projects, and now you can host your application on the same platform.

GAE is designed to host web-based applications and elegantly handle request/response communications. Understanding how to achieve this on Google Cloud will be central to building consistent and efficient applications that can delight end users with their responsiveness.

Before delving into the details of GAE, let's spend some time discussing the rationale behind the application platform. For the following paragraphs, we will outline the main elements of GAE, which will provide us with sufficient knowledge to make intelligent decisions around what types of application would benefit from being run on GAE and, conversely, what applications would not.

To begin our journey, let's commence by answering the following questions to build a shared understanding of what the GAE application platform provides:

- Why go serverless with App Engine?
- What is the underlying App Engine framework?
- How does App Engine handle auto-scaling?
- Who is the target audience?

Why go serverless with App Engine?

Making a service available on the internet requires a lot of thought to minimize the potential for system compromise and associated security risks. All application traffic to App Engine is propagated via the **Google Front End** (**GFE**) service to mitigate access protocol compromise.

GFE provides a **Transport Layer Security** (**TLS**) termination for all GAE-registered routed web traffic. Acting as a protection layer, GFE is capable of performing several essential security services for a Google Cloud project. From a security perspective, it provides the public IP hosting of a public DNS name and **Denial of Service** (**DoS**) protection. Besides, GFE can also be used by internal services as a scalable reverse proxy.

When working on Google Cloud, a term commonly mentioned is **security in depth**. An approach such as this provides multiple concurrent safeguards for your environment that work against bad actors wishing to misuse your service. Many of these security safeguards are built into the platform, so no additional effort is required on the part of the developer.

GAE provides a fully managed application platform that enables developers to only concern themselves with building their application. Concerns regarding the management of lower-level infrastructures, such as compute and storage, are automatically managed by the service. In this respect, serverless solutions such as GAE offer the ability to devote focus to the development process and leave operational matters to the provider of the service.

GAE enables developers to take advantage of a simplified serverless environment that addresses hosting the web application and API services on Google Cloud. By providing a significantly simplified environment, the intent is to increase the adoption of the cloud platform by bringing more developers to the cloud. In most instances, when a developer uses such a system, they can immediately see the vast potential for efficiency to be gained by working within an environment such as this.

In the following diagram, we outline a logical view of the typical workflow of an environment based on GAE. From the illustration, we can see that all external communication is performed using the HTTP(S) protocol and is routed via **Cloud Load Balancer** (provided by GFE). In this scenario, the frontend device exposes a single service name that encapsulates the application resource deployed. The service enables GAE to direct traffic received to multiple backend resource components dynamically. GAE maintains responsibility for establishing which role these components performed and ensures that each of them remains distinct for the purposes of identification:

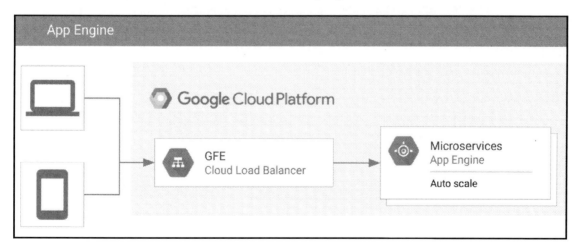

Backend service communication use the HTTP/HTTPS protocol, which means that GAE assumes an internet-based environment (that is, it assumes that you have access to a public-facing internet connection). Application request processing is performed by the default instance that's deployed, and this instance is subject to autoscaling based on system workload thresholds.

Taking the described approach enables workloads to be seamlessly load balanced across application instances, again without any additional configuration needed from the developer. Standard workload operational activities such as TLS termination and DNS resolution require no further user configuration. The addition of these activities provides a significant benefit to the developer. Application workloads being subject to isolated instances means the application is also capable of massive scale without any substantive work.

In addition to standard protection, the addition of GFE also provides seamless compatibility with secure delivery protocols such as gRPC (`https://grpc.io/blog/principles/`). The gRPC protocol uses the RPC framework to provide layer isolation when forwarding requests for the service. Also, communication remains encrypted by default to avoid the nuisance of communication eavesdropping or device compromise when performing inter-service communication.

The more recent adoption by the industry has seen broader adoption of gRPC developing more extensive compatibility across a range of services. The RPC security protocol is used extensively at Google, for example, to secure API access. When working with communication protocols across the internet, many standards exist. Having all service-related traffic routed through GFE means an incredibly flexible and scalable frontend is available without any additional work.

There are two versions of the App Engine available:

- App Engine Standard
- App Engine Flex

Both versions share many commonalities, and the majority of what's outlined in this chapter will apply to both equally. However, there are some key attributes to call out when thinking about the two environments, highlighted in the following diagram:

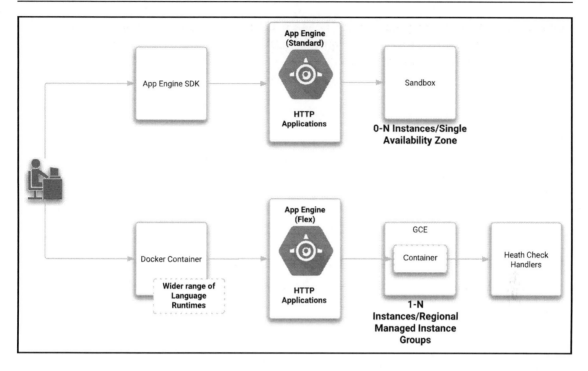

One of the main things to call out in the preceding diagram is that App Engine Standard scales down to zero. However, an App Engine Flex environment scales down to a minimum of one instance. Therefore, if your primary consideration is cost, use App Engine Standard. Being able to scale down to zero provides a real advantage over the App Engine Flex environment, which will always have a cost associated with it.

The ability of GAE Standard to scale to zero is due to the use of a sandbox environment. Using a dedicated sandbox provides quicker responses, that is, quicker start-up times and auto-scaling responses. Having deployment time measured in seconds may also be an advantage that appeals when considering the level of flexibility that may be required by different application growth patterns.

Unlike the standard environment, GAE Flex uses **Google Compute Engine (GCE)**, more specifically **Managed Instance Groups (MIGs)**, to enable auto-scaling. An overhead of one compute instance is always present for GAE Flex when working within this environment. Resultant costs also need to factor in how many compute resources GAE Flex requires. Maintaining an application in this environment will also mean a slower initialization time (that is, cold boot) due to the requirement to spin up a GCE instance plus a container environment for any flexible-based deployed application.

There are further differences evident in the application environments. However, the preceding characteristics are the ones that commonly impact decision making when starting to build an application on GAE.

Who is the target audience?

Working on the GAE fully managed serverless application platform removes many of the historical constraints associated with building internet-scale applications. Using this new paradigm, developers can focus on building sophisticated web applications and APIs without needing to learn about backend services and low-level networking or infrastructure.

Building serverless applications means that agile code is quickly deployed to the cloud. Web apps (for examples, see the following list) are most definitely the sweet spot for this type of solution:

- Web applications
- Mobile backends
- HTTP APIs
- **Line of Business Applications (LOB)** applications

If that sounds like an area that your workload would benefit from, then you are the target audience. Working in an environment where it is not necessary to concern yourself with creating or maintaining infrastructure is highly desirable to most developers. GAE is built on this premise and provides an excellent experience for developers to develop and deploy without reference to underlying technologies.

Having outlined the differences in the environments provided for App Engine, we can start to explore what makes this such a fascinating product.

Understanding the App Engine framework

Exploring the general architecture of App Engine brings to light how much of the underlying framework has been put in place to deliver integrated workflows for web application development.

Google has bundled many internal services to minimize the effort needed by developers to make their applications cloud-native. Added to that is the innate ability of the GAE service to automatically scale without any additional actions required on the part of the service creator.

Creating a web application on this platform can be as simple as deploying your code to the App Engine environment. However, behind the scenes, there are several activities taking place to ensure that the application is deployed successfully, the infrastructure is provisioned, and the whole thing is ultimately able to scale intelligently. So, what is happening in the underlying App Engine framework is illustrated in the following diagram, in which we introduce the optional components supporting App Engine:

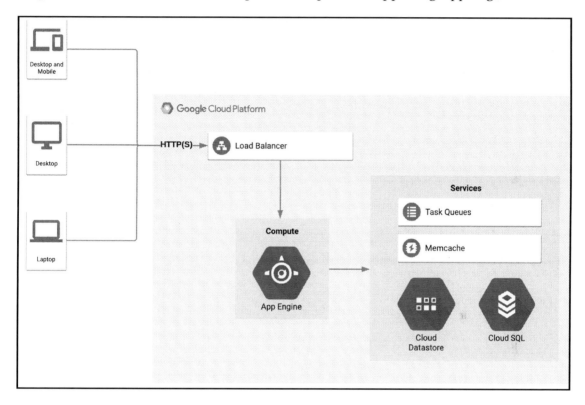

Examining GAE from a broader perspective shows that there are many high-level components used to establish the fully managed application platform. Of course, being a serverless environment, there is no real need for you to understand what is happening behind the scenes.

Having a conceptual understanding of what is occurring on any platform is useful during the development process. No matter how much a service tries to abstract information from you, it is immeasurably easier to resolve technical issues when you have some understanding of how the various components integrate.

In addition to the standard environment, GAE Flex supports custom container runtime environments. Custom containers are deployed on GCE and enable the developer to build their environments. In doing this, a higher level of customization was suddenly available and significantly broadened the appeal of GAE to a broader audience. The ubiquity of containers has made the introduction of the GAE Flex environment a compelling option where greater control is required.

There are, however, some performance and cost implications to using GAE Flex over the standard environment. Understanding these constraints is crucial for the application developer and they are clearly outlined in the specification for GAE. Having clarity regarding the various advantages and disadvantages of design considerations will help address any concerns and make the selection of the most appropriate environment easier. For more details on the differences, refer to the *Runtime languages supported* section of this chapter.

In addition to the GAE environment outlined previously, some other essential constituent components are working in the background. A service layer adds to the compute function of GAE and provides the ability to store, queue, cache, and perform authenticated communication with the Google Cloud API.

App Engine components

Over the next couple of sub-sections, we will explore the main points related to these service layer components.

Task queues

Systems remain responsive through the use of additional decoupling algorithms that manage the flow of information. GAE uses message queues to maintain a sub-second response rate for web traffic. Long-lived processing is handed off to the task queue system to free up the request/response cycle.

At a more granular level, task queues use two approaches to manage the asynchronous processing of information associated with a web request/response cycle:

Service dispatch	Description
Push Queue (HTTP request)	Dispatch requests. Guaranteed task execution. Use case: En-queue a short-lived task that can be fulfilled over time or in a situation that involves a time-specific action, similar to a diarized event task execution.
Pull Queue (Request handler)	Lease mechanism. Provides additional flexibility beyond dispatch requests. Provides a lifecycle for tasks. Use case: Batch processing that can be used to achieve an outcome at once, without needing to process information one item at a time.

Task queues provide a dispatch mechanism that is isolated from the web traffic transaction. In this service, we segregate the processing element of information related to the web request to minimize the time to complete between request and response. Adding a task queue provides the HTTP request/response cycle with the ability to maintain a high level of efficiency.

Memcache

A vital feature of the GAE environment is the inclusion of memcache. Memcache is abstracted from persistent storage to provide a buffer for fast data access. Adding a low-latency data tier for applications establishes a consistent mechanism for repeatable access requests. Memcache provides a convenient data access tier based on the memory-resident (in-memory) temporary storage of transient data.

There are two levels of the memcache service defined for the service layer:

- **A shared memcache**: This is the default setting for GAE. Shared memcache provides a default access mode. In most situations, there is no requirement to change the cache level applied to your application as the default will suffice for the majority of work to be performed.

- **A dedicated memcache**: This is an advanced setting used to reserve a dedicated application memory pool.

A dedicated memcache service provides additional scope for getting greater efficiency in an application. As a cache represents a quick data retrieval mechanism to access temporary data, if data access is central to an application, it may well be useful to investigate this option.

 Be aware that this latter option is a paid offering, unlike the default cache setting. However, this option guarantees the reservation of a larger memory footprint for applications that might require high-frequency data access.

When working with an application primarily used in read mode, on the data to be consumed, it is beneficial to keep both memcache and the data storage in sync. Read mode is perhaps the most common use case that most GAE developers will encounter and, for this type of scenario, GAE is more than capable of meeting most of the application demands faced.

More sophisticated use cases exist, such as database modes requiring both read and write synchronization. Between the cache layer and backend database, there needs to be consideration of how to manage the cache layer and Datastore integration. For situations where interaction with the Datastore is a priority, Cloud NDB caching provides a configuration for more advanced requirements. An element of the investigation will be beneficial in this use case to optimize the data management and refreshing of data. In this situation, the underlying system will only be able to provide limited optimizations, and further efficiencies will need additional design as part of the iterative application development life cycle.

Data storage

GAE has multiple options for data storage, including schemaless and relational database storage. Backend data storage, such as Datastore/Firestore or Cloud SQL, enables developers to deliver consistent access across a wide range of use cases that integrate seamlessly with GAE.

The following table provides a high-level overview of the mapping between schemaless and relational databases:

Cloud SQL (relational)	Cloud Datastore (schemaless)
Table	Kind
Row	Entity
Column	Property
Primary key	Key

App Engine provides multiple options to give developers the ability to work with backend storage that suits the purpose of the application. In most instances, it is also essential to consider how to store information within the Datastore selected. As with any development, it is also crucial to understand the underlying data and how it will be accessed.

Cloud Datastore

Cloud Datastore will be a standard component for any GAE development performed. As per the rest of the application platform, very little understanding of database management is required upfront. Datastore, as a managed schemaless (NoSQL) document database, will be sufficient in most instances.

The following high-level points are most pertinent to using Datastore with GAE:

- Datastore is a NoSQL schemaless database.
- App Engine API access.
- Designed to auto-scale to massive datasets (that is, low-latency reads/writes).
- Stores information concerning the handling of requests.
- All queries are served by previous build indexes.

As a core component of App Engine, Cloud Datastore caters to high performance, application development, and automatic scaling. Once the Datastore has initialized, it is ready for data. Working with data persisted in Cloud Datastore is very easy as no upfront work is required to attach the data to the backend. However, this may be potentially off-putting if you are from a relational database background.

When creating a database, it is worth considering how to index information to ensure that access remains performant regardless of the use. There are many good references on building suitable mechanisms for accessing data, for example, how to create fundamental indexes and composite indexes. Becoming familiar with this will provide ongoing benefits should issues arise, for example, performance latency with an application hosted on GAE.

 It is essential to consider how the information within Datastore will be stored. In the instance where your Datastore is not central to your application, the data management question will not be relevant when creating a data-centric application. Datastore performance degradation resulting from an inefficient data layout requires consideration of how the data representation may save the significant effort of refactoring at a later stage.

At this point, knowing that schemaless databases are a good match for most App Engine requirements and that Cloud Datastore is a document database, provide a massive clue to their use cases. Going beyond the initial conditions of storing document data (for example, entities and kinds) is where putting some thought into the proper access methods will yield benefits as the application increases in complexity.

Cloud SQL

When working with Cloud SQL, there are two products currently available on Google Cloud, that is, MySQL and Postgres. Both options provide managed relational databases used in conjunction with GAE. To clarify, *managed* in this context means the service provider is responsible for the maintenance of backups and updates without requiring user interaction.

Cloud SQL provides a relational model that supports transactions. If you have a relational requirement for your application deployed to App Engine, then consider using Cloud SQL. Working with multiple database types can be confusing, so, before development activities begin, aim to be clear as to how the Datastore selected is to be used. A key priority is to ensure that the design is representative of how the application uses information.

Attempting to make Datastore into an **Online Transactional Processing (OLTP)** backend is an unnecessary task. Similarly, trying to utilize schemaless data in a Cloud SQL database without a relevant schema or normalization will not result in optimal performance.

While it is vital to invest time to define the correct normalization for the schema to be applied, this requirement may change over time. Working with data is never as simple as uploading content and then forgetting about it, so pay particular attention to this part of your application development life cycle to generate the most benefit.

Handling auto-scaling on App Engine

In this section, we look at how App Engine handles autoscaling. In most instances, GAE will handle any workload using its distributed architecture. Of course, if you have more advanced requirements, then it is worth the effort to understand how GAE performs instance auto-scaling.

Within GAE, instance scaling definitions are within the configuration files. Two configuration items are specifically relevant and outlined here (that is, scaling type and instance class):

Scaling type	Instance class	Description
Manual	Resident	Several upfront instances are available. Amending the number of instances would require manual intervention by the system administrator.
Auto-scaling	Dynamic	In response to telemetry data (for example, response latency, and request rate) gathered from the system, autoscaling decides whether it should increase/decrease the number of instances.

When thinking about auto-scaling a service, it is imperative to consider how to design your application to take advantage of the constituent components. Here are some considerations concerning building a scalable solution:

- Load testing is essential to establish the best performance design for your application. In most instances, working with real-world traffic provides the best scenario for testing system bottlenecks.
- Google Cloud imposes quota limits on all projects, so be mindful of this when creating an application. Quota limits apply to API calls as well as compute-based resources.
- In most instances, a single task queue will be sufficient. However, GAE does provide the ability to shard task queues when long-lived tasks require higher processing throughput.

In the next section, we move away from the general architecture of App Engine to discuss the specifics of implementation. As part of this discussion, there will be an overview of the languages supported.

Defining App Engine components

The objective of this section is to describe the details of GAE. The nature of the GAE application platform is to provide a serverless application environment that is capable of supporting multiple language runtimes. Runtime support requires that there are two versions of App Engine in existence. A critical difference between these environments relates to the language runtimes supported.

Runtime languages supported

Historically, the GAE runtime only supported a limited number of languages, but this has expanded over time to provide a broader range. A limitation on runtime languages was one of the most common criticisms of the original version of GAE when it was released over a decade ago. This situation has improved significantly in the intervening years, and today an expanded range of runtimes are now supported, including the following:

- Python 2.7/3.7
- Java, Node.js 8/10
- PHP 5.5/7.2
- Go 1.9/1.11/1.12

App Engine – Standard

In this environment, a sandbox wrapper provides application isolation and constrains access to specific external resources. Depending on the runtime selected, security measures enforce the sandbox environment, for example, the application of access control lists, and the replacement of language libraries.

In the following diagram, GAE Standard uses a sandbox environment, supporting 0-N instances within a single availability zone:

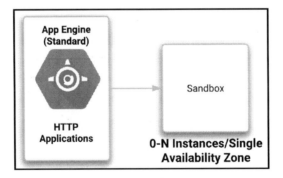

When working with applications that require a runtime language such as Python, Java, Node.js, or Go, GAE Standard is the optimal choice. GAE Standard works within a sandbox environment and ensures instances can scale down to zero. Scaling to zero means a meager cost is incurred with this type of situation.

App Engine – Flexible

In the GAE Flex environment, a container resides on a GCE instance. While in certain respects, this provides the same service access as GAE Standard, there are some disadvantages associated with moving from the sandbox to GCE, specifically instance warm-up speed and cost.

In the following diagram, GAE Flex uses a container environment for the creation of resources to support 1-N instances within a regional MIG:

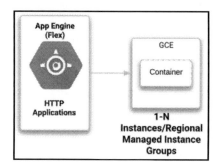

The container residing on GCE is based on a Docker image and provides an alternative to the sandbox environment mentioned earlier. Using GAE Flex requires some compromise on both speed and cost. The speed sacrifice is attributed to initiating the container through the Cloud Build process necessary to deploy the code into the GAE environment. As at least one instance needs to be active at any point in time, this means this type of situation will always incur some degree of cost.

Although GAE hides the build process from you, the associated lead time for building a custom runtime versus the sandbox approach is not insignificant. On completion of the build process, the image is posted to Google Cloud Build and is ready for deployment within the application. So, what are the main characteristics of GAE? The following sections will cover the main attributes of GAE.

Understanding App Engine features

Throughout the next few sub-sections, we will describe some of the critical facets of GAE, starting with application versioning.

Application versioning

GAE uses a configuration file to manage application versions to deploy. The configuration file for the runtime selected, for example, `app.yaml` for Python deployments, contains the version ID associated with your application. In addition to the version, an application default denotes the primary instance to the system.

Each application version deployed will maintain its distinct URL so that the developer can view multiple versions at the same time. Similarly, releases can be upgraded or rolled back depending on the deployment scheme selected. As new code deploys, a unique index is applied to the configuration code to ensure that each application revision can successfully distinguish between the old and new version deployed.

In the following diagram, three versions of the application have deployed on GAE. However, traffic will only be routed to the default version, unless otherwise stated by the application administrator:

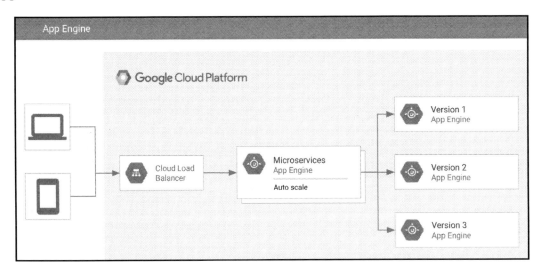

The approach taken by GAE means that deployments are straightforward to manage as the administrator of the system can make updates at the touch of a button. Similarly, they can also perform more complex deployments via the console without losing access to previous revisions of the application.

In addition to the built-in tools, App Engine supports source version control. Working with code stored in version control happens in much the same way as using local files. Deciding where system code access resolves is up to the developer; for example, they may choose to have code deployed using Cloud Source Repositories.

If you are unfamiliar with Google Cloud Source Repositories, it is essentially a Git repository directly associated with the project environment. If you are familiar with Git, then you will be able to get up and running using Google Source Repositories quickly. From here, it is entirely possible to mirror code from external sources such as Bitbucket, GitLab, or GitHub.

For more uncomplicated use cases, deploying from a local file may be satisfactory for most instances. However, moving to a more consistent approach can help with the management of code across a project. Once the application successfully deploys, a decision on how to manage the traffic flow to this new deployment is the next step in the process.

Traffic splitting

Traffic splitting provides a useful way to move between versions. GAE offers several options to make this process easier. Also, you don't need to keep track of the application version that is currently deployed.

The options available for GAE traffic splitting are these:

- **IP traffic**: Using the source IP to determine which instance to serve responses from
- **Cookie splitting**: Applying session affinity to the web transaction based on a cookie named GOOGAPPUID with a value between 0-999
- **Random**: Using a randomization algorithm to serve content found with the preceding options

In the following diagram, traffic routed to GAE is split between two instances. In this case, a 50% split is evident based on IP addresses:

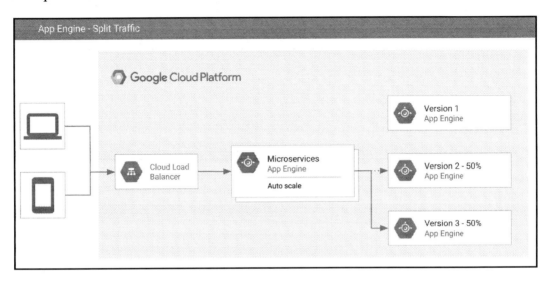

The command to deploy ensures that a simple process is available that enables moving from one version to another. As a fully managed application platform, the onus is on App Engine to simplify how the application will be deployed based on defined traffic splitting preferences observed.

In an instance where a new deployment takes place, it is possible to tell App Engine how much of the traffic should be sent to the updated application deployment. A technique such as this is useful, for example, to perform A/B testing against two different deployed versions. Using this capability enables many different deployment and testing approaches to become available when looking to deploy a new release. Should there be an issue with the code that is implemented, there are numerous tools available to assist with this investigation. One such tool is Stackdriver, and we will be looking at the product more closely in the next section.

Monitoring, logging, and diagnostics

Stackdriver is the default monitoring solution for Google Cloud. When observing information relating to GAE, in Stackdriver, the resource type gae_app can be used to filter information specifically associated with the environment data. In the following diagram, we see traffic to the project is managed by GCE, and it is this that is responsible for connectivity to other services such as **Task Queues**, **Memcache**, and **Stackdriver**:

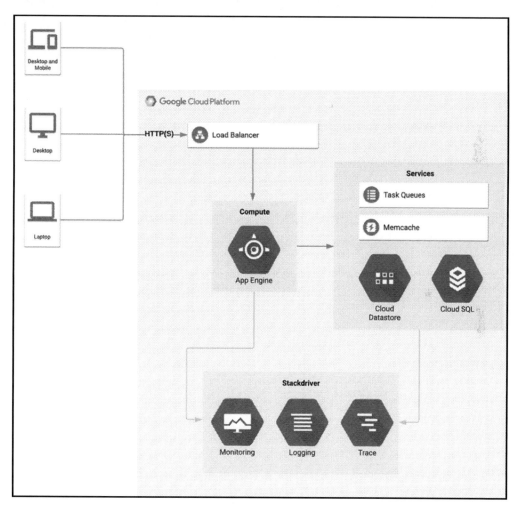

Stackdriver logging is available as standard for any GAE environment, providing the ability to see what operations are being performed in your application in real time. Logs generated via the application are available to interrogate as required. This logging process does not require any additional configuration and is available for all the application-related logs that are made available. For reference, when using records with GAE, it is essential to note the following data sources available in Stackdriver:

- **Request logs**: These provide the default information associated with requests made to the application. The resource for this log is named `request_log`. You can observe this in the **Stackdriver Logs Viewer** under the `appengine.googleapis.com/request_log` filter.
- **App logs**: These provide additional application information supplemental to the request log.
- **Third-party logs**: These are application-specific and in addition to the preceding logs. There may be package-specific information sent to the system logs. Where present, there will be an entry available via the API accessible via the **Logs Viewer**.

Stackdriver Trace also doesn't require any additional instrumentation to work with App Engine. Working with this solution is automatically enabled to allow the monitoring of application trace data. The data is incorporated into the default GAE settings and will be accessible within the Stackdriver environment.

When working with App Engine Flex environments, logs use either Google Cloud Client Libraries or `stdout/stderr` to capture application-related information and push it to the centralized Stackdriver logging system.

Summary

In this chapter, we covered a high-level introduction into the fully managed application platform App Engine. Working in this environment illustrates many of the usual infrastructure tasks related to development are performed automatically without recourse to the developer.

In general, GAE deployment is a fully managed activity that requires very little interaction to build, host, or execute code. The environment typically consists of a load balancer, a compute tier, and a services layer, all working in tandem to provide an integrated application platform. GAE provides a low-effort development environment built to do much of the heavy lifting for developers.

Now we have a general understanding of the App Engine environment. The next chapter will focus on introducing code samples to flesh out our experience and skill level.

Questions

1. What type of service dispatch is supported by task queues?
2. What are the two levels of service supported by memcache?
3. What type of database is Cloud Datastore?
4. Name a runtime language supported by GAE.
5. What forms of traffic-splitting algorithms are supported on GAE?
6. What is the purpose of GFE in relation to GAE?
7. Name the three types of scaling supported by GAE.
8. What mechanism is used to isolate long-lived workloads for efficiency purposes from the HTTP request/response life cycle?

Further reading

- **Choosing an App Engine environment**: https://cloud.google.com/appengine/docs/the-appengine-environments
- **gRPC**: https://grpc.io/blog/principles/
- **NDB Caching**: https://cloud.google.com/appengine/docs/standard/python/ndb/cache
- **Datastore and Firestore modes**: https://cloud.google.com/datastore/docs/firestore-or-datastore
- **Cloud Source Repositories and App Engine**: https://cloud.google.com/source-repositories/docs/quickstart-deploying-from-source-repositories-to-app-engine

Developing with App Engine 2

When working on Google Cloud, you will naturally require access to a cloud environment. In the upcoming chapters, we will learn how to build App Engine applications that reside in Google Cloud.

As we now have a good understanding of the various components that make up a **Google App Engine (GAE)** environment, in this chapter we will look at how to use GAE to engineer applications that meet defined requirements. We will begin by building a simple app to demonstrate the process of deploying code on App Engine. We will then learn how to perform application updates. Finally, we will explore how to use the features of Stackdriver Logging to assist with the analysis of defects. All of these lessons will be accompanied by examples and activities so that you can apply these GAE concepts and principles on your own.

GAE supports a number of language runtimes; in this chapter, we will utilize Python to demonstrate Google Cloud's capabilities. Working with different languages can be intimidating; however, the purpose of this chapter is not to teach you Python, but rather to explore using GAE in different scenarios.

In this chapter, we will cover the following:

- Building an application on GAE
- Understanding deployment strategies
- Troubleshooting App Engine deployments

Building an application on GAE

To get started, we will consider what tools and assets we need to commence building our first GAE example application.

For this section, we will be taking our source code and deploying it on GAE. As part of this process, we will explore the application structure and how this relates to the deployed system. While using the code, we will observe what information is available and displayed within Google's Cloud Console.

In addition to this, we will look at deploying the application (to discuss what is meant by the default version), how this relates to code, and deploying multiple versions. Finally, we will perform a rollback on the system code deployed to illustrate accomplishing this task and what it means in terms of available versions. But first, let's learn about the Qwiklabs environment that we will be using in this chapter.

Qwiklabs

Qwiklabs (`https://qwiklabs.com`) provides a Cloud sandbox in which Google Cloud projects can run. The aim of using an environment such as Qwiklabs is to give you a close representation of real-world tools and services. A transient Google Cloud account, to facilitate this process, assigns a time-restricted sandbox environment. Once created, the Google Cloud project will provide you with access to all of the relevant access permissions and services that you can expect in a project that has been provisioned in a typical manner.

Getting started

We will assume you have either registered on Google Cloud or have a valid Qwiklabs account that enables you to access a Google Cloud sandbox environment. Feel free to follow along without an account, but it will be more interesting if you can join in the exercises as we discuss them.

Our first look at Google's Cloud Console might seem intimidating; however, the interface provides an excellent way to navigate the numerous services on offer. Launch App Engine from the left-hand navigation menu, and we will take a tour of it.

To commence development, let's use the existing App Engine code provided by Google to understand how a basic application should appear. To do this, follow these steps:

1. From your Google Cloud account, select the **App Engine** menu item to begin creating an application.
2. The initial screen will be displayed, called the **Dashboard**, and from here you can see an aggregation of all things associated with App Engine; for example, services, task queues, and firewall rules.
3. Now select the **Create Application** button:

The next thing we need to decide is which region our application will reside in. Let's take a look at how to do this next.

Selecting a region

Looking at the following onscreen list, it is clear that there are many options available. Typically considered the standard practice is to select a region as close as possible to where the data is to be accessed. In this example, that criterion won't apply for our demonstration, so perform the following steps:

1. Choose **us-east1** as the region.

2. Select the **Create app** button:

Now we need to decide which language runtime we are going to use.

Selecting a language runtime and environment

For our first simple example, we will use the Python runtime. To do this, perform the following steps:

1. Select the **Language** drop-down list.
2. From the various languages that appear, click on **Python**.
3. From the **Environment** drop-down list, select **Standard** (this is the default option, but it can also be changed later in the development cycle):

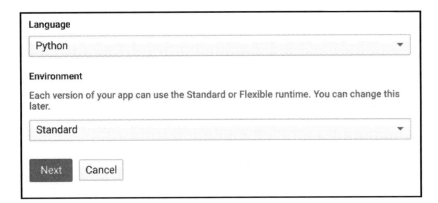

Be aware that there are multiple language runtimes available. If you are unfamiliar with Python, don't worry: its layout and features are very accessible. In most instances, using an alternative language will follow the same process we've outlined; however, the language specification will be different from that described for the Python example.

Once completed, we can explore using the **Google Cloud SDK (GCloud SDK)**.

Working with the GCloud SDK

The GCloud SDK provides a simple way to authenticate against Google Cloud. Having the SDK available locally (that is, local to your environment) provides significant benefits, so it is an excellent option to include if you wish to integrate with other Google Cloud services:

1. Select the **App Engine** menu option from the left-hand side of Google's Cloud Console.

2. In the following screen, we will need to choose the required resources for our project:

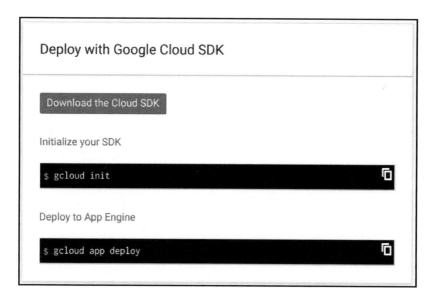

3. We will not be needing the Cloud SDK, as we will be using Cloud Shell, which includes a preloaded cloud SDK. So skip this screen by selecting the **I'LL DO THIS LATER** option.

From the preceding deployment screen, you will also be given a command-line prompt to deploy code using `gcloud` commands. Learning how to use the `gcloud sdk` command to perform different tasks is highly recommended.

Congratulations! At this point, you have successfully created your first GAE application on Google Cloud. As you can see, this process is pretty simple and is aimed at ensuring developers minimize the time necessary for infrastructure management:

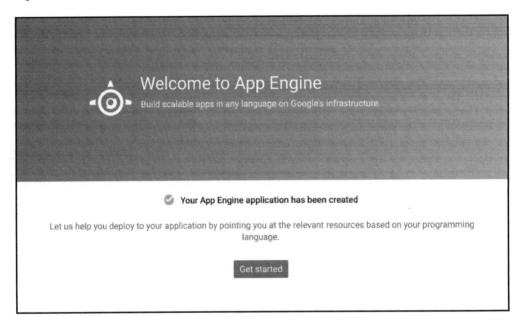

Take a moment to remember that, for each application created, a similar process to create your infrastructure will be required. As you can see, there is nothing complicated about this process; on successful completion, it produces an important message that indicates the overall status.

Building and deploying a sample application

In this section, we will deploy a standard `Hello World` application to GAE. Luckily, the engineers at Google have our back, and we can use some sample code. For the next build and deploy stage in this process, we will examine this sample code.

To commence the process, follow these steps:

1. Open a Cloud Shell window in your project and clone the sample code for App Engine from the Google Cloud repository.

> If you ever need to code an application on Google Cloud, it is more efficient to check the Google sample repository first to see whether the sample code exists as a template.

2. From the open Cloud Shell window, enter the following on the command line:

```
git clone
https://github.com/GoogleCloudPlatform/python-docs-samples
```

3. The code location is in a directory named `hello_world`. So, enter the following to move to the correct source directory:

```
cd python-docs-samples/appengine/standard/hello_world
```

4. Now that we have some source code available, let's investigate what is in this directory by performing a directory listing from the Cloud Shell prompt:

```
ls -la
```

Notably, there are two Python files and the `app.yaml` file. A structure such as this is common, so it's worth outlining what these files do:

Filename	Purpose	Description
`main.py`	Application	This file, written in Python, represents the source code to be run, and outputs a `Hello, World!` message to the user.
`main_test.py`	Unit testing	This file is a test case for the main source file to ensure a managed response is returned as expected.
`app.yaml`	Configuration	This file is the configuration file for the application. The contents of the data include a reference to the language runtime, API version, and URL to be accessed.

5. To deploy the source code to GAE, enter the following on the Cloud Shell command line to use your code:

```
gcloud app deploy ./app.yaml
```

6. As the deployment command processes configuration information, on completion it will provide a URL from which you can access the running application:

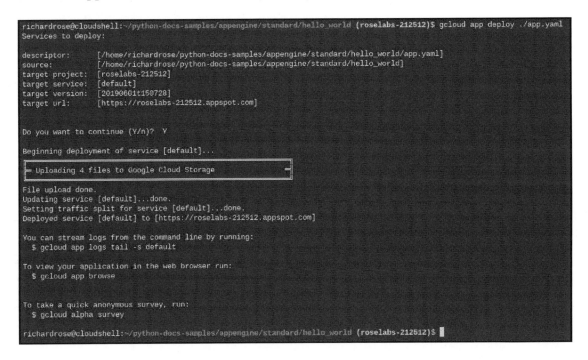

To view the application deployed use `gcloud app browse` from Cloud Shell or use the App Engine Dashboard to see the assigned URL.

Once App Engine has completed its deployment, the application is accessible from the browser. Typically the URL to access your deployed application will be in the form `[PROJECT_ID].appspot.com`. If you have used a custom domain, the `PROJECT ID` section will be replaced with the custom domain.

7. Access this URL via the browser; this should display the `Hello, World!` message from our application, as shown in the following screenshot:

8. Now take a look at the updated GAE dashboard to observe what changes are apparent once the application is deployed:

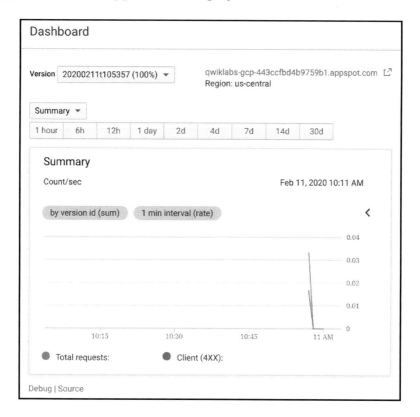

9. From the dashboard, we can see all the relevant telemetry for our application. We now have an excellent working knowledge of GAE and how to deploy a simple application on Google Cloud.

Great job! We have gone through a lot of information quickly, so let's slow down a little and recap what we have learned so far in this chapter.

Wrapping up

In the `Hello World!` example, we learned about the following aspects of deploying code on GAE:

- We looked at how to create a simple GAE application; we did this using the Google Cloud console to initiate the build and deploy process.
- We saw there were multiple regions available and where this information can be accessed.
- We selected a GAE Standard environment and the Python language runtime for our application, noting that we can also use alternatives if desired.
- We cloned the Google Cloud repository to gain access to some Python-based example code.
- We explored the system within the catalog and saw that we have three files available, taking the time to outline the purpose of each of the source files used.
- Finally, we deployed our code via Cloud Shell and accessed the running application via a browser interface from the URL presented on completion of the deployment process.

As you have seen in this first section on App Engine, it is a very straightforward process to deploy code. Within this environment, working with GAE provides a level of simplicity that developers crave.

The ability to avoid infrastructure management overhead can significantly improve efficiency and lends itself to a greater emphasis on specific development activities. Throughout the next section, we will explore how GAE handles various deployment strategies.

Understanding deployment strategies

GAE allows new versions to deploy and more besides, performing more complex operations such as traffic splitting. As we have already deployed a simple application from the command line, let's continue with this code base and look at how to implement a new version using the GAE management console.

Understanding the mechanism behind the GAE console used to control the flow of code is invaluable. Being able to deploy a new system via a rollout provides a good layer of control over the application environment. Taking this to the next level, we can also split traffic between versions to perform sophisticated A/B testing.

Creating a new version

Back in the Cloud Shell, still working with our source code, we will edit the main.py file and change the message to read as follows: Hello, Serverless World!. These simple changes will represent our new version of the application.

Google Cloud Shell also includes a code editor based on Eclipse Orion to perform straightforward file edits. The inclusion of this editor can be tremendously helpful for situations where you need to view files within a project. Alternatively, Cloud Shell also includes other editors (for example, Vim and Nano), so feel free to use something that reflects your personal preference.

In the previous section, you will have noticed that, after editing our source file, we then used the GCloud SDK to deploy the code. Now that we have amended the source code, follow the same process again:

1. From the Cloud Shell, run the following command:

    ```
    gcloud app deploy ./app.yaml
    ```

2. A new application version has been deployed without needing any additional work.
3. Look back at the Google Cloud Console and the **Versions** menu.

We can see that a new version of the application has been deployed and is available from the list:

Versions		C REFRESH	🗑 DELETE	◼ STOP	▶ START	↗ MIGRATE TRAFFIC

	Version	Status	Traffic Allocation		Instances ❓	Runtime	Environment
☐	20200211t110726 ↗	Serving	▬▬▬▬▬▬▬▬	100%	0	python27	Standard
☐	20200211t105357 ↗	Serving	▬▬▬▬▬▬▬▬	0%	1	python27	Standard

Note that, in the preceding output, the traffic allocation has automatically switched to the new version. This behavior is acceptable in most situations; however, if you don't want the traffic to be automatically promoted to the latest version for the deployment of new code, use the `--no-promote` flag option.

Observe that the version string used represents a timestamp for the application. Additionally, both versions of the application remain easily accessible from the console—the default version tracks which revision traffic used. If you wish to switch to a specific version string, you can specify this as part of the deploy process using the `--version` flag option.

At this point, you might want to contrast this simple deployment process with a typical infrastructure project where this ease of use is not as apparent. The ease with which GAE is deployed is stunningly effortless and exquisitely modeled so it only exposes an element of the development that is required.

Now that we have a deployment, we can look at some of the excellent features App Engine provides as standard, starting with traffic management.

Traffic splitting

Now that we have two versions running, wouldn't it be great if we could divide the traffic between them? Consider how useful this option is when working with an environment such as testing (for example, A/B) or production (for example, phased rollout). Again this level of simplicity should not be misunderstood; this is an incredibly powerful option and will undoubtedly be one that is used time and time again.

To split traffic, follow these steps:

1. Go into the GAE Cloud Console and, under the **Versions** menu, look for the **Split traffic** option for the specific version and select it.
2. Now a list of options will be available to split our traffic, as outlined in the previous chapter (that is, **IP address**, **Cookie**, or **Random**):

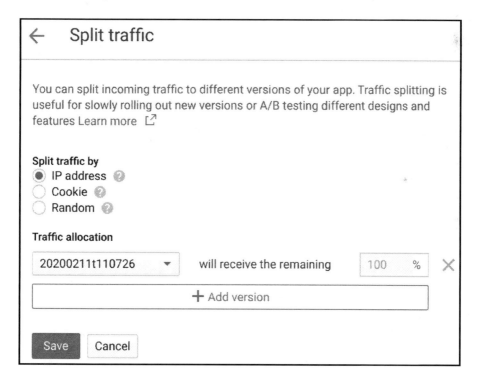

We can see that our new application version has defaulted to accept 100% of the traffic allocation. For demonstration purposes, we would like it to only receive 25%. To do this, perform the following steps:

1. Select an alternate application version that will consume 75% of traffic by clicking on the **Add version** button. You will see that we still have the original version of the deployed application available, so let's divert the traffic to that.

2. Now select the remaining percentage from the box next to the versions:

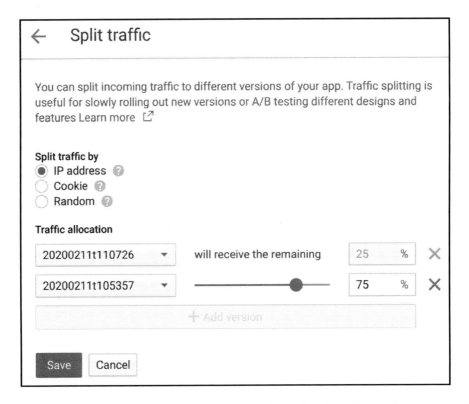

3. Once the traffic splitting ratio has been selected, select the **Save** button and GAE will indicate that it is dynamically updating the traffic splitting configuration in your project.

4. Return to the **Versions** screen to see the project actually dividing traffic between the applications chosen, in the proportions previously selected:

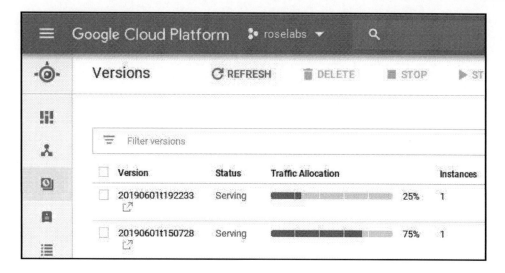

 As we expected, the preceding actions, for example, traffic splitting, are also achievable using the GCloud SDK. To achieve the same result with the SDK, use the `gcloud app set-traffic` option to provide a flexible way to get the desired outcome from a script or command-line interface.

Now that we know how to initiate traffic splitting between application versions, let's move on how to migrate traffic.

Migrating traffic

Finally, for this section, we want to migrate all traffic back to the original deployed version of our application. By now, I suspect that you already have an idea of how to achieve this.

At the top of the **Versions** screen, there is a **MIGRATE TRAFFIC** option. We will use this to move all of the existing traffic flow back to the original version, as shown in the following screenshot:

 Note that the original application currently accepts 75% of the traffic and the new version only accepts 25% of traffic.

The migration will ensure traffic is directed to the selected default version. In this type of migration, the destination instance can only be a single version:

	Version	Status	Traffic Allocation	
☐	20200211t110726 ⤢	Serving	▬▬▬▬▬▬▬	0%
☐	20200211t105357 ⤢	Serving	▬▬▬▬▬▬▬	100%

The migration of traffic between application versions is straightforward using GAE. To reinforce what we have learned, we will summarize our understanding next.

Wrapping up

In this section, we learned how to control deployment on GAE. We used several built-in tools and learned how to use them when working with our application:

- We saw how GAE instigates version control on the application.
- We observed real-time traffic splitting on GAE, accessed at the push of a button.
- We utilized the migrating traffic option to perform a simplistic application rollback.

In this section, we explored how traffic splitting can be an invaluable developer tool for testing application functionality. In this regard, working with GAE is refreshingly simple as it provides a sophisticated means of performing A/B testing without any additional setup or requirements.

Additionally, we performed a version rollback that allowed us to quickly move between traffic-serving versions to a designated default version. In this scenario, we did not need to think about how to manage the underlying infrastructure; the heavy lifting was performed for us by GAE. In the next section, we will look at how we can make the build and deploy process more consistent and less error-prone.

Troubleshooting App Engine deployments

In this section, we are going to undertake a more detailed examination of troubleshooting an application by using Stackdriver Logging. Stackdriver collates application information in a *single pane of glass* to enable data to be analyzed by developers.

Debugging an application can be time-consuming and requires a great deal of skill to establish the signal from the noise. Logs for GAE are fully available in Stackdriver, and learning to use this tool can prove to be a valuable aid for identifying defects within an application.

Building and deploying

Open Stackdriver Logging from Google's Cloud Console to present the main page of information relating to logs collated on Google Cloud. Stackdriver Logging has two modes:

- Basic mode
- Advanced filter

Basic mode is the default, and, in our example, we will use this to display some vital information about the application deployed. The advanced filter provides the user with the ability to build bespoke filters for use against logged information.

Basic mode

The first thing we need to do in Stackdriver Logging is filter the information and restrict it to the GAE application, so that it relates specifically to the part of the system we have an interest in:

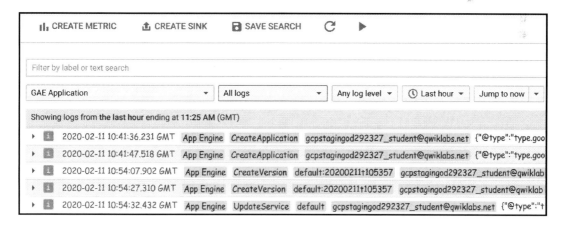

In the preceding screenshot, the filter amendment includes **GAE Application** and **All logs**. As is evident from the information displayed, this is a very detailed overview of the activities that have occurred on GAE. For example, we can see several references to, for example, `CreateApplication`, `CreateVersion`, and `UpdateService` activities. Each of these activities has an associated payload with more detail, so gleaning further information where necessary is supported.

Additionally, the (HTTP) response codes received for the pages are also displayed in the logs, meaning a metric to monitor the availability of the application can easily be created based on the log information. A metric such as *How many times have I received a 404 in the past hour* is quite useful. Aggregating metrics is a smart way to perform application analysis, so only the frequency of incident occurrence provides the basis for investigation.

Advanced filter

In some instances, a more bespoke filter is required to investigate an operation on GAE. In this instance, use the advanced filter. The advanced log filter is accessed via the drop-down filter and presents a more productive interface from which you can select information from the logs consumed within Stackdriver.

For example, in this mode, selecting the `CreateApplication` item populates the advanced filter and enables a more targeted list of entries to be displayed based on the criteria submitted by the user.

Stackdriver is an enormously valuable service when used to manage an application proactively:

- **Stackdriver Logging**: Access log information for the analysis of issues
- **Stackdriver Monitoring**: Access monitoring information for general questions
- **Stackdriver Trace**: Access trace information for latency issues
- **Stackdriver Debug**: Access application details for defect issues

The first defense layer involves integrating logging to supply a detailed and accurate view of deployed applications. Examples of this include Stackdriver Monitoring, Trace, and Debug, which utilize information about the application to assist ongoing maintenance activities and enhancements to deployed artifacts.

Wrapping up

In this section, we highlighted the first steps in using Stackdriver Logging in conjunction with GAE. We will be exploring this Stackdriver capability in further detail as we move on to more advanced topics:

- We created a *basic* mode filter to see specific GAE information.
- We switched to an *advanced* filter to take a more granular view of GAE application log information.
- We outlined some Stackdriver functionality and discussed at a high level how to use the key features.

Learning how to use Stackdriver on Google Cloud is fundamental to increasing developer productivity. The ability to aggregate information from multiple services in an easy-to-access dashboard is both compelling and useful as application complexity increases over time.

Summary

In this chapter, we covered a lot of material in order to work through some typical examples of using GAE. By now, you should have a good understanding of how the architecture and its associated components interact and can prevent the situational reinvention of the wheel.

We began with a discussion of how to deploy an application within the GAE environment. Working with version control and source configuration to support multiple environments was also covered. Finally, we looked at different deployment strategies and took our first look at Stackdriver Logging.

We have seen that GAE is very good at hosting applications that are responsible for managing solutions requiring HTTP(s)/API access. Both GAE Standard and Flex provide compelling cases for serverless applications in Google Cloud. From a developer perspective, there is very little in the way of infrastructure management required.

In the next chapter, we will expand our view of Google Cloud serverless products and start looking at event-based options. When looking at alternatives, it is always good to consider how one type of use case is more beneficial than another. Now that we have explored applications, we will take a look at more granular requirements and introduce event processing via functions.

Questions

1. There are three versions of GAE. True or false?
2. What traffic splitting options are available with GAE?
3. What filter logging options are present for Stackdriver Logging?
4. When creating an App Engine application, you need to select a Zone. True or false
5. Traffic migration offers a simple way to perform an application rollback. True or false?
6. What is the command to perform a command-line deployment of GAE?
7. What common properties does an App Engine deployment contain in its URL?

Further reading

- **Google Cloud Shell**: `https://cloud.google.com/shell/docs/launching-cloud-shell`
- **Google Cloud Shell Editor**: `https://cloud.google.com/blog/products/gcp/introducing-google-cloud-shels-new-code-editor`
- **Google app services**: `https://cloud.google.com/sdk/gcloud/reference/app/services/`

Section 2: Google Cloud Functions

In this section, you will learn about Cloud Functions and the features that make it such a compelling product for building lightweight functions. The initial discussion outlines the central properties of working with functions on Google Cloud. The remaining chapters provide an overview of the product capabilities and integration with services such as Stackdriver and Cloud Build. Finally, we build on the examples presented to create a small application to augment the concepts covered across the four chapters on Google Cloud Functions.

This section comprises the following chapters:

- Chapter 3, *Introducing Lightweight Functions*
- Chapter 4, *Developing Cloud Functions*
- Chapter 5, *Exploring Functions as a Service*
- Chapter 6, *Cloud Function Labs*

3
Introducing Lightweight Functions

Following on from a general introduction to **Google App Engine (GAE)**, we can now turn our attention to fully managed event processing. In this chapter, we will start working with Google Compute Engine and discover how to integrate serverless operational management tools in our environment. More specifically, coverage of event processing including Cloud Functions begins here.

This chapter will begin with a quick overview of Cloud Scheduler and Cloud Tasks, which are services that provide support to Google Cloud, followed by an introduction to Cloud Functions, after which we will develop a small application to utilize these services.

Throughout this chapter, we will discuss the following topics:

- Operational management tools
- Cloud Tasks and Cloud Scheduler
- An introduction to Cloud Functions
- Developing a Cloud Functions application

Technical requirements

In order to complete the exercises in this chapter, you will require a Google Cloud project or a Qwiklabs account.

You can find the code files for this chapter in the GitHub repository for the book in the `ch03` subdirectory at `https://github.com/PacktPublishing/Hands-on-Serverless-Computing-with-Google-Cloud/tree/master/ch03`.

While you are going through code snippets in the book, you will notice that, in a few instances, a few lines from the code/output have been removed and replaced with ellipses (. . .). The use of ellipses only serves to show relevant code/output. The complete code is available on GitHub at the preceding link.

Operational management tools

Being capable of responding to externally generated events provides a flexible mechanism on which to build systems that can be easily scaled and augmented. Consider how you might design a solution to create a thumbnail image based on the submission of a graphical representation. First, we need some disk storage to hold the image, then we need to process the image to generate a thumbnail, and then we need some more disk storage to keep the output.

Each stage of this activity requires a state change and response. The state change is a notification tied to the service call to indicate the state of the resource; for example, an image has been deposited, a picture has changed, or processing has completed.

In the example of Cloud Functions (introduced later in this chapter), an event triggers a new item deposit in **Google Cloud Storage (GCS)**. The function is alerted by an event trigger and can then perform a series of instructions in reaction to this event. At the outset of these instructions, the transformed image (now a thumbnail) is made available to the end user.

At this point, having been through the earlier chapters based on GAE, you will already have some familiarity with Cloud Tasks. It is always important to consider the objective before selecting a service. Taking this step will tell you whether the technology is appropriate for your needs.

As a result, this section will not be a detailed exploration, as these are ancillary services that enable serverless workloads on Google Cloud. Instead, we will include an overview of the critical points to provide the context and likely use cases. In this way, working through this section should help intelligent decisions to be made regarding the appropriateness of incorporating these services. In many instances, there will be grey areas, as well as circumstances in which there is no clear choice. Thankfully, these situations will be outliers, and we can, therefore, generalize to a large extent on how to address these rate type of circumstances. Our discussion begins with Cloud Tasks.

Cloud Tasks

We have already reviewed the benefits of using Cloud Tasks with GAE in `Chapter 1`, *Introducing App Engine* and `Chapter 2`, *Developing with App Engine*. Many of these advantages remain when working with HTTP targets, for example, decreased application latency by offloading long-lived requests to a worker, or minimizing traffic spikes in user-facing tasks.

Distributed tasks on Google Cloud have their service dedicated to managing the execution, dispatch, and delivery of jobs. The idea here is that it is preferable to be able to offload, isolate, and manage HTTP requests to minimize latency. This asynchronous workflow is especially useful when dealing with user-facing applications that require responsive interfaces. The message payload request made for the task must include POST or PUT as the HTTP method to be processed with this method.

Cloud Tasks provides several benefits beyond the advantage of asynchronously offloading tasks. Also, it allows the developer to configure the various properties associated with the transmission of data. This could include sophisticated policies such as the application of retries or rate limits established on any data contract created.

In brief, the following elements are vital characteristics of Cloud Tasks and provide a compelling reason to use this service:

- Async task offload
- Configurable retry policy
- Configurable rate limit
- Deferred scheduling
- Decouple services
- Increase resilience against failure
- Scalable and fully managed
- HTTP targets
- Guaranteed delivery
- Supports several popular languages

By building a queue of data elements, Cloud Tasks establishes an efficient way for workers to process information. Each queue is subject to rate limits, which determine how many tasks will be executed per queue. Due to the guaranteed delivery mechanism applied, there will be a retry if the response to the message published is not adequate for the application. In general, response codes follow HTTP norms, with a status code in the 2xx range indicating success.

Distributed task queues make applications more responsive when performing async execution. Task queues are capable of organizing and controlling requests by exploiting key product features such as scheduling, de-deduplication, retry policy, and version redirection.

Decoupled services (for example, Cloud Tasks and Cloud Pub/Sub) allow for better structure and application scale, especially when working with microservices. In this instance, task handlers will reside in each dedicated service to enable the microservices to scale independently. Consequently, this control of the management of resource consumption ensures better load dynamics, resulting in smoother service access, for example, rate-limiting queues.

Furthermore, when handling releases and incidents gracefully, requests can be paused, retried, and redirected to a new version. If you have worked with Cloud Pub/Sub, this decoupling may all sound very familiar. The main difference between the two services involves invocation. Cloud Tasks provides the publisher with the ability to control execution, that is, the endpoint. Conversely, Cloud Pub/Sub enables the subscriber to control message delivery.

To learn more about the differences between these two services, read the *Choosing between Cloud Tasks and Pub/Sub* documentation reference at `https://cloud.google.com/tasks/docs/comp-pub-sub`.

Cloud Scheduler

Think of Cloud Scheduler as cron jobs for the cloud. If you are not familiar with cron jobs, they represent an easy way to schedule activities on a machine based on a schedule. Acting as a single pane of glass, Cloud Scheduler enables users to manage all their automation needs from a single place. Creating a Cloud Scheduler job only requires a few elements to be up and running.

If you are in a situation where you wish to automate some cloud infrastructure operations, then this is a perfect way to achieve that outcome. As a fully managed service, there is a simple interface through which you can set up and configure your automation needs as follows:

1. Establish the frequency with which to run and trigger a task.
2. Determine how Cloud Scheduler is to be invoked (that is, Pub/Sub, App Engine HTTP, or HTTP).

3. Deploy the service and the task will be invoked automatically when the scheduled time occurs.

4. Consult the Cloud Scheduler console page to see the results of each invocation or access it via Stackdriver Logging.

Cloud Scheduler provides a simple and effective way to run regular jobs on schedule. If you have ever needed to run things such as backups or download updates, you will already know how useful and powerful this application is. Being an enterprise-grade product, Cloud Scheduler provides what is essentially a cloud-based crontab. The beauty of this product is that it enables users to trigger jobs across existing Google Cloud target services. Having these integration targets available provides a highly reliable mechanism to ensure that tasks run on a schedule can support existing usage patterns.

In addition to this, Cloud Scheduler also provides some key elements that are covered in the following list:

- Reliable delivery guaranteed that is, delivery of at least one of the job targets (this does come with its own complications, where ordering data may be a concern, similar to using a messaging solutions such as Cloud Pub/Sub).
- A wide range of service support targets such as App Engine, Cloud Pub/Sub, and HTTP endpoints.
- The retry and backoff mechanism determines a suitable retry policy for job requirements.
- Integration with Stackdriver Logging captures information relating to the performance and execution of your task
- Supports the Unix cron formation, so your existing knowledge is transferable.

So now we know all of that, we can create a quick Cloud Scheduler demonstration on how to use it. In the following example, Cloud Scheduler will use Cloud Pub/Sub to illustrate how it can interact with a defined endpoint.

The first task is to create a Pub/Sub topic. A Pub/Sub topic will collate the messages ready for distribution based on allocated subscribers as follows:

1. From the Google Cloud Console menu, select the **Pub/Sub** option.
2. From the **Pub/Sub** screen, select the **Create Topic** menu option.
3. On the **Create a topic** screen, enter the **Topic ID** as `cron-topic`.

4. Leave the **Encryption** settings at the following default option: **Google-managed key**; then select the **CREATE TOPIC** button:

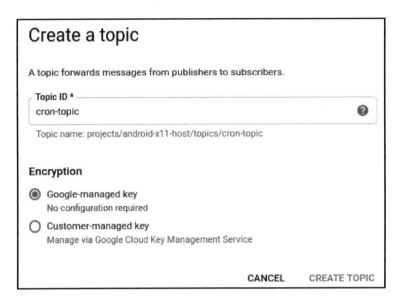

Once we have a topic defined, we now need to establish a subscription to it. For any available messages, we will be able to use either the pull or push mechanism to access the data payload associated with the topic:

1. Now we need to create a subscription for the topic, so select the **Subscriptions** option from the left-hand menu.
2. At the top of the screen, select the **CREATE SUBSCRIPTION** option.
3. Enter the **Subscription ID** as `cron-sub`.
4. Enter the **Topic name** as `projects/<project-id>/topics/cron-topic`, replacing `<project-id>` with the Google Cloud project ID on your system.
5. Then select the **CREATE** button at the bottom of the screen.

Finally, we need to define the Cloud Scheduler that will use the Pub/Sub created earlier as an endpoint. Each time the Cloud Scheduler task invokes, it will send a payload to Pub/Sub:

1. Select the option for **Cloud Scheduler** (located under **Tools**) and choose the **CREATE JOB** option.

2. The result should look similar to the following screen:

3. Complete the fields as per the following table:

Field	Content
Name	cron-task
Description	Demonstration of Cloud Scheduler on Google Cloud Platform
Frequency	* * * * *
Time zone	United Kingdom (GMT)
Target	Pub/Sub
Topic	cron-topic
Payload	Yeah Cloud Scheduler Rocks

4. Once you've finished filling in the preceding fields, select the **CREATE** button to add your Cloud Scheduler task to the list of active jobs.

The example code will run every minute, but for the sake of brevity, press the **RUN NOW** button. From the **Cloud Scheduler Jobs** page, you will see the result category logged as successful, and it also indicates the last time the job was run. If you now look at the Cloud Pub/Sub queue and click on the **cron-topic**, under the **View Messages** option, you can pull the payload information added in Cloud Scheduler. Alternatively, you can use the Cloud Shell to access Pub/Sub subscriptions using the `gcloud` command as follows:

```
gcloud pubsub subscriptions pull cron-sub --limit 10
```

Congratulations! As you can see, Cloud Scheduler enables straightforward integration with Pub/Sub, App Engine, and HTTP.

Now that we have discussed the means to initiate both tasks and scheduled activities, we can begin to consider more extensive system requirements for processing information with functions.

Introducing Cloud Functions

The Cloud Functions platform provides an effective way to run single-purpose code in the cloud. Remember that standalone services remove the need to manage a server or its associated runtime. The occurrence of an event notification then triggers single-purpose functions. The lightweight Cloud Functions platform then provides the basis for event-driven serverless compute.

Building single-purpose functions that are independently called provides a highly available architecture for building your services. Compounding these functions presents an excellent way to extend cloud services. These single-purpose functions deliver lightweight components that, in turn, can be a more natural way to maintain your application. The simplicity of deployment and maintenance devoid of server provisioning and patch/update cycles can be an effective way to design your solution.

The ability to connect to cloud services and interact with different interfaces such as webhooks, APIs, and **Internet of Things** (**IoT**) devices is desirable. Google has made the interface to Cloud Functions extremely simple to use; you can build single-purpose functions that are limited only by your imagination.

Later in the book, we will discuss how to develop code using the Functions Framework to create lightweight functions. The Functions Framework is an open source project that enables seamless compatibility across several environments (for example, Google Cloud Functions, Cloud Run, and Knative). For now, be aware that, when building functions, this approach provides an element of compatibility that enables you to switch between technology stacks seamlessly.

The wide variety of scenarios in which a serverless compute platform deploys makes this an attractive offering. Often deployed as the glue between services and APIs, Cloud Functions establishes an extensible layer for anyone wishing to use Google Cloud in the following areas:

- Real-time file processing
- Event-driven extract, transform, and load pipelines
- Serverless IoT backends
- Third-party integration via APIs

Typical use cases might include the following:

- **The IoT**: Serverless engagement with devices to process information via an event stream. Cloud Functions provide a simplistic interface that can provide a powerful tool with which to gather and disperse batch or real-time information using services such as Cloud Pub/Sub.
- **APIs**: HTTP triggers can design aggregated logic to respond to application calls. This lightweight API is perfect to abstract more complex processing in the event chain, such as storage or queue requirements. Building an API of this type can be achieved with an event-driven interface and over HTTP.

To illustrate how to create a simple Cloud Functions application, in the next section, we will walk through the main steps of this process.

Developing a Cloud Functions-based application

To help build our understanding of the services previously discussed, we will develop a small application to utilize these services. Our Cloud Function will present a simple web page, in which some web-based information displays the output. To illustrate the power of each of the functions previously discussed, each of the *Requirement* milestones in the following table will alter and improve the overall design incrementally.

Our application will be developed with Google Cloud Functions and will display some information on the screen. Incidentally, if you need to host something like a static website, this can quickly be done by using a GCS bucket. Storage buckets are very versatile. For more information on how to implement them, check the documentation at `https://cloud.google.com/storage/docs/static-website`.

The application we will develop over the next couple of sections will be an RSS reader. Our high-level requirement is to present information from a particular site as an HTML web page. Our high-level requirements are as follows:

Ref	Requirement	Description
1	Develop a Cloud Function.	Deploy a single function application.
2	Read content from an RSS site.	For the example, we use a BBC RSS feed.
3	Render data as HTML.	Present the information to be consumed as HTML.
4	Refresh the data.	Enable data to be refreshed on an automated schedule.

Now that we have all our requirements in place, we can progress to building our first iteration of the application.

App version 1 – introducing Cloud Functions

In this example, we will step through the process for using Cloud Functions as the basis for the application. This process consists of the following steps:

1. **Creating a function**: Start out with a simple Cloud Function.
2. **Adding Functions Framework**: Understand how to add other libraries when migrating code to Cloud Shell.
3. **Deploying the resultant code**: Learn how to deploy code from the command line.

Starting with Cloud Functions is made more accessible by the fact that it provides template code in several languages. The inclusion of this template code is beneficial when starting and enables developers to quickly try out the service without having to spend any time setting up an environment.

When working through the high-level requirements, retrieving an RSS feed from an external site seems like a critical activity. This task also seems like something that should have an existing pattern with which to achieve the desired outcome.

As a first development step, it is always worth doing a quick scan of the internet for inspiration. For the identified task, there are quite a few existing packages capable of accessing an RSS feed. Coming up with an initial design can help us to think through what we want to design:

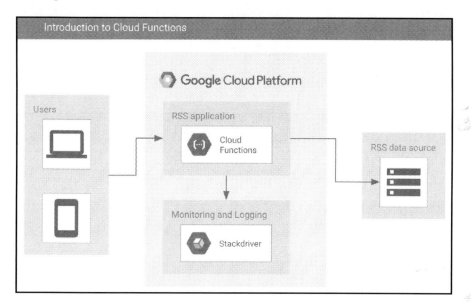

In the preceding diagram, we can see that Cloud Functions is used to access the backend RSS data source. Also, users can access an HTTP endpoint to retrieve RSS information consumed from the backend.

The following example will use the Cloud Functions option in Google Cloud. To speed up the development cycle, we will use available components to build our application and minimize the amount of code we need to write. To handle the RSS feed, we will use a pre-existing package to handle all the processing. The package also needs to be capable of accessing elements within the RSS feed. In this example, I am going to use Node.js; however, feel free to use an alternative language such as Python or Go.

At this point, we will use Cloud Console to write and deploy code to Cloud Functions:

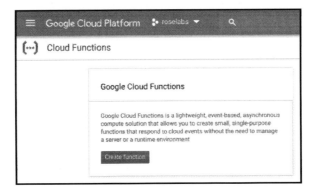

We begin by using the standard boilerplate code provided by Cloud Functions to create an application. Using this template will enable the creation of Cloud Functions together with different properties:

Having selected the **Cloud Functions** option from Google Cloud Console and then opened a new Cloud Function, select Node as the runtime language to have the application code pre-populate with the example boilerplate code, as shown in the following screenshot:

To print some arbitrary text to the console log with Cloud Functions, we can do the following:

1. Edit the `index.js` file presented in the Cloud Functions template. We will start our application by amending the blueprint code provided by Google and add some code to perform the following task:

```
/**
 * Responds to any HTTP request.
 *
 * @param {!express:Request} req HTTP request context.
 * @param {!express:Response} res HTTP response context.
 */
exports.helloRSS = (req, res) => {
  console.log('helloRSS - display some info');
  res.status(200).send('helloRSS');
};
```

   In the preceding code, we introduce the `console.log` statement, which writes information to the logging infrastructure. In the case of Google Cloud, this will be Stackdriver Logging.

2. To deploy the preceding code, we need to click the **Create** button displayed at the bottom of the screen.

   Deploying this code results in a `helloRSS` message being returned as the HTTP response. In addition, the information will also be available under Stackdriver as this acts as a centralized repository for all captured logging.

3. To retrieve information from Stackdriver, use a filter on `resource.type = cloud_function` to access specific data relating to program execution.

 Chapter 2, *Developing with App Engine*, has a section outlining the process of filtering in Stackdriver. Check that out if you need a reminder on how to perform this task.

We now have a very basic function. To add to this in the next section, we will incorporate some external packages to render a view.

App version 2 – migrating to Cloud Shell

As our code becomes more complex, we should take the opportunity to move our development to somewhere more convenient. By convenient, I am, of course, referring to the command line. Now that we have seen how to use Cloud Functions from the console, our next step is to use Cloud Shell on Google Cloud:

```
cloudshell x   + ▾

Welcome to Cloud Shell! Type "help" to get started.
To set your Cloud Platform project in this session use "gcloud config set project [PROJECT_ID]"
richardrose@cloudshell:~$
```

When we use Cloud Shell, it will provide lots of helpful tips. For example, in the preceding screenshot, Cloud Shell is indicating that it doesn't know which Google Cloud project it should be associated with. To remedy this, use the `gcloud config set [PROJECT_ID]` command.

If you don't know the correct `PROJECT_ID` to include, you can find this information on the home screen of the Google Cloud Console under the **Project Info** heading.

If you ever get stuck on any of the application code in this book, you can also use the code repository version link at the beginning of each chapter. Now that we have Cloud Shell open, follow these steps to recreate the application from scratch:

1. First, make a new directory for your Node code to hold your code. Let's call it `ch03`.

    In the Cloud Console, two code files, `index.js` and `package.json`, are deployed as part of our Cloud Function. The content of each can be observed in the Cloud Functions console. Using your favorite editor, we are going to recreate this application.

In later chapters, we will look more closely at other options for local development but, for now, we will focus on how to migrate our code to Cloud Shell.

2. In the new directory, copy the existing function code for `index.js` from the Cloud Functions console window and place this into a new `index.js` file located within the `ch03` subdirectory in Cloud Shell.

3. Do the same for the `package.json` file and you now should have two source files (`index.js` and `package.json`) in your `ch03` development directory.

4. In addition, we will also need to install any packages required. Let's add the `functions-framework` package:

```
npm install @google-cloud/functions-framework
```

If you take a sneaky peek at the directory, suddenly we see more than the two source files we created. Don't worry about that for now. The critical thing to mention is the inclusion of `functions-framework` in the `package.json` configuration file. We will cover what this is in more detail in the next chapter on Cloud Functions.

Now we have our code nicely packaged in Cloud Shell, we can do fancy things such as saving it to a repository to help with version control. But we will continue to test that the files are working as expected, which means deploying our code.

5. Let's stay in the Cloud Shell, using the following command to deploy our code:

```
gcloud functions deploy tempest --entry-point helloRSS --runtime
nodejs8 --trigger-http
```

You will be asked if you want to allow unauthenticated invocations; answer Yes. Excellent, congratulations! You have deployed a Cloud Function named `tempest` from the command line! At the moment it doesn't do much, but take a bow anyway. Next, we are going to expand the application to do something a bit more useful.

App version 3 – adding a view

In our application, we want to extend the code to read an RSS feed. To build upon the existing code, we should incorporate a few additions to move closer to our application requirements:

- Display some static content.
- Utilize an HTTP response to display as HTML page.

To achieve this, we will perform the following steps:

1. Introduce an NPM peer package to perform the necessary RSS interaction. A peer package is a Node dependency declared in the `package.json` file. Performing a quick search of NPM packages shows `rss-parser` as the right choice for our requirements.

An advantage of using a package is that it will include all the relevant information about configuration. Node establishes an automatic update of the package.json file when an install completes. By adding the RSS component, we are quickly able to meet the requirement to read RSS feeds with a minimal amount of code.

A good practice to adopt is to check the available source code/library. We should never implicitly trust packages and therefore must remain vigilant when incorporating third-party code into our projects. Always heed vulnerabilities and warnings displayed that relate to security.

Looking at the rss-parser page on the NPM website (https://www.npmjs.com/package/rss-parser), under **Versions**, we can see that the most current version (at the time of writing) is version 3.7.2.

2. From the command line, we can install this package by issuing the following command:

```
npm install rss-parser
```

3. Now by viewing the package.json file, we can see it has been updated to include the relevant package and version.

```
{
  "name": "sample-http",
  "version": "0.0.1",
  "dependencies": {
    "@google-cloud/functions-framework": "^1.3.2",
    "rss-parser": "^3.7.3"
  }
}
```

4. Now that the package.json file has been updated to incorporate rss-parser, in the JavaScript file, index.js, we will declare a new asynchronous function to do all the heavy lifting and retrieve the RSS code to output the results.

We are using an asynchronous function as network calls may take a while to process; we don't want to incur an unnecessary delay in the UI processing of the request/response life cycle.

5. In this new function, we first want to introduce the rss-parser package (https://www.npmjs.com/package/rss-parser) to consume the RSS data source by declaring a new object. We also add a new background asynchronous function to handle the parsing of the relevant RSS feed.

We don't pass back this data to the original function, `helloRSS`. Instead, we process all network-related activity in the `asyncBBCFeed` function.

6. Add the following code to `index.js` as shown as follows:

```
let Parser = require('rss-parser');
let parser = new Parser();
// New background function - Async
async function asyncBBCFeed(req, res) {
    let feed = await
parser.parseURL('http://feeds.bbci.co.uk/news/rss.xml');
    console.log (feed.title);
    var testString = '';
    // Title
    testString = '<h1>RSS Lab</h1></p>'
    // Loop through the content
    feed.items.forEach(item => {
      console.log(item.title + ':' + item.link);
     // Create a link per title
     testString = testString + '<a href="' + item.link +
'">'+item.title + '</a>' + '</br>';
    });
    // Display the feed returned
    res.status(200).send(testString);
}
```

7. Now update the `helloRSS` function to look like the following code:

```
/**
* Responds to any HTTP request.*
* @param {!express:Request} req HTTP request context.
* @param {!express:Response} res HTTP response context.
*/
exports.helloRSS = (req, res) => {
 var testMessage = '';
 console.log('helloRSS - display some info');
 asyncBBCFeed(req, res);
};
```

8. Back in Cloud Shell, deploy the updated code:

```
gcloud functions deploy tempest --entry-point helloRSS --runtime
nodejs8 --trigger-http
```

Once the code is deployed, look at the Cloud Functions interface in the Cloud Console. Here we can see the application has been incremented to version 2. Go ahead and trigger the function to see the result of the asynchronous call we added. Awesome! Some lovely headlines are retrieved from the RSS feed, as shown in the following screenshot:

RSS Lab

Ian Paterson: Surgeon wounded hundreds amid 'culture of denial'
Coronavirus: UK tells all Britons to leave China 'if they can'
Petrol and diesel car sales ban brought forward to 2035
COP26: PM 'doesn't get' climate change, says sacked president
Ikea announces first big UK store closure
Stillbirth: The woman who found my baby's grave
Streatham stabbing attack victim named as Monika Luftner
Hashem Abedi: Manchester Arena attack brother 'equally guilty'
Iowa caucus: 'I'm the winner' says Trump amid Democrat chaos
Lesotho First Lady Maesaiah Thabane faces charge of murdering rival
Caption mix-ups 'show lack of respect' for black MPs
Stuck in Syria: 'Can you forgive your IS father?'
Shannen Doherty: 'My cancer came back'
Coronavirus: 'We may have no clothes left to sell'
'I was sent racist abuse over the coronavirus'
Bang Bang: The artist who's tattooed LeBron James, Lewis Hamilton and Thierry Henry
'Exploding meteor' caught on doorbell camera in Derby
Derrick Nnadi pays dog adoption fees after Super Bowl win
The changing industrial landscape of Britain
The Chinese doctor who tried to warn others about coronavirus
Mayhem and mishaps during Norway's gruelling dog sled race
Lupita Nyong'o: 'Books don't have to be about white people'
Bubble tea: A sweet treat that went global
Lesbos: Tear gas fired as migrants hold protest over conditions
Bafta Film Awards 2020: 10 things we learned at the ceremony
Ukraine MP's advice to sell dog to pay bills causes outcry
How will the petrol and diesel car ban work?
'I didn't know it was abuse until I nearly died'
Streatham attack: Will terror sentence changes stop offences?
Nkosi Johnson: The child campaigner who changed South Africa
The shelter giving wine to alcoholics
Manasi Joshi: The accident that created a world champion
Keeping rats out of kitchens and bedbugs out of hotels
Oscars 2020: The lowdown on international film nominees
Yalta: World War Two summit that reshaped the world
Warnings over British independent film scene's 'spiral of decline'
Coronavirus: British Chinese people reveal prejudice amid outbreak
England's Tuilagi to miss Scotland game with groin strain
More than two-thirds of fans say VAR makes Premier League less enjoyable, survey finds
Israel Folau: Hull KR lead Super League revolt over new Catalans Dragons signing
Honesty Cards: Jamal Lewis & Todd Cantwell worst hair, driver and fashion at Norwich
What is climate change? A really simple guide
Climate change: How 1.5C degrees of global warming could change the world
All you need to know about electric cars
Climate change: Where we are in seven charts and what you can do to help
Amazon rainforest: The 90-year-old trying to stop destruction
Who is Greta Thunberg, the teenage climate change activist?
What does healing the Brexit divide mean?

Working with external data sources will be an everyday use case, so it is essential to understand how to do this and also to think about crucial aspects of the associated design. Iterating to the second version of our application, we want to output HTML to our site. Again, this remains an everyday use case and, rather than developing additional code, we used an existing Node component to handle the processing for us. Introducing an asynchronous task will minimize the associated latency for network interactions.

Looking at the code, the HTML remains tightly coupled with the system code, so that needs addressing. Before embarking on that particular challenge, it's time to move our code from the Cloud Console to the command line. In the next section, we start to work with Cloud Shell exclusively.

App version 4 – decoupling HTML output

As we now know from working with Node, it means we have access to a wealth of packages to do cool stuff. For our application, let's utilize a package named pug to render our HTML in a more manageable way. Decoupling the given text from the RSS data presents us with an opportunity to display the information in a less convoluted way and without having to recode significant elements of the Cloud Function:

1. In Cloud Shell, in line with the previous example, we need to add a new peer dependency to the package.json file:

    ```
    npm install pug
    ```

2. Pug will enable HTML previously embedded within the JavaScript to be segregated into a separate file:

    ```
    {
        "name": "sample-http",
        "version": "0.0.1",
        "dependencies": {
            "@google-cloud/functions-framework": "^1.1.1",
            "rss-parser": "^3.7.2",
            "pug": "^2.0.4"
        }
    }
    ```

3. In the `index.js` file, we need to add a reference to the pug object within our application:

```
let pug = require('pug');
```

4. Next, we initiate a programmatic view (that is, how the page will look) when rendered against our HTML output using the `index.pug` file. In the `asyncBBCFeed` function add the following:

```
const pugInputFile = pug.compileFile('index.pug');
```

5. We also need to update the response object to indicate:

- Successful processing
- The view to be rendered, that is, `index.pug`
- Interpolation of values, in our case, the `feed.items` returned from the async call:

```
res.status(200).send(pugInputFile({
    items: feed.items
}));
```

6. Finally, let's get rid of some of the boilerplate code that is no longer required to process the feed items.

After updating the changes outlined in the preceding step, our `index.js` should look as follows:

```
let Parser = require('rss-parser');
let parser = new Parser();
let pug = require('pug');

// New background function - Async
async function asyncBBCFeed(req, res) {
    let feed = await
parser.parseURL('http://feeds.bbci.co.uk/news/rss.xml');
    // Use an external pug file
    const pugInputFile = pug.compileFile('index.pug');
    // console.log(feed.items)
    // Display the feed returned
    res.status(200).send(pugInputFile({
        items: feed.items
    }));
}
/**
* Responds to any HTTP request.
```

```
 *
 * @param {!express:Request} req HTTP request context.
 * @param {!express:Response} res HTTP response context.
 */
exports.helloRSS = (req, res) => {
    asyncBBCFeed(req, res);
};
```

7. To render a view, we now need to create a new file named `index.pug` within the view directory and add the following to it:

```
html
  head
    title Template - This is a Pug generated output
  body
    header
      p RSS Lab
    section
    each item in items
      a(href='' + item.link) #{item.title} <br>
```

8. Back in Cloud Shell, deploy the updated code:

```
gcloud functions deploy tempest --entry-point helloRSS --runtime
nodejs8 --trigger-http
```

Testing the deployed code should result in the same output as shown in the *App version 3 - adding a view* section previously.

However, take note that our application complexity has significantly decreased. Also, we haven't even needed to write much code. Once you have updated the application with the preceding code updates, take this opportunity to try another form of deployment:

1. From the Cloud Shell, compress the contents of the development directory into a ZIP file.
2. Let's make a Cloud Storage bucket in your project (bucket names need to be globally unique, so pick one that works for you and replace [BUCKET_ID] with your unique identifier).
3. Upload the file to your bucket.
4. From the Cloud Function interface, choose the Create function and select the ZIP file from Cloud Storage.
5. Select the ZIP file from the bucket location and don't forget to change the **function to execute** setting—we are using a function named helloRSS.

6. Finally, select the **Create** option and **Create a new function** option for the code taken from the storage bucket.

> If you are anything like me, the joy of deploying code manually will be short-lived. In this case, using Cloud Build will be of interest to you.

Working with event processing provides a simple and effective mechanism to set up an action to be taken in response to a stimulus. In the initial revision of our application, we introduced Cloud Functions. Working with the template code, we were able to adapt the system to consume an RSS feed and output the content to application logs.

In the example code, I used the BBC RSS feeds site as the source material because it has plenty of options and is a suitably stable site on which to base a demo. However, feel free to replace this site with one of your choosing as long as it adheres to the same standard specification; this should not impact the code presented.

Great job: working on Google Cloud provides a lot of options. In the next section, I will set you an optional challenge to build on all the things you have learned so far.

App version 5 – extending the RSS reader

In this final revision of the application, I am going to set you a challenge! Our application can already retrieve RSS feed data and display it as HTML. However, it would be nice to have the ability to show even more information and perhaps include another feed or two.

By extending the requirements, we now have the following task list:

Ref	Requirement	Description
1	Develop a Cloud Function.	Deploy a single function application.
2	Read content from an RSS site.	For example, the BBC RSS feed.
3	Render data as HTML.	Present the information to be consumed as HTML.
4	Refresh data.	Enable data to be refreshed on an automated schedule.
5	Read content from an RSS site.	Find another RSS site and add it to the application.
6	Improve the HTML layout.	Add some images to the output and add some more data from an RSS feed.

The majority of the code should already be familiar to you but don't worry if it is not. The point of the challenge app is to test your understanding and build your confidence so you can take on increasingly complex code.

 Remember, if you find it challenging to perform this exercise, a solution can be found in the book repository in the ch03/solution subdirectory.

In this example, do note that building an application within a single function can be viewed as an anti-pattern for serverless functions. An alternative approached might be to create a reader function for data access, and a presentation function for data rendering. This could lead to the state being migrated to other services such as Firestore (or even just saved to GCS). Also, the addition of a Cloud Scheduled job might be used to refresh the data. The refreshed data might then be stored in the backend, such as on Firestore. We could then use a trigger on write for an event-driven function to render the updated HTML, possibly even writing the data to GCS or some other cache. With this approach serving thousands of frontend requests without the slow-down associated with getting the RSS feed, we've decoupled our workload into small and easy-to-understand code.

Summary

Throughout this chapter, you will have realized that building solutions on Google Cloud does not require a vast amount of knowledge to get to a **minimum viable product (MVP)**. Investing time to be able to iterate over numerous revisions quickly is worthwhile and can lead to significant improvements in the overall design.

Through this chapter, you should now have an appreciation of the nature of the services available. You will find it much easier to think about combining different products, almost like building blocks. In this regard, it is imperative, at the outset, to have a clear view of how the end solution should look. Taking the opportunity to build lightweight functions, as opposed to a monolith, can generally simplify the overall design; however, be sure that this is what your solution requires. As you will now be aware, there are many situations in which serverless event processing can be beneficial.

That concludes our initial overview of the three event processing services for serverless workloads. The versatility of the functions discussed fulfills a wide variety of use cases. When looking to design an application using these services, it is worth considering the desired use. Design iteration is a good thing and should bring about better efficiencies in your application. As we move on to more complex systems, having a working knowledge of the appropriate use cases and associated design patterns will make building systems feel more natural. In the next chapter, we will be turning our attention specifically to Cloud Functions. There is lots more to cover in terms of usage, and we also need to discuss trigger events that make them so useful.

Questions

1. Does Cloud Tasks support rate limiting? (True or False)
2. Describe deferred scheduling for Cloud Tasks.
3. Does Cloud Scheduler support a retry and backoff mechanism? (True or False)
4. Does Cloud Scheduler operate in a similar way to cron? (True or False)
5. What trigger do we use to deploy an HTTP endpoint?
6. Where does Cloud Functions send its logs?
7. What command enables Cloud Functions to be deployed from the command line?
8. What is the entry point for Cloud Functions and why is it important?

Further reading

- **Choosing between Cloud Tasks and Pub/Sub**: https://cloud.google.com/tasks/docs/comp-pub-sub
- **Static website examples and tips**: https://cloud.google.com/storage/docs/static-website
- **The NPM pug package**: https://www.npmjs.com/package/pug
- **Distributed computing**: https://en.wikipedia.org/wiki/Fallacies_of_distributed_computing

4
Developing Cloud Functions

In this chapter, we will deliver an overview of Google Cloud Functions. It will provide you with a good understanding of the what, why, and how of Google Cloud Functions. Knowing the basis for any technology and its use case will assist with integration and application in the real world.

To achieve this outcome, we will again build an application throughout the chapter to illustrate some critical aspects of Cloud Functions.

The topics covered in this chapter include the following:

- Introducing Google Cloud Functions
- Developing with the Functions Framework
- Exploring the Cloud Functions workflow
- Understanding the HTTP protocol

Technical requirements

In this chapter, to complete the exercises, you will require a Google Cloud project or a Qwiklabs account.

You can find the code files of this chapter in the GitHub repository for the book under the `ch04` **subdirectory** at `https://github.com/PacktPublishing/Hands-on-Serverless-Computing-with-Google-Cloud/tree/master/ch04`.

 While you are going through code snippets in the book, you will notice that, in a few instances, a few lines from the code/outputs have been removed and replaced with ellipses (. . .). The use of ellipses is to show only relevant code/output. The complete code is available on GitHub at the preceding link.

Introducing Google Cloud Functions

The description of Cloud Functions on Google Cloud indicates an event-driven serverless compute platform. What this means is that functions are triggered either by HTTP endpoints or via a background service (for example, Google Cloud Storage or Cloud Pub/Sub and other sources within Google Cloud). Operationally, Cloud Functions are *single-use* pieces of code that are quick to deploy and provide the *glue* between multiple services. The exciting aspect of Cloud Functions is that they can be stitched together quite easily in the same way a traditional application would be. It is entirely feasible to create a couple of HTTP endpoint functions that link through to a Cloud Pub/Sub backend, and by keeping your service simple, the build can quickly complete.

While the default setting for functions is public, authentication can be enabled for features to secure the environment in which they operate. Cloud Functions are executed using a service account and are, therefore, configurable via Google Cloud **Identity and Access Management (IAM)**. It is important to note that functions do not share memory space, which means an isolated context for each instance executed.

Additionally, it is essential to note that functions are stateless in nature; they are therefore not expected to persist information within the Cloud Function.

 The exception to this is scenario is something like persisting a database connection that should be stored globally in code. Doing this means the next Cloud Function invocation doesn't need to introduce any additional latency retrieving the connection information.

Further to this, the following properties are central to the DNA of Cloud Functions:

- They operate in a secure operation context.
- They don't share memory across functions.
- No state is maintained.

Working with Cloud Functions provides an excellent way to execute single-purpose Cloud Functions without needing to spend a lifetime coding an application. Further use cases exist and are denoted in the following section.

Defining the use cases

As developers have become more exposed to cloud infrastructure, an exciting outcome is the evolution of lightweight functions. Consider the applications you use daily and how they have matured over time. How many of these now feature an HTTP endpoint that can be used independently from the application? What would happen if everything became an API; how cool would that be? Situations such as these are analogous to the processing of logs in which records were held internally in a proprietary format. Then someone had the bright idea to export application data to a centralized solution to capture information. A tipping point occurred, and we all adopted this typical pattern as the de-facto mechanism for the management of logging.

Back to Cloud Functions – consider how much more convenient it is to develop an application when you have standard solutions and patterns that can easily integrate with your resolution. Also, consider the level of design required upfront to ensure that an application retains a degree of compatibility. Working with a protocol such as HTTP provides a very well-understood interface that is recognized by a wide range of people. Having a typical frame of reference provides an excellent method of moving the industry forward, and HTTP provides just the vehicle for adoption and propagation of the development of abstracted interfaces. So, we'll reflect on the types of use cases that Cloud Functions are most appropriate for over the next couple of sections.

Processing with backend services

Backend serverless compute is triggered by services such as Cloud Pub/Sub and Cloud Storage. The scope of these services is made more interesting by the prospect of being able to integrate different Google Cloud services with your Cloud Functions.

We already know that we can use Cloud Functions for many scenarios. As outlined previously in the use case introduction, serverless backend processing is an excellent use case for this solution. In this situation, the Cloud Function design addresses a request to provide specific information. This request presents a particular signature of the service that encapsulates the information necessary to complete processing some arbitrary data. At the outset of this processing, the function responds to indicate it has completed the assigned activity. The response can note success or failure; however, in terms of the service, its life cycle is complete, and it will fade out of existence.

Processing with real-time data

Another scenario that sits well with serverless compute is that of real-time data processing. In this situation, Cloud Functions' on-demand provisioning enables them to meet processing requirements for a service designed against minimal latency. As we discussed earlier in the book, it may be useful to understand several attributes before the development of a solution. The ability to quickly provision infrastructure in a short amount of time is a significant factor for solutions requiring real-time processing. Cloud Functions support a startup time of less than 2.5 seconds for memory allocations of less than 1,024 MB and this can be highly beneficial where an application requires immediate processing. As many systems move from batch to near real-time processing, the adoption of these types of capabilities will become more prevalent. Accordingly, it is therefore increasingly important to understand how to adapt and incorporate these patterns in the services designed.

Beyond the example scenarios laid out in the preceding section, many other use cases exist. Working with Cloud Functions minimizes the work needed to integrate your code and removes the obligation to provide the associated infrastructure.

To use Cloud Functions requires very little in the way of additional knowledge of the backend architecture. In truth, as long as you are comfortable in one of the language runtimes, you can be up and running very quickly. Having said that, we should take the time to explain what is happening in the background and how you can go about extending this to meet your needs.

In the next section, we move on to cover the Functions Framework. One thing Google Cloud is keen to ensure is that developers get an excellent experience. To achieve this typically means allowing them to work in their existing environment. So how about being able to work locally but being still able to deploy code to a cloud environment?

Developing with the Functions Framework

At this point, please take a moment to consider the benefit of the Functions Framework we have been discussing – the various options available on Google Cloud, meaning we can run code in different environments. As a platform that prides itself as being developer-centric, allowing engineers to pick up and use their code in different contexts is highly advantageous.

Introducing the Functions Framework

The Functions Framework is an open source project that enables you to build your functions in multiple environments, for example, locally. As with any magic trick, the beauty is not understanding the mechanics of the illusion, but with how it makes you feel. In this instance, let's pull back the curtains to see how this particular trick is done and also what it means in terms of Cloud Functions.

So why do we need something like this? Well, working in a local, often highly customized environment provides a friendly comfort zone for developers. The context you are working in will be familiar, and the tools, locations, and access can all easily be checked and validated. There is an inherent comfort associated with working in this way. Moving to the cloud removes some of those psychological comforts from the user.

Having the ability to work locally, despite being counter to the end objective of running code in the cloud, is something folks want to do. Being able to work across a variety of environments using Cloud Functions leads us to the Functions Framework. The framework is a lightweight dependency that allows developers to run simple interfaces in a range of settings, such as the following:

- Cloud Functions
- Local development
- Cloud Run and Cloud Run for Anthos
- Knative environments

Building on the **Functions as a Service (FaaS)** platform for Google Cloud, the availability of this framework provides a simple mechanism to achieve portability across multiple environments. To incorporate the code is as simple as adding the relevant package to your project. In the next section, we will walk through a simple example to demonstrate its usage in a project. In the following case, we create a basic Node application to process some web-based information.

Deploying an application locally with the Functions Framework

Most developers prefer the local experience of working within a development environment. The Functions Framework provides Cloud Functions developers with the ability to continue to use this local work environment and propagate their code to the cloud in a seamless manner:

1. First, create a directory for the example code to be built and initialize the environment. In my example, I have created a directory named `functions-framework` and will be using this to develop my code.

 It is important to note that in my local environment I am using Node v10+, as this is a requirement to use the Functions Framework. Also, I have npm v6.9.0 installed on my testing machine.

2. To check the Node version on your environment, run the command:

   ```
   node -v
   ```

3. Using an editor, create a file named `index.js` and add the following content to it:

   ```
   exports.helloWorldLocal = (req, res) => {
       res.send('Hello, Functions Framework from a local machine');
   };
   ```

4. To create a template `package.json` file, run `npm init` from the command line. Edit the content as necessary:

   ```
   {
       "name": "lab01_FF",
       "version": "1.0.0",
       "description": "Example use of the Functions Framework (FaaS)",
       "main": "index.js",
       "scripts": {
       "test": "echo \"Error: no test specified\" && exit 1"
       },
       "author": "Rich Rose",
       "license": "ISC"
   }
   ```

As you can see from the above code extract, I have the bare minimum added to my file.

5. Next, install the functions-framework package. My assumption here is that this is not already present on your local machine. To install this package, you will use npm to get the necessary package information:

```
npm install @google-cloud/functions-framework
```

6. Once this command has been completed, you will see that the package.json file has been updated to include reference to the Function Framework under the dependencies category, as follows:

```
{
    "name": "lab01_FF",
    "version": "1.0.0",
    "description": "Example use of the Functions Framework (FaaS)",
    "main": "index.js",
    "scripts": {
        "test": "echo \"Error: no test specified\" && exit 1"
    },
    "author": "Rich Rose",
    "license": "ISC",
    "dependencies": {
        "@google-cloud/functions-framework": "^1.1.1"
    }
}
```

Now our environment is ready to build functions, so let's make a really simple application to test our environment.

7. With our new code, we need to tell the application to run a script when the application is run. In the existing package.json, add the following reference to the code to call the Functions Framework and pass a target function:

```
{
    "name": "lab01_FF",
    "version": "1.0.0",
    "description": "Example use of the Functions Framework (FaaS)",
    "main": "index.js",
    "scripts": {
        "start": "functions-framework --target=helloWorldLocal"
        "test": "echo \"Error: no test specified\" && exit 1"
    },
    "author": "Rich Rose",
    "license": "ISC",
```

```
        "dependencies": {
            "@google-cloud/functions-framework": "^1.1.1"
        }
    }
```

Great job; we now have our `index.js` and `package.json` ready to use the Functions Framework.

8. Run the application locally using the standard calling method `npm start` from the command line.
9. Note that, in our example environment, the running application is bound to port `8080` over the HTTP protocol. Open your browser and access this URL, `http://localhost:8080`, to see the output from your application as shown in the following screenshot:

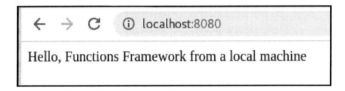

Building code to run locally on a development machine is trivial using this framework. However, how would this scenario differ if we wanted to deploy to the cloud? In the next section, we look at how to deploy code to the cloud.

Deploying an application to the cloud with the Functions Framework

When migrating our local application to a cloud environment, surprisingly, there is little that we need to do in terms of preparation. In this example, I will assume you have already installed and initialized the Google Cloud SDK to enable you to connect and provision resources on Google Cloud.

For the sake of clarity, I will create another function that says something slightly different; however, you can use the same Cloud Function defined in the code created previously:

1. In the `index.js` file, create a second function named `helloWorldCloud`.

2. Give this new function the attributes as defined previously; however, we will use a different message to illustrate that a different function is called:

```
exports.helloWorldCloud = (req, res) => {
    res.send('Hello, Functions Framework from a Google Cloud
project');
};
```

3. Save the new content for the application and test to ensure it continues to work as per the previous run.

4. Run `npm start` from the command line. Remember, the only thing we have changed in this iteration is the code base.

5. Running the `npm start` command allows us to browse to `localhost:8080` and see the message from our application.

6. Now we want to run our code base in the Cloud by deploying the Cloud Function. For this instance, we rely on the Cloud SDK to get our code running in a Google Cloud project. Run the following command:

```
gcloud functions deploy helloWorldCloud --runtime nodejs10 --
trigger-http --region us-central1
```

7. To confirm that the information created from the source uploaded successfully, take a look at the running Cloud Function source code. Here, we can see it includes the same source code that has been archived and uploaded to Google Cloud. However the resulting display is showing the message specifically relating to our new function.

At this point, we now know how to deploy code to our local environment and also to a Google Cloud project using Cloud Functions. But what exactly are Cloud Functions for and what can it do? In the next section, we go into some further details on the relative benefits and use cases for this service.

Exploring the Cloud Functions workflow

So, it seems like Cloud Functions are pretty useful, and together with the Functions Framework, it would appear to be a match made in heaven. Besides, the overall approach seems very extensible, and working with other products and services within Google Cloud seems greatly simplified. So, if you are already in *team Google Cloud*, using Cloud Functions is a no-brainer.

For those of you who are not in *team Google Cloud* or may be sitting on the fence, there is more to this story. Serverless is a general term that has taken some critical feedback over the years. For most folks, serverless relates to the lack of requirement-driven infrastructure management when deploying code. For others, it means, services being available immediately and being capable of achieving sizing appropriate to the needs of the application used, with the ability to self-heal.

Depending on your perspective, Cloud Functions may or may not meet your needs. The main concern that people highlight is the time taken to deploy code. *Why isn't the function available immediately?*, *Why is the memory constrained?*, and so on – *When I use provider X, the services are available immediately, the memory isn't constrained, and they serve tea and cakes for every deployment!*

So before we go into the details on Cloud Functions, it feels like a good time to bring up what is happening behind the scenes as we deploy our code to the cloud. Google has laid out an excellent architecture in terms of mapping out the leading products regarding capability for a data processing pipeline. The data life cycle is useful from an architecture perspective as it outlines the produce available to render specific aspects of your pipeline. In terms of the common topics of ingestion, storage, processing, and analytics, this approach provides an exciting way to break down the component architecture.

So how do you create a function? Let's examine this in the next section.

Cloud Function properties

As discussed earlier, Cloud Functions provides support for several runtimes on Google Cloud, including Node.js, Python, Go, Java, and Ruby. Getting started with Cloud Functions is as easy as accessing the Google Cloud console and selecting the most appropriate runtime. Each runtime includes template code that presents the blueprint for a primary Cloud Function plus all the ancillary system code necessary to get an example up and running in no time.

A key consideration for code is how much time an algorithm will take to process and how much this matters. For example, if the algorithm is part of the UX, then any delay in processing will likely be noticeable to the end user. Asynchronous code permits long-lived processing actions to be offloaded from the main thread and executed in the background. Taking this action is key to maintaining performance across the application space as it provides the ability to delineate between resources requiring fast or slow responses.

Besides, as you are now aware, functions are generally stateless applications that should not persist any information. As a general rule, this means that the service utilizes a short life-cycle in which data processes and the task comes to an end. To minimize potential latency reduce long-lived request and response cycles, by using asynchronous calls within code.

For stateful applications, the need to maintain information presents an issue in terms of the potential latency associated with the persistence of data. It should be clear that anything requiring the read/write cycle outside of memory will introduce some level of delay. Trying to minimize this delay presents an interesting design problem that ultimately depends on what you want to give up and to what degree you want to move away from the performance, loose coupling, data design, and so on.

To call a function, the event notification mechanism on Google Cloud is a trigger. The trigger is an important consideration when starting out developing a Cloud Function. Design of a function does require some thought to determine what pieces are needed to deliver a suitable model. As an event-driven architecture, there are some options available, as indicated in the following table:

Trigger	Event	Destination
HTTP	HTTP	URL
Cloud Pub/Sub	Topic	
Cloud Storage	• Finalize/create • Delete • Archive • Metadata	Bucket
Cloud Firestore	• Write • Create • Update • Delete	
Google Analytics for Firebase	Log	Log Event Name
Firebase Authentication	• Create • Delete	

Firebase Realtime Database	• Write • Create • Update • Delete	Database
Firebase Remote Config	`remoteconfig.update`	

In addition to the runtime, there are also additional properties included when commencing creating a Cloud Function. Memory allocation is an essential consideration as the expectation is that the processing performed exists in-memory. Cloud Functions provide memory allocation from 128 KB to 2 GB that can be adjusted by the developer based on the requirement of the application developed.

Before moving onto the more general options, it's worth having a brief overview of authentication and how this relates to Cloud Functions.

Authentication

The default authentication for Cloud Functions represents public access; that is, it can be accessed by anyone, anywhere. From the Cloud Functions configuration screen, select **Allow unauthenticated invocations** to create a publically exposed endpoint. The `allUsers` IAM setting provides public access assignment to the service account associated with the Cloud Function. An invocation of a function relies on the association of a service account. A service account is a particular account used for non-interactive access, as in the entrance is for another computer rather than a human. The user account is assigned role permission, and this is bound to the service. By default, Cloud Functions binds an `allUser` permission, but alterations before and after the creation of a function are possible.

Note that the initial function designation allows adjustment through IAM settings. This approach brings Cloud Functions into line with other services on Google Cloud. Later in this book, Cloud Functions security will be discussed, and it will cover the configuration of service accounts concerning Cloud Functions to limit privilege.

For now, let's move on to the options available regarding accessing the source versions for a function.

Source control

Working with source code presents many challenges. Thankfully, Cloud Functions provides several options to integrate source code. The Cloud Functions source code can be accessed from the sources such as those outlined here:

- **Inline editor**: Create and amend the function code in the Google Cloud Console.
- **ZIP upload**: Upload a local ZIP file to an intermediary staging Cloud Storage bucket.
- **ZIP from Cloud Storage**: Use an existing ZIP file located in a Cloud Storage bucket.
- **Cloud Source repository**: Use source version control.

For a quick bout of development, the inline editor can be quite useful; however, it will probably make more sense to use one of the many other options when writing more intricate code. In most instances, you can continue to use your favorite editor and upload code with whichever method meets your needs.

Knowing how to upload source code takes us nicely onto the next topic, that is, selecting a language runtime.

Working with different runtime languages

Throughout the next few paragraphs, we will outline the baseline functions using Node, Python, and Go, and discuss the high-level differences between the various runtime languages.

Node.js

Our discussion begins with Node.js (v10). In this template code, we can see that the actual function consists of a couple of lines of code. In terms of Node.js, the exact flavor is Express.js. Express.js is a concise framework that works in conjunction with Node.js to enhance functionality through additions such as routing middleware and HTML rendering.

Looking at the following example code, we can see a function definition based on `exports.helloWorld`. The `exports` keyword indicates the function executes (that is, exposed as a callable function) once deployed. Note also that the service to be exported takes two parameters mapped to the HTTP request and response values.

The default Google Cloud Function written in Node.js is illustrated as follows:

```
1. /**
2. * Responds to any HTTP request.
3. *
4. * @param {!express:Request} req HTTP request context.
5. * @param {!express:Response} res HTTP response context.
6. */
7. exports.helloWorld = (req, res) => {
8.     let message = req.query.message || req.body.message || 'Hello
World!';
9.     res.status(200).send(message);
10.};
```

The body of the function examines the request made to determine the addition of a query message or message body.

Reviewing the Express.js documentation tells us a bit more about the access requirement for the message assignment statement. For a GET message, we understand that a query can pass additional data to the function.

If not, the default message of `Hello World` will be returned in the message variable. Next, `res.status` is set to the value of 200 and the message variable added to the response. Remember from the previous discussion on HTTP response codes that a 200 represents a successful transaction.

Python

The current revision of Python supported on Google Cloud is version 3.7. From the example code, what we do not see is that the Flask package handles HTTP communication. At first glance, there is undoubtedly a lot more code present than in the example for Node.js.

To start, we define our function and can see an immediate difference in the naming convention. In Python, we have named our service `hello_world`, which is different from the sample Node.js template. Feel free to change the name to be consistent, but it does not ultimately matter. Ensure you use the correct name for the function to execute, as this can be a frustrating error to fix:

```
def hello_world(request):
""" Responds to any HTTP request.
    Args:
        request (flask.Request): HTTP request object.
        Returns:
        The response text or any set of values that can be turned into a
```

```
        Response object using
        `make_response
        <http://flask.pocoo.org/docs/1.0/api/#flask.Flask.make_response>`.
    """
    request_json = request.get_json()
    if request.args and 'message' in request.args:
        return request.args.get('message')
    elif request_json and 'message' in request_json:
        return request_json['message']
    else:
        return f'Hello World!'
```

In the body of the function, we can see a call to return a JSON object. Similar to the Node.js Cloud Function, we check the argument for the message to indicate if we are to override the default message. To cover the bases, we again ensure this example works for both GET and POST messages. Finally, if the user has not added a message in the required format, we return the default message of Hello World!.

Go

Go is currently supported on Google Cloud for version 1.11+. As you would expect, the revision compatibility is maintained as each version is released, so the recommendation is to maintain compatibility with newer versions.

In the following example code, we import some packages to enable our application to perform the necessary access to HTTP and JSON. The function signature remains the same with request and response arguments, both used as an entry point to the function.

For the body of the function, our code will default to a standard message if the program does not provide one:

```
// Package p contains an HTTP Cloud Function.
package p
    import (
        "encoding/json"
        "fmt"
        "html"
    "net/http"
)
// HelloWorld prints the JSON encoded "message" field in the body
// of the request or "Hello, World!" if there isn't one.
func HelloWorld(w http.ResponseWriter, r *http.Request) {
    var d struct {
        Message string 'json:"message"'
    }
```

```
    if err := json.NewDecoder(r.Body).Decode(&d); err != nil {
        fmt.Fprint(w, "Hello World!")
        return
    }
    if d.Message == "" {
        fmt.Fprint(w, "Hello World!")
        return
    }
    fmt.Fprint(w, html.EscapeString(d.Message))
}
```

Working with Cloud Functions, we see that irrespective of the runtime language chosen, many of the properties are shared nonetheless. In terms of languages, we also observed the different forms of example code used for Node, Python, and Go.

In terms of coding our functions, looking for design patterns will help us to avoid reinventing the wheel. We know a bit more about the available language runtimes and have seen an example of the boilerplate code associated with each one. To test the function, we would need a triggering event, and, in the next section, we will discuss an approach to this situation.

Testing the runtime triggering event

To test the function, we can craft some data with which to confirm the success criteria of our service. Again, Cloud Functions can assist with this task by allowing the entry of JSON data to be passed directly to the function at runtime in the testing window:

1. A typical URL for a cloud function will resemble syntax of the following link. Hitting the endpoint will access the default information associated with the Cloud Function:

   ```
   https://[REGION]-[PROJECT].cloudfunctions.net/[CLOUD-FUNCTION]
   ```

2. For the template code, we can supplant a new message by adding some additional information to the URL, as follows:

   ```
   https://[REGION]-[PROJECT].cloudfunctions.net/[CLOUD-FUNCTION]?mess
   age=Yo%20Gabba %20Gabba!
   ```

   In this example, the `req.query` property returns an object with information, in this case, a message to be displayed in place of the default `Hello World!`.

3. If you go ahead and run this function without entering any additional parameters, a message of `Hello World` will be displayed and a response code of `200` generated. Triggering the event in this way is similar to accessing the function URL directly, in that no additional information will be incorporated into the query:

Message	Triggering Event	Output	Response return code
1	{}	Hello World!	200

4. Alternatively, by adding some parameters to the triggering event, we can output a specific string when running the function.

Message	Triggering Event	Output	Response return code
2	{"message":"Yo Gabba Gabba!"}	Yo Gabba Gabba!	200

In the preceding example shown, the triggering event has a JSON string added. In this instance, the output to the function changes to display the string entered earlier. As before, the return code generated is `200`.

Being able to test an application is fundamental to any developer workflow. However, it is just as essential to be able to reference the logs and application-specific information for monitoring purposes. To achieve this on Google Cloud, we use Stackdriver.

Stackdriver

Each time traffic reaches the endpoint, information relating to the Cloud Function will be captured automatically in Stackdriver. If you are not familiar with Stackdriver, it is a centralized logging and monitoring system for Google Cloud. We will discuss Stackdriver in greater depth later in the book in `Chapter 10`, *Cloud Run Labs*; however, for the time being, it is essential to know that this is where to access real-time information for a function. To search for function execution, use a filter in Stackdriver, as follows:

Field	Example content
resource.type	cloud_function
resource.labels.function_name	function-1
resource.labels.region	us-central1
labels.execution_id	4ubpvdgz7c8w

The determining factor for which runtime language to use will largely depend on your personal experience. I have used Node.js throughout this book as it is very accessible. The interface is straightforward and efficient and doesn't take too much head-scratching to understand the code. Of course, you may have your personal favorite, and, hopefully, similar packages are available in those runtime languages.

Working with the boilerplate code is the beginning of your journey, so do not be afraid to experiment with different approaches and techniques. In the next section, we provide an overview of the HTTP protocol.

Understanding the HTTP protocol

In the context of our discussion on Cloud Functions, it is essential to consider how the HTTP protocol works—learning the necessary foundation of the API to enable communication between request and response.

HTTP verbs, such as GET, PUT, POST, DELETE, and so on, provide the basis for the HTTP protocol to perform its various functions. The design of the contract is one that has generally stood the test of time as more advanced use cases have been more prevalent over time. Typically running over TCP, the protocol requires a reliable medium on which to transmit messages—utilizing a contract such as TCP establishes some level of resilience for the data transmission and acknowledgment when performing machine-to-machine communication. In terms of commonality, GET and POST represent the most common methods used for applications.

In the next section, we provide a quick overview of these methods to understand their use.

Defining GET/POST methods

Accessing a web page typically uses the GET method to gather content stored on remote servers. Whenever you are surfing the internet and looking at the contents of various websites, the HTTP GET method is used to achieve this. The GET method is, at its most basic, an idempotent retrieval mechanism for HTTP. Think about the GET method as a simple retrieval mechanism, that is, *get this information from the remote server*. Sending this command to a remote server tells it to provide a message response.

The GET method also allows query information to be sent to the remote server; however, this information is displayed as part of the URL. The message payload is typically served as a stream of bytes, after which the remote server will close the open TCP connection indicating the completion of the transaction.

When working with web pages, in addition to retrieving information from a website using the GET method, there is also the POST method. The POST method provides the ability to supply additional information as part of the query sent to the remote server. In contrast to the GET method, there is no exposure via the URL of query information, and the request made is non-idempotent. These attributes make the POST method more useful for incorporating information that should not disclose content via the URL and is susceptible to change. A typical use for this type of arrangement is web forms, in which field values are sent as part of the HTTP request query.

Once the request/response cycle has completed, a status code indicating the status of the transaction is returned. In the next topic, an overview of HTTP codes outlines the general categories.

Unmasking HTTP response codes

An HTTP response's three-digit response code indicates the success of the communication performed. These response codes are vital to ensure the smooth running of any HTTP-based application server.

If you have ever needed to configure or maintain a web server, the following information will undoubtedly be very familiar to you:

Return Value	Type	Description
1xx	Information	An informational response code indicating the request was understood.
2xx	Success	The more common method of confirming the success of the request is by returning this status code.
3xx	Redirect	Redirection associated with the client request; typically no user interaction is required as a redirect is automatically enacted to complete the action.
4xx	Client Error	A request-based error that indicates something was wrong with the information sent from the client to the server.
5xx	Server Error	An error relating to the response from the server-side communication has occurred, meaning the request could not be fulfilled.

The full list of HTTP status code is maintained by the **Internet Assigned Numbers Authority (IANA)**. The broad categories associated with the HTTP status code ensure that most situations are catered for when working in this area.

Another area that may be of use in extending your understanding is how to work across domains with web content. In the next section, we'll look at a concise overview of cross-origin resource sharing.

Working with Cross-Origin Resource Sharing (CORS)

Enabling CORS in the HTTP header enables a range of actions to be performed across domains. The addition of this provides an extra capability beyond that of traditional single-domain, client-to-server information exchange. As you would expect of the client, their responsibility is to initiate a request that includes indicating the method and header requirements. From a server perspective, the range of header properties is more numerous, allowing the achievement of a richer set of functionality.

An application may not always be in a situation where execution takes place in the same domain. For these types of situations, there is CORS, and this provides the ability to enable communication across domains:

Client	Server
• Origin • Access-Control-Request-Method • Access-Control-Request-Headers	• Access-Control-Allow-Origin • Access-Control-Allow-Credentials • Access-Control-Expose-Headers • Access-Control-Max-Age • Access-Control-Allow-Methods • Access-Control-Allow-Headers

Finally, we outlined the event-driven triggers associated with Cloud Functions. Looking at the options, it's clear that these triggers are capable of meeting many of the use cases related to building systems. Thinking of events and triggers like *glue* or *lego* pieces is a good metaphor for the use of these components. When it comes to building new components or designing a serverless application, it is often surprising how easy it is to use these building blocks together. But it doesn't stop there – imagine extending beyond Google Cloud to other cloud providers and using their services. Serverless provides a real and exciting disruption to the existing design and application development process. Single-use functions focused on delivering a clean interface with defined inputs and outputs make for a more efficient delivery and maintenance experience.

Working through each of the options, we discussed how each could be used to significant effect when building a serverless application. To achieve this, an adaptive type of architecture requires more than Cloud Functions, for example, when incorporating authentication (via Firebase), proxy access (via Cloud Endpoints), or temporary storage (via Google Cloud Storage). Working with best practices and combining different approaches isn't a one-size-fits-all affair, and you have the ability to utilize both open source and commercial software seamlessly, moving beyond the serverless platform and looking out to the broader aspects of your system. While serverless provides a simple method of achieving scale, introducing network scale in other aspects of your portfolio will still require careful planning.

Summary

In this chapter, we walked through a broad overview of Cloud Functions and where it sits within the Google Cloud Serverless portfolio. Also, we looked at a few tangential aspects that are relevant to the use of FaaS, such as HTTP2 and the data life cycle.

By exploring the runtimes and observing the associated code throughout the chapter, we are now aware of how to structure Cloud Functions in multiple languages. We also are aware of how to test and resolve issues by incorporating monitoring and logging into our development workflow. As you will know, Google provides a full array of tools and services to get you to the point where you can quickly develop a **minimum viable product (MVP)**.

In the next chapter, we will cover some more examples in greater depth. Building an application provides an excellent way to learn the critical elements of a serverless application environment.

Questions

1. What port does Cloud Functions run on?
2. What trigger is used by Cloud Pub/Sub?
3. What runtime languages are supported by Google Cloud Functions?
4. What is the HTTP response code for success?
5. What is the HTTP response code for a client-side error?
6. What is the HTTP response code for a server-side error?
7. What is the purpose of CORS?
8. How is CORS enabled?

Further reading

- **Introduction to HTTP/2**: `https://developers.google.com/web/fundamentals/performance/http2`
- **HTTP/2 for load balancing with Ingress**: `https://cloud.google.com/kubernetes-engine/docs/how-to/ingress-http2`
- **Functions Framework**: `https://cloud.google.com/functions/docs/functions-framework`

5
Exploring Functions as a Service

In this chapter, we will take a deep dive into Cloud Functions on Google Cloud. We have covered a fair bit already; however, there is still so much more to know and learn. Our primary focus so far has been to understand HTTP endpoints and to build some simple applications in order to demonstrate their associated capabilities. In addition to exciting HTTP event functionality, there are also background functions, that is, those functions that do not require access to an external HTTP endpoint.

To increase our understanding of these types of functions, we will be building several tools throughout this chapter to illustrate various concepts and techniques. We will continue to utilize the Functions Framework to create our code, and start to integrate the external system in order to showcase the ease of building a tool that meets our requirements.

Later in this chapter, we will build a simple application based on creating a `SignedURL` function by utilizing Google APIs, which provides a way to establish a time-constrained URL. The source data for this will reside on Cloud Storage, and we will extend our function to have a simple frontend. Finally, we will continue to use the Functions Framework to enable us to work locally and to maintain compatibility with Google Cloud Functions.

In this chapter, we will learn about the following topics:

- Developing an HTTP endpoint application
- Exploring Cloud Functions and Google APIs
- Exploring Google Cloud Storage events
- Building an enhanced signed URL service

Technical requirements

To complete the exercises in this chapter, you will require a Google Cloud project or a Qwiklabs account.

You can find the code files of this chapter in the GitHub repository for the book under the ch05 subdirectory at https://github.com/PacktPublishing/Hands-on-Serverless-Computing-with-Google-Cloud/tree/master/ch05.

 While you are going through code snippets in the book, you will notice that, in a few instances, a few lines from the code/output have been removed and replaced with dots (. . .). The use of ellipses is only to show relevant code/output. The complete code is available on GitHub at the previously mentioned link.

Developing an HTTP endpoint application

Working with Cloud Functions allows isolated and standalone components to create extended functionality. These components or microservices offer an excellent way to build your applications as decoupled architecture. In this example, we will go back to basics and learn how to extend our knowledge to call Google Cloud APIs.

Events provide the ability to react to system notifications associated with a provider. As outlined in earlier chapters on Google Cloud, these providers present multiple options in which to extend services through defined provider interfaces such as Cloud Pub/Sub and Cloud Storage.

We have already looked at the HTTP functions invoked using a URL. Utilizing the same semantic notation (for example, GET/POST) and signature (for example, request/response) for HTTP communications, these types of functions are well understood and can build upon existing knowledge. Due to the abstraction of HTTP complexities over time, the general understanding of the HTTP construct represents a well-understood API.

However, not everything will support an HTTP endpoint; therefore, another approach for integrating providers with existing services is required. Background (that is, asynchronous) functions enhance the Cloud Functions model beyond parameters to establish middleware interfaces that are capable of passing data between disparate components. Examples of these types of providers include Cloud Pub/Sub and Cloud Storage, which both offer a rich interface for messaging and event notifications. In both instances, any data presented must conform to the standard supported schemas to be capable of responding to the provider interface.

Additionally, a trigger needs to be defined in order to invoke background Cloud Functions. However, the integration mechanism changes depending on the trigger used. Over the following sections, we will focus our discussion on the different types of triggers available on Google Cloud. For background functions, Cloud Pub/Sub and Cloud Storage will be the primary areas of discussion; however, there many other trigger types that are available for an application.

Triggering Cloud Pub/Sub

A Cloud Pub/Sub trigger is based on a message queue in which information is passed between the publisher and the subscriber:

- The *publisher* is responsible for the schema associated with the message to be propagated using a topic.
- A *topic* indicates the available queue on which information consumption takes place.
- The *subscriber* (consumer) of the message queue can read the associated information in the queue.

It's worth pointing out that, in general, subscriptions are either pull or push subscriptions, as shown in the following diagram:

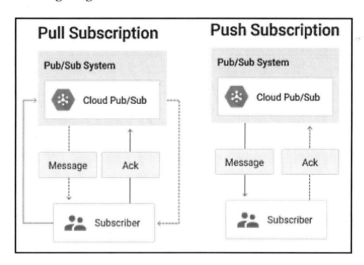

In the preceding diagram, you can see an overview of the pull and push subscription types.

For scenarios that require high levels of throughput, a pull mechanism is currently the most effective way to manage this type of requirement.

Having the publisher and subscriber together enables both sides of the message queue deliver a payload from the origin to the destination. Cloud Pub/Sub uses several scenarios in order to provide information to and from sources consistently. As you might expect, there are many design patterns associated with Cloud Pub/Sub that ensure the transmission of data occurs with a regularity scheduled for the service that is required.

The distribution of messages uses a globally distributed message bus that enables the exchange of information between systems. In this instance, an event system for Cloud Pub/Sub uses a push mechanism with Cloud Functions to trigger messages. A trigger type of `google.pubsub.topic.publish` is defined to manage events used by Cloud Functions, allowing you to have complete control over the publishing of events. For each message published, the notification of the event establishes the message payload to be published.

Besides this, Cloud Pub/Sub supports different design patterns depending on where you want to go. Subscribers will provide an acknowledgment for each message that is processed for every subscription. If a subscriber cannot acknowledge a message within the `ackDeadline` threshold, then the message payload is re-sent. Based on your own use case, the following patterns are good examples to consider when thinking about incorporating Cloud Pub/Sub into your design:

Pattern	Description
Straight-through processing	A simple queue mechanism—from topic to subscription.
Multiple publishers	Multiple publishers of the same topic—this enables the concurrent processing of a source message.
Multiple subscribers	Multiple subscribers to the same subscription—this enables you to have different subscribers for the originating topic consumed through subscription.

An event for Cloud Pub/Sub has the defined trigger value of `google.pubsub.topic.publish`. The event notification is triggered when a payload message publishes to the event type associated with a Cloud Function. Input data will take the message payload that is passed and execute the named Cloud Function to establish data to any subscriber set to receive information.

The following example illustrates how you can use a background function with Cloud Pub/Sub; the blueprint code that is shown represents the default function used by Google:

```
/**
 * Triggered from a message on a Cloud Pub/Sub topic.
 *
 * @param {!Object} event Event payload.
 * @param {!Object} context Metadata for the event.
 */
exports.helloPubSub = (event, context) => {
  const pubsubMessage = event.data;
  console.log(Buffer.from(pubsubMessage, 'base64').toString());
};
```

As you can see, the signature relating to the background function definition remains consistent. We define an `exports` function onto which the trigger establishes a corresponding action. The service related to the event information to be used requires parameters, that is, event payload data and event metadata. In the Cloud Pub/Sub Cloud Functions example, the function will take the input to the message queue and display the content as a log entry.

Creating an event type trigger of the Cloud Pub/Sub type requires a topic to be created as part of the initiation of the function. Once created, testing the service presents the same properties that we saw previously with the HTTP trigger, for example, region, memory allocation, timeout, and last deployment. However, here, the HTTP endpoint is replaced with the trigger type of Cloud Pub/Sub and the associated defined topic.

To test the function, an important thing to remember is that Cloud Pub/Sub expects its data to be formatted as `base64`. Follow these two steps:

1. Transpose the data to `base64` to trigger an event from the Cloud Functions testing page. Thankfully, you can do this from Google Cloud Shell by entering the following on the command line:

   base64 <<< "Rich"

2. The output of the preceding command shows the `base64` equivalent of the text entered:

```
rosera@cypher      ☛ ~/Development/hands-on-serverless-wip/ch05    base64 <<< "Rich"
UmljaAo=
rosera@cypher      ☛ ~/Development/hands-on-serverless-wip/ch05
```

In the preceding example, we need to convert the information using `base64` manually. If you were to use the Cloud Pub/Submenu item or the `gcloud pubsub topics publish` command, both of these tools will automatically convert your text message.

From the preceding, you may discern the raw power of this event type, as it can pass information between multiple services. For example, Stackdriver supports Cloud Pub/Sub interfaces (a Stackdriver sink). Understanding this means that it is possible to use Cloud Pub/Sub to invoke a coupling across services, such as publishing information in Stackdriver and consuming this data in services such as BigQuery or Cloud Storage.

Now that we know a bit more about the power and versatility of Cloud Pub/Sub, we can turn our attention to Cloud Storage.

Triggering Cloud Storage

As indicated in earlier chapters, Cloud Storage is an object data store that has an associated life cycle and event notification. More commonly referred to as a bucket, Cloud Storage adds a highly functional notification mechanism to your arsenal. Having the ability to incorporate intermediary storage into your application opens up greater possibilities, and it provides the means to apply stage gating as part of any processing via the associated event types that are supported. The flexibility of this solution means that it is a useful service to familiarize yourself with, as the storage can be adopted for multiple scenarios.

The typical use cases for storage is that of either temporary storage (that is, where an application might need to store an intermediary file such as audio or text output) or as a cheap form of storage for something like a static website. Later in this chapter, we will present an example for building a simple website that can be used to show information, based on a defined template.

Cloud storage can be used in a number of different ways; however, here, we will primarily focus on using this as storage. Event types focus on the notification of actions such as `finalize`, `delete`, `archive`, and `metadataUpdate`. It should be noted that the notification mechanism for storage leverages Cloud Pub/Sub notifications to ensure scalable and flexible messaging.

Over the course of this section, we will cover a few of the most common use cases for Cloud Storage. In addition to this, the event type mentions that you are still able to retain all the existing benefits, for example, life cycle access, API access, support of different storage classes, and secure/durable storage.

Google provides a wealth of APIs and learning how to access these APIs gives you the opportunity to access different services. Due to the richness of the Cloud Storage API, there are a number of event types that are supported. The most common, perhaps, is the creation of an object within Cloud Storage:

```
/**
 * Triggered from a change to a Cloud Storage bucket.
 *
 * @param {!Object} event Data payload.
 * @param {!Object} context Metadata for the event.
 */
exports.helloGCS = (event, context) => {
  const gcsEvent = event;
  console.log(`Processing file: ${gcsEvent.name}`);
  console.log(`Event Type: ${context.eventType}`);
};
```

In the preceding example, a notification occurs when an *object creation* event is generated from the bucket object. When setting up the function, an essential requirement is to specify a storage bucket on which the action will respond.

Notably, there are several parameters supported that enable an application to derive further information about the state of the calling object. If an event has passed additional metadata, this high-level event metadata (of the type invocation information) is also accessible. Additionally, background functions can utilize other properties, such as data that contains the message to be processed.

A notification emitting from the function has a similar pattern across each of the notification types. This event structure is one that you should aim to become familiar with, as the use of functions is very consistent, irrespective of the kind of service used.

The specific function referenced by the Google Cloud Storage event is captured in the event parameter, which is passed to the Cloud Function when the service is run. The blueprint code listed previously will log the event notification that has been processed along with the name of the file residing within the bucket. Outside, more essential services include additional triggers such as Firebase Authentication. However, the patterns outlined follow for these functions, and it should be a smooth and easy transition to be able to work with any of these other function triggers as they become available:

- Google Cloud Firestore
- Google Analytics for Firebase
- Firebase Authentication
- Firebase Realtime Database
- Firebase Remote Config

At this point, you will hopefully be thinking about how to incorporate some of these trigger types into your application. When working with functions, it is essential to remember that the services should be short-lived and built around lightweight components. Clearly, there are many cases and examples that are both innovative and useful that will show how to use the code in a real-world example. The documentation for Cloud Functions is amazingly detailed and can provide answers to many of the queries you may come across in your implementations.

Later in this chapter, we will be looking at some use cases that utilize these notification types. First, we will look at how to utilize the vast software library of Google APIs.

Exploring Cloud Functions and Google APIs

In this example, we will build an application that will use Cloud Pub/Sub to provide resilient access to a document. Earlier, we introduced our new friend, Google Cloud Pub. Now we will get to see how we can utilize this feature as part of a simple solution.

Our application will create a time-constrained link to a text file, which can only be accessed by an authenticated source. This type of functionality is actually an everyday use case for transferring data securely across the internet.

General architecture

To create a signed URL, we will need an existing file that has been uploaded to a storage bucket. For the sake of this example, we will take the following approach in terms of the types of functions to be developed:

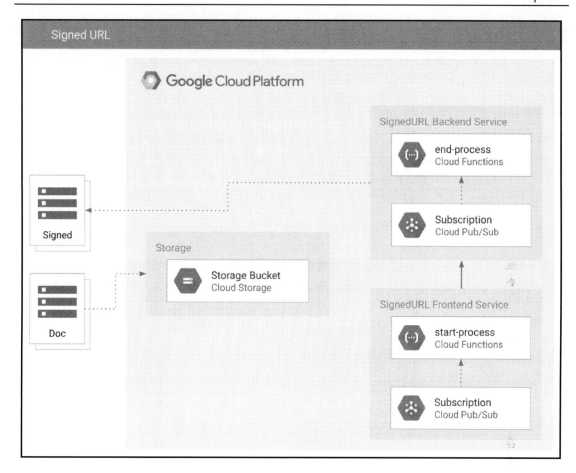

From the preceding diagram, we are going to create two services in order to create a signed URL:

1. **Frontend service**: A straightforward service that will be based on an HTTP endpoint and be made publically available.
2. **Backend service**: A second service that will be used to perform the background function of creating the signed URL.

Let's understand each service in more detail next.

Frontend service

Our primary export function named `gcpSecureURL` accepts a request and response parameters, indicating that this is an HTTP function. This signature is consistent across all Cloud Functions and provides a common way to pass and receive information in an application.

From the architecture diagram previously presented, it should be apparent that our frontend service uses Cloud Pub/Sub. As described earlier in this chapter, we can use Pub/Sub to provide information to our application. In this example, we are using the initial request information and adding this to the message queue of Cloud Pub/Sub.

To start, we need to initialize our environment once more:

1. Create a new directory called `ch05` and make this the current directory.
2. Create a new subdirectory called `frontend-service`.
3. Create a second new subdirectory called `backend-service`.
4. At this point, you will have the following directory structure:

```
.
└── ch05
├── backend-service
└── frontend-service
```

5. Make `frontend-service` the current directory.
6. Initialize the `npm` package for this directory, that is, `npm init --yes`.
7. Then, add the `pubsub` package, that is, `npm install @google-cloud/pubsub`.

In order to process the information presented at the frontend, we need to create a new application:

1. Create a new file called `index.js`.
2. Add the following code to `index.js`:

```
const {PubSub} = require('@google-cloud/pubsub');
const pubsub = new PubSub();

async function gcpCreatePayload(message) {
 const payload = Buffer.from(JSON.stringify(message));
 console.log ('Information passed: ' + message);
 await pubsub.topic('start-process').publish(payload);
}

exports.gcpSecureURL = async(req, res)=> {
```

```
const message = req.query.message || req.body.message || 'google-
cloud.png';
await gcpCreatePayload(message);
res.status(200).send('Creating a secure URL for:' + message);
}
```

The entry point for the code is the `gcpSecureURL` function. Here is an overview of this application's activities:

1. From here, we call the `gcpCreatePayload` function with an example filename, for example, `google-cloud.png`.
2. The `gcpCreatePayload` function performs a single task in order to establish a new topic and publish the filename to it.
3. After this action has been taken, the application will return a 200 HTTP response code and output a message indicating that a secure URL has been created for the filename.

To deploy the function, we take the normal steps for an HTTP endpoint, that is, the following:

```
gcloud functions deploy gcpSecureURL — trigger-http --runtime nodejs8
```

As mentioned previously, we are going to use Cloud Pub/Sub; therefore, we need to create a topic to enable communication to take place:

```
gcloud pubsub topics create start-process
```

Congratulations! The frontend application has been successfully deployed and is ready to serve filenames to Cloud Pub/Sub.

Backend service

Now that we have the frontend service created, what is left to do? Well, so far we have essentially been creating a queue of files to be processed. In this section, we will set about processing the filenames that have been added to the message queue.

Once again, we need to reinitialize our environment—this time, focusing our efforts on the `backend-service` subdirectory:

1. Move to the `backend-service` subdirectory created earlier.
2. Initialize the `npm` package for this directory, that is, `npm init --yes`.
3. Add the `pubsub` package, that is, `npm install @google-cloud/pubsub`.
4. Then, add the Cloud Storage package, that is, `npm install @google-cloud/storage`.

In order to process the information presented at the backend, we need to create a new application:

1. Create a new file called `index.js`.
2. Add the following code to `index.js`:

```
exports.gcpCreateSignedURL = (event, context)=> {
  // Get the file to be processed
  const payload = JSON.parse(Buffer.from(event.data,
'base64').toString());

  // Debug message
  console.log ('Creating a Signed URL: ' + payload);
}
```

In the preceding code, we will take information from a message queue and convert it from `base64`. The information presented should represent the example filename passed. Using a console log message, we can confirm that it has been correctly accessed. Deploy this initial revision of the code in order to check our assumption:

```
gcloud functions deploy gcpCreateSignedURL --trigger-topic start-
process --runtime nodejs8
```

At this point, we now have two Cloud Functions deployed on Google Cloud:

Name	Function type
gcpSecureURL	HTTP endpoint function
gcpCreateSignedURL	Background function

Testing the functions can be done via the Cloud Console using the `trigger` commands. Go to the Cloud Functions option in Google Cloud and select the function for accessing the required command:

1. Select the trigger from the menu and choose the URL associated with `gcpSecureURL`.
2. The function will display the message `Creating a secure URL for: google-cloud.png`.
3. Now select the second `gcpCreateSignedURL` function.
4. From the invocation list, it can be seen that this function has been called.
5. Then, select the view logs options to see the associated log messages.
6. Observe the message, `gcpCreateSignedURL: google-cloud.png`, in the logs.

Congratulations! The `gcpCreateSignedURL` (backend) service has been successfully deployed and is receiving messages from the `gcpSecureURL` (frontend) service.

At this point in the development, we are unapologetically using unauthenticated invocations of our functions, as this makes the development process more straightforward. In a production environment, this approach would be unacceptable. As there are components for both the frontend and the backend, one approach would be to amend the permissions so only the `gcpSecureURL` is able to call the `gcpCreateSignedURL` service. Toward the end of the chapter, we will come to a different conclusion on how to address this particular issue.

Our application is really progressing quite quickly. Now we need to add the signed URL processing capability to our existing `gcpCreateSignedURL` backend code.

To process the information presented at the backend, we need to create a new application:

1. Edit the `index.js` file.
2. Add the following code to the top of the existing `index.js` file:

```
async function gcpGenerateSignedURL() {
  // Get a signed URL for the file
  storage
    .bucket(bucketName)
    .file(filename)
    .getSignedUrl(options)
    .then(results => {
      const url = results[0];

      console.log('The signed url for ${filename} is ${url}.');
```

```
    })
    .catch(err => {
      console.error('ERROR:', err);
    });
}
```

In the preceding code, we make some assumptions regarding the bucket and filename for the purposes of brevity. As you can see, the function performs one task, which is to create a signed URL. Again, we use the `console.log` function for debugging purposes.

Additionally, we also need to add some definitions to our code.

3. Add the following code to the top of the existing `index.js` file:

```
const {Storage} = require('@google-cloud/storage');
const storage = new Storage();

const bucketName = 'roselabs-cloud-functions';
const filename = 'google-cloud.png';

// These options will allow temporary read access to the file
const options = {
        action: 'read',
        // MM-DD-CCYY
        expires: '11-23-2019',
};

async function gcpGenerateSignedURL() {
...
}
```

In the code extract, we need to ensure that the both variables' names `bucketName` and `filename` exist in your project before running the application. In addition to this, **make sure that the expiration date is set to a future date**, taking note of the expected format. We will fix that in a later revision; however, for now, just remember that these attributes are valid for your project.

Finally, we want to reference our new `SignedURL` function within the subdirectory `backend-service`:

4. Edit the `index.js` file and amend the entry point function:

```
...
exports.gcpCreateSignedURL= (event, context)=> {
  const payload = JSON.parse(Buffer.from(event.data,
'base64').toString());
  console.log ('gcpCreateSignedURL: ' + payload);
  gcpGenerateCreateSignedURL();
}
```

5. Based on the preceding enhancements, we are now ready to deploy the updated version of `gcpCreateSignedURL` (that is, the `backend-service`)

```
gcloud functions deploy gcpCreateSignedURL --trigger-topic start-
process --runtime nodejs8
```

To test the newly deployed `backend-service`, we replicate the process that we followed earlier. Go to the **Cloud Functions** option in Google Cloud and invoke the `frontend-service` by pressing the associated URL available in the Cloud Console. Then, observe the logs for the `backend-service` as the information is processed and logs messages.

Congratulations! The logs contain a reference to the signed URL for the file presented. We have covered a lot of important context in this section. Continue to the next section to work on an example using Cloud Storage.

Exploring Google Cloud Storage events

In this example, we want to expand our understanding of background functions. In particular, we will be integrating with Cloud Storage in order to automate object life cycle management.

Taking advantage of existing functionality (for example, packages and libraries) is an excellent way to build your application. In this example, we will leverage Google Cloud Storage encrypted by default to develop a secure data solution.

General architecture

The main difference from our Cloud Pub/Sub example will be the notifications that we attach to Cloud Storage. In this example, we will want the storage bucket to initiate the request to provide a `SignedURL` function, rather than having to invoke our function manually. Remember, in the first version of our application, there was no event notification between the storage bucket and the `frontend-service`—let's fix that:

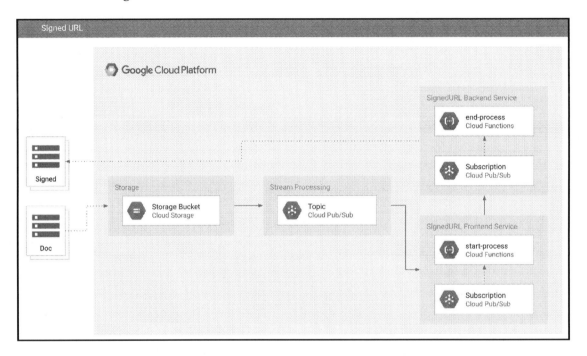

From the diagram, we will introduce an additional service to react to storage event notifications (that is, create/finalize):

- **Storage**: A file is uploaded to the storage bucket.
- **Stream Processing**: A notification is generated as well as a payload containing the filename.
- **SignedURL Frontend Service**: This maintains a subscription to a topic and invokes its function on receipt of a new payload.
- **SignedURL Backend Service**: This performs the background function of creating the signed URL.

We need to make two changes to our existing code to enable this functionality. First, we need to amend the frontend service:

1. **Frontend service**: Amend the code.
2. **Storage service**: Set up a new notification.

Frontend service

As you may have guessed, the signature for a Cloud Storage trigger is different from an HTTP endpoint. Therefore, the code in `frontend-service` subdirectory will require a small amendment to retain compatibility. We need to change our application code so that we can process the information correctly:

1. In the `frontend-service` subdirectory, edit the `index.js` file.
2. Remove the existing `gcpSecureURL` function as this relates to an HTTP endpoint.
3. Add the following code so that the Cloud Storage trigger can be processed:

```
exports.gcpSecureURL = (data, context) => {
  // Get the file to be processed
  const message = data;

  // Create a pubsub message
  gcpCreatePayload(message.name);
};
```

 Note how the signature for `gcpSecureURL` is now using data and context as we are now referencing information from Cloud Storage. Compare this to previous examples that use request and response for HTTP based triggers.

Congratulations! The `gcpSecureURL frontend-service` is now able to accept notifications from Cloud Storage. Let's move on to establishing a suitable trigger for the storage bucket used in our project.

Storage service

To enable the storage service, unlike the previous section, we need to let Google Cloud Storage know that we want to receive notifications. Due to the richness of the API associated with storage, there is also another command that we need to use, `gsutil`.

From the command line, we need to tell our storage bucket which notification event we want to monitor. Besides that, we also want it to inform us when something has happened. Chapter 4, *Developing Cloud Functions*, contains the Cloud Storage triggers that are supported. Specifically, the one relevant to our task is google.storage.object.finalize (that is, the finalize/create activities), which includes the events based on the creation of an object within a bucket:

1. Delete the existing gcpSecureURL Cloud Function.
2. Deploy the frontend function with a trigger based on the bucket resource:

```
gcloud functions deploy gcpSecureURL \
  --runtime nodejs10 \
  --trigger-resource gs://roselabs-signed-upload \
  --trigger-event google.storage.object.finalize
```

 In the above code my bucket is defined as roselabs-signed-upload which is unique to my application. In your project, the bucket should be named appropriately based on your Google Cloud project settings.

3. Upload a file to the bucket. This can be any file you have handy.
4. The gcpSecureURL will now be invoked through a Cloud Pub/Sub notification.

Congratulations, integrating notifications within an application is a huge time-saver. In the next section, we will enhance the function in order to learn how to integrate it with Google Cloud Services.

Building an enhanced signed URL service

In the final revision of the application, we will fix some of the apparent issues with the Cloud Function. The main thing that needs addressing is the hard coding of the bucket reference, filename, and expiration date. One option would be to provide a nice graphical frontend for the application. However—spoiler alert—we won't be taking that approach here.

To conclude the application, we need to correct three things to make the Cloud Function super useful:

1. Filename
2. Bucket reference
3. Expiration date

Small changes can have a substantive impact, and these three things will make the application significantly better. To make the changes, we need to amend both services and pass additional variables from one service to another. Remember, we have previously implemented Cloud Pub/Sub to pass information between our services. Now we need to expand this approach. But will this make the task more difficult? By enhancing the components in turn and discussing the impact it has, we will answer this question as we start our enhancement journey with the frontend service.

Frontend service

In terms of the frontend service, the application currently sends the filename as the payload. However, we are missing a trick here, as the Cloud Storage data object actually includes some really useful information.

Cloud Storage context object:
The following table contains the information associated with a context object.

Object	Field
Context	eventId
Context	eventType

Cloud Storage data object:
The following table outlines the information associated with a data object. As you can see there is some useful information available here that we can use in our application.

Object	Field
data	bucket
data	name
data	metageneration
data	timeCreation
data	updated

Based on the preceding information, much of what we need is available in the data object. In this case, we can pass this object to our message queue for further processing by the backend:

1. Go to the `frontend-service` subdirectory.

2. Amend the `entrypoint` function, which is outlined as follows:

```
exports.gcpSecureURL = async (data, context)=> {
    // Get the file to be processed
    const message = data;

    // Create a pubsub message based on filename, bucketname
    await gcpCreatePayload(message);
}
```

3. Then, amend the `gcpCreatePayload` function as follows:

```
async function gcpCreatePayload(message) {
    // Process a Pub/Sub message - amend to a JSON string
    const payload = Buffer.from(JSON.stringify(message));

    console.log ('Information passed: ' + payload);

    // Pass the Topic and the payload
    await pubsub.topic('start-process').publish(payload);
}
```

Congratulations! The `gcpSecureURL` function is now forwarding the data object to Cloud Pub/Sub. Rather than creating additional potentially complex code, we simply pass data between services utilizing Cloud Pub/Sub messaging.

Backend service

The backend service will not have a data object presented to the `entrypoint` function. Instead of accessing a filename, we need to extract both the filename and the bucket name from the data object:

1. Go to the `backend-service` subdirectory.
2. Amend the `gcpCreateSignedURL` function, which is as outlined as follows:

```
exports.gcpCreateSignedURL= (event, context)=> {
    // Get the file to be processed
    const payload = JSON.parse(Buffer.from(event.data,
'base64').toString());

    // Debug message
    console.log ('gcpCreateSignedURL: ' + payload.name + ' ' +
payload.bucket);

    // Call the function
```

```
            gcpGenerateSignedURL(payload.name, payload.bucket);
        }
```

3. Amend the `signedURL` function:

```
    async function gcpGenerateSignedURL(filename, bucketName) {
        // Get a signed URL for the file
        storage
          .bucket(bucketName)
          .file(filename)
          .getSignedUrl(options)
          .then(results => {
            const url = results[0];
            console.log('The signed url for ${filename} is ${url}.');
            // gcpMessageQueue(url);
          })
          .catch(err => {
            console.error('ERROR:', err);
          });
    }
```

While we are in the `backend-service` subdirectory, we can also fix the hard coded expiration date. One simple way to correct the issue with expiration dates is to add a standard duration for signed URLs. Adding a duration means that we can automatically supply a future date on which the URLs supplied will automatically expire:

1. Go to the `backend-service` subdirectory.

2. Add an expiry date function above the `gcpGenerateSignedURL` function:

```
    function gcpExpirationDate(duration) {
        const ExpirationDate = new Date();

        ExpirationDate.setDate(ExpirationDate.getDate() + duration);
        futureDate = ((ExpirationDate.getMonth()+1) + '-' +
    ExpirationDate.getDate() + '-' + ExpirationDate.getFullYear());

        console.log ('Expiration date: ${futureDate}');

        return (futureDate);
    }

    async function gcpGenerateSignedURL(filename, bucketName) {
        ...
    }
```

3. Amend the `options` object in order to call the `gcpExpirationDate` function:

```
const MAX_DURATION_DAYS = 7

const options = {
        action: 'read',
        // MM-DD-CCYY
        //expires: '11-23-2019',
        expires: gcpExpirationDate(MAX_DURATION_DAYS),
};
```

Rather than adding complex code, we pass the current information provided by Cloud Storage, and that enables our services to take advantage of a complete dataset. Additionally, we now have a set duration for signed URLs, so the process is completely automated from start to finish.

Go ahead and delete the existing Cloud Functions from your project, and delete any content from the storage bucket. We will redeploy our functions one last time. However, this time, when asked whether you want to allow unauthenticated invocations, select **No**:

1. Deploy the updated frontend service:

```
gcloud functions deploy gcpSecureURL \
  --runtime nodejs8 \
  --trigger-resource gs://roselabs-signed-upload \
  --trigger-event google.storage.object.finalize
```

2. Deploy the backend service:

```
gcloud functions deploy gcpCreateSignedURL --trigger-topic start-
process --runtime nodejs8
```

3. Once the Cloud Functions are deployed, upload a new file to the storage bucket.

Once the user uploads a document to the bucket, the automated process takes over. Our functions still work, as they use the service account associated with the project. The Cloud Functions are no longer externally accessible to unauthenticated invocations.

The data object for Cloud Storage provides all the information we need for our service to be completely self-reliant (that is, a filename and a bucket name). With the application now seamlessly passing information between services using a service account, we no longer have to worry so much about the following:

- The security of the Cloud Functions, as a service account manages them
- User validation, as the information in the storage bucket is provided automatically on file upload
- Scaling our function, as the data uses Cloud Storage and Cloud Pub/Sub

Congratulations! The `backend-service` is now using the data object consumed from Cloud Pub/Sub. Before we conclude this topic, please take a minute to consider how flexible our solution has become. We started with a simple requirement, and by making some small incremental changes, we now have a fully automated service. Due to the inclusion of both Cloud Pub/Sub and Cloud Storage, we also have a solution that will scale and has a level of resilience built-in. The architecture maintains loose coupling between the functions, so we can continue to iterate our design without fear of breaking links to components, thanks to the inclusion of Cloud Pub/Sub messages.

Summary

At this point, you should have a reasonable understanding of the general architecture and components provided by Cloud Functions. While the typical use case of Cloud Functions is to use HTTP endpoints, it is also incredibly useful to have background functions (for example, Cloud Pub/Sub and Cloud Storage) available to integrate different services using a standardized interface. Our use of HTTP endpoints and background functions has enabled us to prototype a simple service application to create a `signedURL` function. Building on the knowledge we have gathered over the previous chapters, we have been able to perform the majority of this work from a local development environment.

The Cloud Functions process of developing an application demonstrates how a simple solution can be quick to build and extend. Cloud Pub/Sub requires a message queue to be defined that provides the capability to integrate different services. Being able to decouple the background processing of data allows solutions to be loosely coupled and more open to integration with a broader range of technical solutions. In many instances, Cloud Pub/Sub operates as the glue for Google Cloud, delivering data exchanges between a variety of services. Cloud Storage offers a simple, yet effective, means for users to upload data without needing to expose portals or create complex life cycle management code.

In the next chapter, we will create some general examples to build on the techniques we have learned so far. Our focus will remain on Cloud Functions and building components to whet our appetite for developing a more complete and challenging application. The emphasis of this content will be to provide a more comprehensive series of examples and also cover some of the elements necessary to incorporate Cloud Functions within your portfolio.

Questions

1. What subscription types does Cloud Pub/Sub support?
2. Name three message design patterns for Cloud Pub/Sub?
3. What verbs are associated with HTTP?
4. If I want to have user data accessible in the URL, should I use GET or POST?
5. What Cloud Storage property maintains information on the data content?
6. If my code responds with an error code of 5xx, where should I expect the error to be?
7. Does Google Cloud support OAuth v2?
8. If a Cloud Pub/Sub message is not acknowledged before its deadline, is the message lost?

Further reading

- **Authentication Developers, Functions, and End Users**: https://cloud.google.com/functions/docs/securing/authenticating
- **Using OAuth 2.0 and Google Cloud Functions to access Google services**: https://cloud.google.com/community/tutorials/cloud-functions-oauth-gmail
- **Understanding OAuth2 and Deploying a Basic Authorization Service to Cloud Functions**: https://cloud.google.com/community/tutorials/understanding-oauth2-and-deploy-a-basic-auth-srv-to-cloud-functions
- **Securing Google Cloud Functions**: https://cloud.google.com/functions/docs/securing/

6
Cloud Functions Labs

In the previous chapter, we picked up some useful skills as we built an application to access signed URLs. One of the most common examples is building a website. So we will move on to expand our repertoire by creating a static website-based example database on Marvel Films. By the end of the chapter, you will understand how to enhance the various techniques presented earlier through rich code samples.

In our example, we will look at some tips on how to incorporate data and also take a first look at security in the context of service accounts. Beyond this, we will look at the main components of a static website and how this might potentially be enhanced.
The following topics will be covered in this chapter:

- Building a static website
- Service account security

Technical requirements

In order to complete the exercises in this chapter, you will require a Google Cloud project or a Qwiklabs account.

You can find the code files for this chapter in the GitHub repository for this book in the `ch06` subdirectory at `https://github.com/PacktPublishing/Hands-on-Serverless-Computing-with-Google-Cloud/tree/master/ch06`.

 While you are going through code snippets in the book, you will notice that, in a few instances, a few lines from the codes/outputs have been removed and replaced with ellipses (. . .). The use of ellipses serves to show only relevant code/output. The complete code is available on GitHub at the preceding link.

Building a static website

In the following example, we will be building an application in which our now familiar function baseline code will consume an external data source (based on JSON) and output a view rendered against an HTML template.

Provisioning the environment

We have seen this type of layout used previously in other Node.js applications (for example, Chapter 3, *Introducing Lightweight Functions* and Chapter 4, *Developing Cloud Functions*), so in this chapter, the focus will be on building the code necessary to build our website.

To begin, follow these steps:

1. Make a brand new directory in which to host our code.
2. Within the new directory, initialize the environment by performing `npm init --yes` at the command line to initialize our new development environment.
3. Complete the resulting `package.json` as per the following table:

Field	Response
Package name:	`marvel-website`
Version:	1.0.0
Description:	This is an example website built with Cloud Functions
Entry Point:	`index.js`
Test command:	blank
Git repository:	blank
Keywords:	blank
Author:	Enter your name
License:	ISC

As highlighted in Chapter 4, *Developing Cloud Functions* and Chapter 5, *Exploring Functions as a Service*), to work locally we can use the `functions-framework` package. In addition, we will also need to install the `pug` package for the view template used to render HTML.

4. From the command line, install the necessary packages by issuing the following commands:

```
npm install @google-cloud/functions-framework
npm install pug
```

5. Next, make a couple of new subdirectories to hold `views` and `data` in relation to the function:

```
mkdir data && mkdir views
```

6. At this point, your directory structure should look similar to the following; that is, two files (`package.json` and `package-lock.json`) and three subdirectories (`data`, `views`, and `node_modules`):

```
.
├── data
├── node_modules
├── package.json
├── package-lock.json
└── views
```

Remember that, to use the Functions Framework within your application, you need to alter the `package.json` file to incorporate a `start` property.

7. Edit the `package.json` file and add a reference to the Functions Framework as outlined here:

```
 0 {
 1    "name": "marvel-website",
 2    "version": "1.0.0",
 3    "description": "This is an example website built on Cloud
Functions with Nodejs",
 4    "main": "index.js",
 5    "scripts": {
 6      "start":"functions-framework --target=filmAPI",
 7      "test": "echo \"Error: no test specified\" && exit 1"
 8    },
 9    "author": "Rich Rose",
10    "license": "ISC",
11    "dependencies": {
12      "@google-cloud/functions-framework": "^1.2.1",
13      "pug": "^2.0.4"
14    }
15 }
```

The information highlighted in *line 6* shows the necessary startup command. Take note that the target entry point is called `filmAPI`, which means the exported function in our application will also need to match this signature.

Excellent! We have now created the basic structure of the application. Now we turn our attention to the data source that provides the information to be presented in our application.

Creating a data source

Turning our attention to the data directory, our next step is to create a **JavaScript Object Notation (JSON)** file to store our data. Using JSON is a quick and easy way to create an external data source, as follows:

1. Create a new file in the `data` subdirectory called `films.json`. This will hold our film information.
2. For the first film, add the content in the following table to it.

   To explain the schema used, let's examine the content of the text. The primary construct is an array in which we will create a number of placeholders for an object representing a film. The film object will expose several fields:

Field	Type	Comment
`title`	String	Title of the film
`director`	String	Name of the film director
`release`	String	Release date of the film
`description`	String	General overview of the film plot
`bgImage`	String	URL for the film post

Looking at the JSON file directly we can see how the data will be represented in the file:

 Note the comma at the end of the code block; this indicates we are going to add further content to the file. If we are not adding further content, no comma is added after the film object (see *The Avengers* object for comparison).

```
{
  "movies": [
  {
    "title": "Iron Man",
    "director": "Jon Favreau",
    "release": "2008",
    "description": "Iron Man",
    "bgImage":
"https://upload.wikimedia.org/wikipedia/en/7/70/Ironmanposter.JPG"
  },
```

3. Adding additional content such as `The Incredible Hulk` can be achieved by appending content at the end of the array record:

```
  {
    "title": "The Incredible Hulk",
    "director": "Louis Leterrier",
    "release": "2008",
    "description": "The Incredible Hulk",
    "bgImage":
"https://upload.wikimedia.org/wikipedia/en/8/88/The_Incredible_Hulk
_poster.jpg"
  },
```

4. Add a new record for `Iron Man 2`:

```
  {
    "title": "Iron Man 2",
    "director": "Jon Favreau",
    "release": "2010",
    "description": "Iron Man 2",
    "bgImage":
"https://upload.wikimedia.org/wikipedia/en/e/ed/Iron_Man_2_poster.j
pg"
  },
```

5. Add a new record based on `Thor`:

    ```
    {
       "title": "Thor",
       "director": "Kenneth Branagh",
       "release": "2011",
       "description": "Thor",
       "bgImage":
    "https://upload.wikimedia.org/wikipedia/en/f/fc/Thor_poster.jpg"
       },
    ```

6. Add a new record for `Captain America`:

    ```
    {
       "title": "Captain America: The First Avenger",
       "director": "Joe Johnston",
       "release": "2011",
       "description": "Captain America: The First Avenger",
       "bgImage":
    "https://upload.wikimedia.org/wikipedia/en/3/37/Captain_America_The
    _First_Avenger_poster.jpg"
       },
    ```

7. Finally, add a new record for `The Avengers`:

    ```
    {
       "title": "The Avengers",
       "director": "Joss Whedon",
       "release": "2012",
       "description": "Marvel's The Avengers",
       "bgImage":
    "https://upload.wikimedia.org/wikipedia/en/f/f9/TheAvengers2012Post
    er.jpg"
       }
       ]
    }
    ```

Based on the preceding code, we have created six new records to hold our data in an array. The intention is for the data to work as input for the Cloud Function we are about to create. In the real world, it is more likely that a database would suffice for this type of access. However, in this example, brevity is our friend, and so is JSON!

Now we have created a data source, we will need to implement an onscreen representation to illustrate the information to be displayed.

Designing a frontend

Making a frontend in HTML should not present too much of a challenge as there are plenty of excellent examples available. In this section, we will take our schema and display it onscreen. The template to be used will be created in the `views` subdirectory and will feature in a new file named `index.pug` with the following content:

- Header definition
- Card definition
- Release definition
- Description definition
- Body definition

From the preceding points, let's look into the contents of each section:

1. The header definition uses standard HTML to incorporate style content. In the example, we create a new header style to alter both the font and alignment of text:

```
#message
html
  head
    style.
      .header {
         text-align: center;
         font-family: roboto;
      }
```

2. The `card` definition creates a new style that will visually look like an onscreen card:

```
.card {
   box-shadow: 0 4px 8px 0 rgba(0, 0, 0, 0.2);
   max-width: 600px;
   margin: auto;
   text-align: center;
   font-family: roboto;
}
```

3. The `release` definition creates color and font enhancements:

```
.release {
    color: grey;
    font-size: 22px;
}
```

4. The `description` definition creates enhancements with reference to the color, font size, and padding for any element associated with this style:

```
.description {
    color: black;
    font-size: 18px;
    padding: 8px;
}
```

5. The `body` definition provides the main layout considerations for importing data via the Cloud Function:

```
body

div.header
    H1 Functions Framework Example
    H3 Google Cloud - Cloud Functions
div.card
    img(src=items.bgImage style="width:100%")
    h1 #{items.title}
    div.release
        h3 Released: #{items.release} <br>
        h3 Director: #{items.director} <br>
    div.description
        p #{items.description}
```

Let's break it down:

Name	Type	Comment
H1	Main heading	The page title
H3	Subheading	A subheading for the page
img	Image link	The URL link for the image
p	Paragraph	Description text

When creating a view, we are using information passed from the Cloud Function to populate the onscreen view. Specifically, we take the title, release date, director, and description from the schema information consumed from the JSON data file.

At this point in our example, we should now have the following directory structure, based on the files created in this example:

```
├──── data
│     └──── films.json
├──── node_modules
├──── package.json
├──── package-lock.json
└──── views
      └──── index.pug
```

We have also created a data source based on a JSON file that holds information concerning films. The methods to add a new movie, remove a film, and alter information relating to a film should be self-evident, and the data file presents a convenient way to manage external data content. Also, the view is isolated from the primary function; thus, as a bonus, the presentation layer acts independently, making alteration easy. Finally, we need to create the service to perform integration between the data and view and generate an appropriate HTTP response.

Analyzing a Cloud Function

The Cloud Function that we've defined doesn't have a significant amount of code associated with it. There are the following elements in our Cloud Function:

- Variable definitions
- The private function
- The public function

To explain the various elements that we've outlined here, let's take a minute to explore each component in a bit more detail.

Variable definitions are as follows:

- **Line 1**: The function starts with a declaration to include our temporary data store in which film information is stored. Again, this is an easy way to incorporate data into an application without needing additional infrastructure to be put in place.
- **Line 2**: Uses `pug` package dependencies and declares them for use within the function:

  ```
  0 // Define dependencies
  1 var data = require('./data/films.json');
  2 var pug = require('pug');
  ```

The private function works as follows:

- **Line 6**: Declares the view to be rendered based on the external view defined in the `index.pug` file
- **Line 11**: Creates the response object based on an HTTP status response code of 200 and an array value based on the item selected by the user when viewing the initial screen:

```
 3
 4 // Function: marvelFilm Detail
 5 // Description: Show the information for the film selected
 6 function filmDetail(req, res, movieRef) {
 7   // Define the view to be displayed
 8   const pugInputFile = pug.compileFile('views/index.pug');
 9
10   // Create the HTML view
11   res.status(200).send(pugInputFile({
12     // Pass data object [movies] to Pug
13     items : data.movies[movieRef]
14   }));
15 }
```

The public function works as follows:

- **Line 31**: A call to the `filmDetail` function passes the request, response, and data objects:

```
16
17 // Entrypoint: marvelFilmAPI
18 // Description: This is the Cloud Function endpoint
19 exports.filmAPI= (req, res) => {
20   // Define the default view to be displayed
21   let filmNum = req.query.film || '00';
22
23   // Translate string to int
24   var movieRef = parseInt(filmNum, 10);
25
26   // Simple validation
27   if (movieRef > 5 || movieRef < 0)
28     movieRef = 0;
29
30   // Display the relevant film
31   filmDetail(req, res, movieRef);
32 };
```

When running the preceding application (that is, `npm start` from the command line), the details of the JSON filmography array will be displayed.

> Note that query string URLs can be used to access information beyond the first film. An HTTP query mechanism like this can be useful when passing additional parameters to sub-components. In this instance, we use these parameters to select alternative pages to be displayed without having to amend the existing function code.

To select another film from the array of available films, use the URL query setting to access any film persisted in the film database, as demonstrated in the following table:

Film	URL
1. Iron Man	`http://localhost:8080`
2. The Incredible Hulk	`http://localhost:8080/?film=1`
3. Iron Man 2	`http://localhost:8080/?film=2`
4. Thor	`http://localhost:8080/?film=3`
5. Captain America: The First Avenger	`http://localhost:8080/?film=4`
6. The Avengers	`http://localhost:8080/?film=5`

> If you are running this from cloud shell, take note that the URL will be different from that shown above. However, you are still able to append query settings, for example, `https://mydomain-dot-devshell.appspot.com/?authuser=0&environment_id=default&film=2` to display the second film.

You will see different pages when presenting different query objects to the application.

This example shows how the GET HTTP verb can be extended through the use of querying parameters. It is this type of flexibility that has made HTTP such a widely adopted approach and outlines the strength of this protocol. Our working example demonstrates how to develop a simple web application using Cloud Functions. The example can, of course, extend to other more intricate use cases. I will leave it to your imagination to build the next big thing based on the accumulated knowledge gathered over the previous chapters.

We will now turn our attention to the crucial topic of Cloud Functions security. In the next section, we will discuss various security techniques that can be applied when working with Cloud Functions.

Service account security

Finally, in this chapter, we will introduce the concept of least privilege with regard to **Identity Access Management (IAM)** and explain how to apply this to Cloud Functions. We will look at some approaches that can secure an application using Cloud Functions.

Later in this chapter, we will discuss service accounts; however, let's take an initial brief look at how to restrict the caller status of the Cloud Functions deployed. Cloud Functions use service accounts rather than a user account to manage services. In this respect, the service account takes on the role of the user without needing an actual human to be involved in the process.

Concerning the user account, each function deployed will be assigned a service account responsible for permissions. The service account is created either manually or automatically; in both instances, the role and permissions need to be defined. When a function deploys, the `cloudfunctions.invoker` permission is typically applied to the service account. This permission provides the service account with the ability to call/invoke Cloud Functions.

Besides this permission, the caller also needs to have the correct authentication for the function. If the default settings persist, then the `allUser/public` interface is bound to the service, meaning anyone can call the function. HTTP functions are typically deployed with the default `allUsers` policy binding, meaning that anyone can invoke the service. In doing this, it enables anyone to invoke our function by using the exposed endpoint. Open access presents a potential vulnerability for our application and needs a solution to mitigate this risk. If you wish to restrict access to the function, limit it to secure account access: for example, `allAuthenticated` or specific users denoted through their IAM account.

Despite a function being available for a shorter amount of time, Cloud Functions are still susceptible to security risks such as malicious code or denial of service.

> Note that, with regard to denial-of-service attacks, Cloud Functions sits behind the Google frontend that is used to mitigate and absorb many attacks on layer 4 and below, such as SYN floods, IP fragment floods, port exhaustion, and so on.

Many different types of vulnerability can be problematic for web-based services. The complexity of this subject means we are not able to provide more than a limited overview of the mitigations in play. There is seemingly an ever-increasing spectrum of potential vulnerabilities, for example, malicious code, denial-of-service attacks, or event resource bottlenecks.

The following section details some techniques to mitigate security concerns with Cloud Functions.

Economic limits

As we are now aware, serverless provides the ability to achieve scalability across the Cloud Functions. However, it may be that a service integrated with Cloud Functions isn't able to cope at these types of level. It is possible to restrict the maximum number of instances available, should such a restriction be applicable within your application.

Applying restrictions against connectivity can ease the burden and prevent a service from experiencing flooding with more requests than can be successfully processed. A threshold setting the available number of instances means that the function can be limited at the point of deployment, as demonstrated in the following command:

```
gcloud beta functions deploy ... \
--max-instances 4
```

In the constrained scenario here, a queuing mechanism is enabled to ensure the constraint applied doesn't impede the processing of information to your service. Limiting the instance threshold is an excellent start to securing service calls. A different variant looks at how to obtain the credentials used to access resources.

Insecure credential storage

Credential storage is an increasingly important topic when attempting to secure various services. Essential credentials (or keys), such as database username/password/publication credentials or secrets stored in code, require a solution that enables this information to be accessible only to authenticated components.

Many industry-based solutions will provide the necessary protections, including Google Cloud **Key Management Service (KMS)**, which supports using Google- or customer-based keys. Also, general products such as HashiCorp Vault provide a similar level of protection for information to be stored securely.

So credentials offer better protection and allow services to be secured. When working with multiple integrated services, how do we manage the workflow to the level of security desired?

Execution flow manipulation

The execution flow essentially outlining how the function workflow for your application. In a scenario where you have multiple functions, there may be an information handoff between components in which they exchange information or provide access to a backend service such as a database.

In this situation, it would not be appropriate for any of the functions in this workflow to be intercepted or accept communications from unauthenticated external sources. To do so would diminish the integrity of the workflow. A situation like this presents a substantive security risk to the application (for example, tainted information).

To prevent this type of vulnerability, we can utilize least-privilege security settings to manage service accounts and establish a per-function authorization mechanism to validate calls. By default, all functions/apps/containers can share the same service identities and have a role assigned, such as project editor. However, identity management can also be set on a per-function basis to establish the least privilege. For Cloud Functions, append a service account to control the function at the point of deployment.

In the following diagram, a service account capable of invoking a Cloud Function is labeled **Function A**:

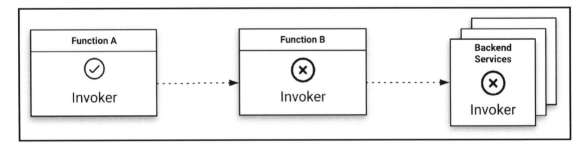

Service account deployment provides a public interface to our other services. We will also create a second service account for **Function B** to manage the backend; this service account will not have invoker privileges and will not be made public. Finally, **Backend Services** do not expose themselves to the public-facing internet. Besides this, they will also be accessible from Function B. An arrangement of this type is relatively common, for example, on a bastion host where the host is internet-facing and only the host has permission to connect with other machines in the estate.

According to Google, a service account is a special account that calls the Google API without the involvement of a user. These computer accounts are an incredibly useful feature and are defined with IAM permissions. We can create a new service account that will provide access to the function by using the following `gcloud` command:

1. Create a service account—`Function A`:

   ```
   gcloud iam service-accounts create publicCloudFunction
   ```

2. Bind a role to the service account that will enable the latter to use the `invoker` role:

   ```
   gcloud functions add-iam-policy-binding SaveData \
   --
   member='serviceAccount:publicCloudFunction@projectid.iam.gserviceac
   count.com' \
   --role='roles/cloudfunctions.invoker'
   ```

   The `cloudfunctions.invoker` role is required to initiate Cloud Functions, and we bind this permission to our new service account. By doing this, our service account can now call Cloud Functions.

   Now that we have created a service account with the necessary permissions, we can deploy our function with the new service account by appending the name of the account.

3. Apply the new service account on deployment of the Cloud Function:

   ```
   gcloud functions deploy ...\
   --service-account account-
   privilege@projectid.iam.gserviceaccount.com
   ```

   To complete our example, we will create a second service account associated with our second function. For this service account, we will not apply the `invoker` (`cloudfunctions.invoker`) role, thereby restricting who can initiate the function.

4. Create a service account—`Function B`:

   ```
   gcloud iam service-accounts create saveData
   ```

   As we did with the first service account, we need to bind some permissions. In this instance, we are using Cloud SQL permissions.

5. Bind a role to the service account:

```
gcloud projects add-iam-policy-binding projectid \
--member='serviceAccount:saveData@projectid.gserviceaccount.com' \
--role='roles/cloudsql.client'
```

Finally, we can deploy the function with the recently created service account.

6. Apply the service account to the function being deployed:

```
gcloud functions deploy saveData \
--service-account saveData@projectid.gserviceaccount.com
```

At this point, we have now made simple changes to our application that ensure that the function execution flow works to our advantage. **Function A** is our entry point function and provides a frontend for our application. **Function B** is now only accessible via **Function A**, which secures the execution flow from A to B. Also note that now the **Backend Services** is only available via **Function B**. With the changes specified in the preceding steps, we now have the following layout:

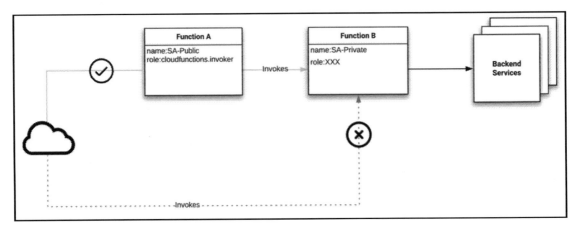

In the final area to be discussed, we'll look at security controls through policy controls.

FunctionShield

Google Cloud Functions also supports third-party solutions such as FunctionShield. With these solutions, strict security controls are employed that ensure the application of a policy to the functions deployed. Specifically, these protections apply to four distinct areas:

- The security policy allows the disabling of egress internet connectivity. Restriction of outbound traffic when not required by the service is a good practice to adopt, as most services will typically only require ingress/inbound traffic to be enabled.
- As previously indicated, Cloud Functions are lightweight functions that are stateless. In this respect, local storage requirements, therefore, should be restricted where possible. FunctionShield can disable read/writes on the `/tmp` directory, typically used for intermediary storage requirements.
- Thread execution for child processes should be minimized and restricted when not required by the function to be invoked. Being able to execute child processes presents a genuine security risk that is difficult to track and trace once initiated without the application of adequate protections.
- Restrict access to the function's source code via the central console. Where the source code has some value or associate **intellectual property** (**IP**), this can be an extra safeguard that applies to the system source code to be deployed.

The FunctionShield solution is a free product that can be deployed to multiple cloud providers, making it a flexible solution we can use to ensure the application of a standard policy within your serverless estate. No function code amendments are necessary to deploy this against your application. A proprietary, behavioral-based runtime establishes protection around the serverless environment. The observability of the cloud functions remains apparent and is available via the standard mechanism: Stackdriver on Google Cloud.

Summary

With this chapter, we have concluded our foray into Cloud Functions on Google Cloud. The last couple of chapters have covered a lot of material on how to develop Cloud Functions. In the first example, we continued on our journey with Cloud Functions to explore how to construct a website based on an external view and data template. In this example, we picked up a couple of tips regarding code organization and dependency isolation.

On completion of the example, we have an easy-to-maintain website that utilizes Cloud Functions to provide a scalable basis for lightweight site access. We learned about the principle of least privilege and how this applies to Cloud Functions. We also learned some fundamental methods that are capable of securing our Cloud Functions by working with Google Cloud service accounts.

At this stage, you should be comfortable building both web applications and services integrated with Google APIs. There is more to learn that we unfortunately don't have the time or space to cover in this book. Cloud Build, GKE, databases, IoT, and third-party services are all possible avenues for further exploration. This concludes our tour of Cloud Functions on Google Cloud. In upcoming chapters, we will turn our attention to the latest iteration of serverless on Google Cloud: Cloud Run and Cloud GKE.

Questions

1. What permission does a Cloud Function require to be invoked?
2. What does Google KMS provide?
3. What does the `allUsers` permission effectively mean?
4. What does the `allAuthenticated` permission effectively mean?
5. What parameter needs to be applied to limit the number of instances available to a Cloud Function?
6. What command allows a role to be bound to a service account?
7. What command is used to create a service account?
8. What is a bastion host and why is it useful?

Further reading

- **Google service accounts**: https://cloud.google.com/iam/docs/service-accounts
- **Least privilege for Cloud Functions using Cloud IAM**: https://cloud.google.com/blog/products/application-development/least-privilege-for-cloud-functions-using-cloud-iam
- **Controlling Scaling Behavior**: https://cloud.google.com/functions/docs/max-instances
- **Google Cloud Key Management Service**: https://cloud.google.com/kms/

Section 3: Google Cloud Run

In this section, you will learn about Cloud Run, Google's latest product for the management of serverless workloads. Cloud Run deploys with or without the Kubernetes platform, so the initial discussion focuses on the basics of a non-Kubernetes environment. Here, we learn about containers and some of the supporting developer tools on Google Cloud Platform (for example, Cloud Build and Container Registry). Following on from this, we take a look at how to use Cloud Run for Anthos in conjunction with Kubernetes. Finally, in this series of chapters, we cover the topic of CI/CD.

This section comprises the following chapters:

- Chapter 7, *Introducing Cloud Run*
- Chapter 8, *Developing with Cloud Run*
- Chapter 9, *Developing with Cloud Run for Anthos*
- Chapter 10, *Cloud Run Labs*

Introducing Cloud Run
7

So far in this book, we have discussed many things relating to building serverless technologies in the cloud. In this chapter, we'll look at the latest offering from Google, which provides a stateless environment for your applications. Unlike Cloud Functions, Cloud Run explicitly utilizes container technology to provide a constrained environment for HTTP endpoints. Cloud Functions, on the other hand, provides an opinionated view of serverless workloads, for example, runtime language limitations. Cloud Run removes many of those restrictions in order to meet developers where they are. If you follow these things carefully, you will know that containers and Kubernetes are both the top skills any cloud professional can have.

To commence our discussion, we will outline the Cloud Run component architecture. In doing so, we will discuss several topics in order to try and set the scene for Cloud Run. The primary objective of this chapter is to present the supporting technologies. You should take the time to understand the use cases and be aware of how Cloud Run leverages each.

Before moving on to the Cloud Run component architecture, we will lay some of the groundwork in terms of outlining some key technologies. To commence this discussion, we'll start with microservices.

In a nutshell, we will cover the following topics in this chapter:

- Working with microservices
- Working with containers
- Introducing Cloud Run
- Cloud Run versus Cloud Run for Anthos

Technical requirements

To complete the exercises in this chapter, you will need a Google Cloud project or a Qwiklabs account.

You can find the code files for this chapter in this book's GitHub repository, under the `ch07` subdirectory, at `https://github.com/PacktPublishing/Hands-on-Serverless-Computing-with-Google-Cloud/tree/master/ch07`.

 While you are going through the code snippets in this book, you will notice that, in a few instances, a few lines from the code/output have been removed and replaced with dots (. . .). The use of ellipses is only to show relevant code/output. The complete code is available on GitHub at the link mentioned previously.

Working with microservices

There has been a lot of discussion about the critical benefits of monoliths versus microservices. The possibility associated with creating smaller code packages has apparent advantages in that they are typically easier to debug, more straightforward to integrate, and have a consistent message interface. Those benefits, by themselves, would not be sufficient to warrant a wholesale migration to microservices.

In the following diagram, we're contrasting a typical monolithic software construct to a microservice architecture. The first thing to notice is that the microservice architecture has a lot more component services available. A key point to note is the deconstruction of the single application into the delivery of services focus on business operation. Over the next couple of paragraphs, we will discuss the reasoning behind this approach and how it is beneficial (and highly relevant) when moving to environments such as Cloud Run:

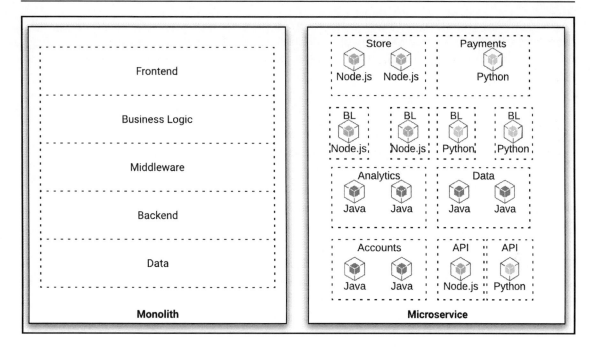

First and foremost, microservices should be autonomous; that is, they provide an isolated and independent component. Providing a standardized interface allows the microservice to participate in the broader ecosystem seamlessly. Ensuring the components achieve inter-component communication provides the basis for building scalable and flexible solutions.

From the perspective of microservices, they typically serve multiple container components that have been deployed within a loosely coupled architecture. Each microservice represents the decomposition of an application into a series of functions. Consider how we focused on building lightweight tasks with a single purpose for Cloud Functions (reference chapters three, four and five). In this conversation, we elevated containers as the artifact of choice. The communication mechanism that's used delivers consistent communication across components in some cases, acting as an **Application Programming Interface (API)**. The use of containers provides a layer of abstraction to ensure compatibility with any runtime language.

Contrast this to a single monolithic application in which tightly coupled constituent components exist. Tightly coupled indicates it would be challenging to pull the various modules apart or create new integrations. Due to the single application structure, the language runtime is typically consistent across the monolith. The inability to use different runtime languages can lead to issues as the best option for the task cannot necessarily be used. Similarly, scaling can also be an issue when incurring specific performance bottlenecks.

The application architecture patterns shown in the preceding diagram are essential considerations since we will be using containers for Cloud Run. In doing so, we'll commit ourselves to continue building lightweight and loosely coupled functions. This will help you to solidify your understanding of building and specific design approaches that are taken while you work through the remainder of this chapter.

Of course, that is not to say that microservices are for every occasion. There are occasions where one size does not fit all. Pragmatically selecting the architecture and the approach lends itself to better-designed applications and increases the skills of the designer. Microservices are far from simple to write and do not give themselves to every occasion. Modeling the services, the correct scope, and the correct content for a microservice is a significant challenge if you wish to deliver the benefits we outlined earlier.

To assist with this process, it is often helpful to consider how microservice design patterns can cater to requirements and help you to build scalable solutions. As you might expect, this subject is both broad and varied and has been covered in many presentations and books to try and define a consensus on the base level of knowledge required for the subject. Since we will be predominantly dealing with HTTP-related communication, we will provide a quick overview of the event processing patterns we will need to consider. These are as follows:

- The asynchronous event processing pattern
- The synchronous event processing pattern

These models are the most relevant types of communication that you will experience.

Asynchronous event processing pattern

While not explicitly called out on the platform, in truth, you will already be familiar with most of the patterns. Asynchronous communication will typically utilize a publisher/subscriber pattern. In this pattern, listeners are activated through an event that they subscribe to. Messages in this partnership are suitable for one-to-many relationships. On Google Cloud, Cloud Pub/Sub provides this service, which is where a defined topic and the subscribers to this topic present information for each matching event on the publisher. A service, such as Cloud Pub/Sub, will need a model like this to provide an asynchronous communication pattern that's suitable for streaming information.

In a situation where a batch-oriented or one-to-one communication flow is desirable, a job queue pattern is more appropriate. In this (winner takes all) model, a queue mechanism is used to hold information while the queue consumer determines when the information will be retrieved.

Synchronous event processing pattern

It is important to note that, with any design method, the design does not create a perfect situation for every situation. Generalizing code in this way may introduce a need to repeat content/code, and this can sometimes be unavoidable. Focusing on keeping microservices isolated and independent should be the primary focus and you need to accept that there will always be exceptional cases. In the case of synchronous event processing, there are two patterns that you need to be familiar with:

- The request/response pattern
- The sidewinder pattern

For synchronous messaging, an immediate response demand by the calling service delivers the acknowledgment. Most commonly associated with the HTTP model, this pattern is the one most people are familiar with. In this request/response situation, the message is to be consumed as part of point-to-point communication.

An alternative state to manage is one where synchronous communication is to be observed rather than consumed. This is known as the **sidewinder** pattern and can be useful if there are multiple endpoints ready to consume the message. However, only a specific endpoint address can be responsible for the generation of a response.

Before diving into more detail on Cloud Run, we will take a quick tour of containers and explain why they are an essential piece of technology. For this discussion, we will focus on Docker containers; however, it is good to know that other containers exist and offer similar benefits.

Working with containers

While applications can run anywhere, working in different environments has traditionally led to issues in terms of general consistency. Deploying code from one environment to another falls foul of a change that renders it incompatible with the underlying infrastructure. The industry's focus on moving away from a monolithic application to small, integrated components (that is, microservices) has, in general, led to the consideration of generating loosely coupled artifacts.

Traditional development in an environment based on virtualized hardware provides a well-understood platform on which many successful deployments exist. However, the inefficiency of deploying microservice components has meant this approach has become less attractive due to the unnecessary replication of underlying resources:

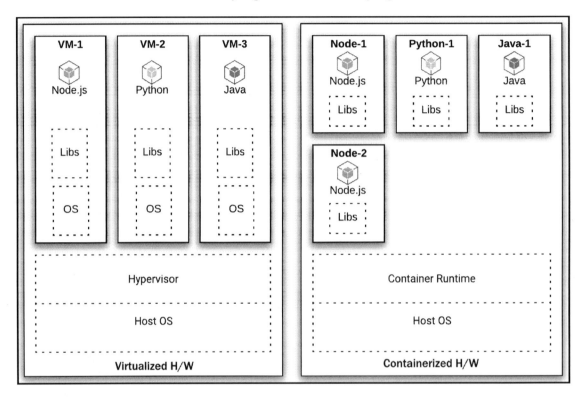

In the preceding diagram, you can see that, with the virtualized hardware, each virtual machine invocation requires replication of resources, both for the operating system and libraries. While virtual machines do continue to provide advantages for large-scale machines, for a microservice-based architecture, a more lightweight approach is desirable.

Containers provide access to the underlying hardware through a shared resource model. An approach such as this, which allows the host hardware to share its existing resources among the containers, is more desirable. Through the use of containers, the host can allocate its resources to the container that will be executed in this environment. If you are working in an environment that utilizes microservices, it is likely that this environment is looking to deliver the efficiencies associated with containers.

Consistently building these components is only half the story; how do you ensure the artifact remains consistent across each deployment? For this, we use containers to define a software package in which we can control the environment (for example, memory, disk, network, filesystem, and so on). The underlying cloud environment utilizes the existing filesystem to create a partition that enacts isolation specifically for your container. So, rather than installing applications directly onto a host, we can install the container and run this on our host. Since the application exists in the host, any incompatibility is likely to be platform-related. A consequence of this is that your application can now provide consistency between deployments.

In the next section, we will go through a lightning-fast overview of Docker and how to use it with Google Cloud. In this discussion, we will cover the basics so that those of you who are unfamiliar with containers can get up to speed.

Leveraging Docker

One of the most common ways to enact containers is by using the Docker container runtime. Docker provides all of the advantages of containers. It presents a simple interface that you can use to manage your application while it's running inside a container. For the sake of brevity, our discussion will focus on using Docker in a Linux environment. However, keep in mind that other options exist and can be just as effective.

In general, the container has three main elements to consider. Primarily, containers utilize a base image that an application is run on. The base image represents the operating system that the application will run on, for example, Debian, Ubuntu, or Alpine. Also, dependency packages for the base image will need to be installed to ensure the environment can achieve compatibility with the application. Packages are typically compatible libraries that are applied to the container, such as SSL, cURL, and the GCloud SDK. Finally, there is command execution, which indicates what runs at the point of execution. The addition of an entry point defines what happens when the container runs.

As we mentioned previously, containers are an excellent way for us to isolate application functionality. However, they also offer an elegant means to define a signature for your application. You may be wondering what I mean by this. Imagine we have an application running inside a container. The image is built using a file that is used to define the environment that the application should run in. In this context, an image represents the executable package and holds the necessary dependencies for the application. By going through the necessary process, we have isolated our application requirements into a transportable environment (container image). Doing this is extremely powerful. But that's enough theoretical discussion—let's build something.

The base element we will start with is the manifest. A manifest represents the image specification, including the application to be created. This environment incorporates a base image (for example, Scratch, Alpine, Ubuntu, Debian, and so on) denoted by a FROM statement. Choosing a base image is a topic in itself, but note that the more lightweight an image is, the easier it will be to deploy the workload.

In addition to the base image, we will also incorporate the packages and libraries that are necessary for the task at hand. If you are working with a modern language, you will potentially have this information already as they will have been installed locally (thank you Node.js). If you are making an image from someone else's application, this is the part where relationships become frayed. In our example, we won't be installing any additional packages; instead, we will be using the existing capabilities of the base Alpine image.

Finally, in our configuration, we will set out what our image should do when the application container starts. The ENTRYPOINT command indicates invocation when the container starts up. The CMD label indicates the parameter to the entry point. Note that this configuration is being used to allow the image to be extended so that it can print other messages. It is highly recommended to read up on the usage of both ENTRYPOINT and CMD as they can save a significant amount of time when it comes to processing commands.

At the end of this process, you will have a manifest file that incorporates each of these elements. For the sake of our example, we can create a simple Dockerfile. Follow these steps to do so:

1. Create a Dockerfile manifest file:

```
FROM alpine
ENTRYPOINT [ "echo" ]
CMD [ "Hello, welcome to Docker!" ]
```

If we were to build the preceding manifest, it would take the instructions we laid out and create an image based on each of the manifest lines. Consider the previous statement for a moment and what that means for us; we have built a host machine for a single application based on a file.

Looking at the preceding manifest content can tell us a lot about the requirements of the application and little about the execution. From the manifest, we can reference the base image (that is, OS), the dependencies (that is, libraries/packages), and the command to be run (that is, the application to be run). The next step would be to run the build process to turn this manifest into an image that is representative of the information contained in the file.

Building a Docker image is managed through the command line. Turning a manifest into something useful means we need to generate an image. The build process goes through each line of the manifest and adds it to the final image. As the build process is running, each line will create an archive layer that represents the command executed. Using the example manifest presented earlier, we can build an image for our application.

2. Build the Dockerfile manifest file:

    ```
    docker build -t hello-docker:1.0 .
    ```

    In the preceding command, we're telling Docker that we want to create an image by initiating the process with the verb build. Docker will, by default, assume there is a local file named Dockerfile present in the current directory. If you wish to use an alternative manifest naming convention, you can, for example, append -f [FILENAME] to the command line, in which case you would need the following command which is technically equivalent to *step 2*.

3. Build a manifest file named myDockerfile:

    ```
    docker build -t hello-docker:1.0 -f myDockerfile .
    ```

    Following the build parameter, we tell Docker to label the images by using the -t [label] command. In this example, we have provided both the name and version to be applied to the image that will be generated.

 It is considered good practice to incorporate a revision of all of the images that are created.

Finally, we indicate where the new image will find the manifest by adding a period (full stop) to the end of the command, indicating that the local directory contains the source information. You can replace this with a more specific destination if you wish to.

Running the preceding command will initiate the Docker tool that will be used to build the local manifest. On successful completion of this process, we can confirm that a new image is present on our machine by asking Docker to list the available images.

4. List the images that are held locally:

    docker images

    Here, you can view how the output looks:

```
rosera@cypher    ~/Development/hands-on-serverless-wip/ch07/hello-docker    docker images
REPOSITORY          TAG               IMAGE ID            CREATED           SIZE
hello-docker        1.0               95b6d18f162c        11 seconds ago    5.59MB
alpine              latest            e7d92cdc71fe        2 weeks ago       5.59MB
rosera@cypher    ~/Development/hands-on-serverless-wip/ch07/hello-docker
```

From the resulting list, we will see that our image has been successfully created and is now available to access. In addition the latest alpine image has been downloaded and used as the base image for your new image. Congratulations—building an image from a manifest is a great thing and increases your general understanding of a range of subjects. For reference, containers are images that run on Linux subsystems and share the kernel of the host machine. In this respect, we can see that containers provide a lightweight mechanism for running discrete processes on a host.

Now that you know how to build an image, we can move on to running a container on the host. A point of confusion when starting with containers is switching between the terms image and container. For reference, an image references a non-running container. Once the image is running, it is a container. These terms are used interchangeably all of the time, but now you know the difference. Please don't lose any sleep over this.

To run a container on our host, we need to tell Docker which image we wish to initiate and state the parameters that are necessary for the application to run. At a minimum, we need the Docker command that will be used to launch a container on the host.

5. Run the image:

    docker run hello-docker:1.0

    Here, you can view how the output looks:

```
rosera@cypher    ~/Development/hands-on-serverless-wip/ch07/hello-docker    docker run hello-docker:1.0
Hello, welcome to Docker!
rosera@cypher    ~/Development/hands-on-serverless-wip/ch07/hello-docker
```

In the preceding command, we're using the verb, `run`, to indicate to Docker that we want to initiate an image. Note that, at this point, the image's location (that is, local or remote) is not important. If the image is not found locally, a remote repository search will proceed automatically. Finally, if the image does not exist locally or remotely, an error will be returned.

Note the preceding application is actually quite useful. If you specify an additional argument, it will print that instead of the default message associated with the command. Try `docker run hello-docker:1.0 "I love working on Google Cloud"`

Earlier in this section, we built our image, meaning it should be accessible to Docker. This process can be seen in the following diagram:

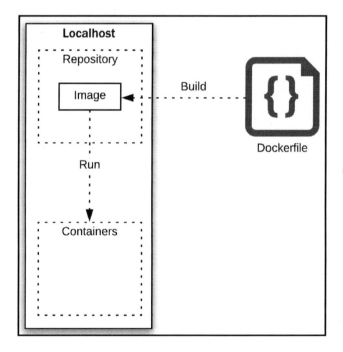

In the preceding diagram, we can see a container, which has a running state and a container ID assigned to it.

So far, we have performed the following steps:

1. Created a manifest file (for example, a Dockerfile)
2. Built the image from the manifest
3. Run the image to create a container

Hopefully, all of these actions are clear to you, and you can see how straightforward it is to incorporate Docker within your development workflow. As the container is running on the host machine, it is sharing its resources with the host. To confirm that the Docker container has been started successfully, you will need to use the Docker process command to list all the running containers.

6. List all the Docker processes available on the host:

```
docker ps -a
```

The ps command option relates to the process that's initiated by the Docker application. In this example, we want to see all of the active containers on the host. Being able to track which processes are currently running on the host is very important. In the preceding command, we're listing all of the processes in the Docker namespace. Doing this allows us to see what is active on a host and gives us valuable insight into the dynamic process that's occurring on the host. Running operations on a localhost doesn't come without a price. The machine resource state that holds the active containers will need to be stopped to restore the machine's overall resources.

Going back to the topic of microservices, in this example, I am outputting information to the screen. It may be more desirable to not output the status on the screen for a majority of situations. Unless you have a genuine requirement to output the status (that is, it's a frontend HTTP application), try and avoid providing feedback via the screen. Sending information directly to the logging infrastructure is a more scalable approach. In the upcoming sections, we will work on more sophisticated examples that require specific network ports to be exposed and information to be written directly to the logs. Adopting this best practice at the earlier stages of using containers is an excellent habit to get into, and minimizes any potential rework associated with removing screen content.

Before releasing the resource associated with the container, take a minute to observe the logs that have been generated by the running application. To do this, we need to use a specific command and insert the actual container ID for the active process.

7. Show the logs associated with a specific container:

```
docker logs <CONTAINER ID>
```

Accessing containers logs in this way is a great strategy if we wish to investigate what is happening during the active life cycle of a container. In an instance where runtime information is not available as a direct output, Docker can be used to ascertain what is happening in the application so that any errors that occur can be addressed. Now that we have examined the properties of an active container, we should look at how to release resources.

To stop an active container, we need to use a specific command that will halt the active process from running. Entering the following at the command line will stop the active container from running on the host.

8. Stop the container running on the host:

```
docker stop <CONTAINER_ID>
```

In the preceding command, the container identifier is the one that was presented by the ps command that we initiated earlier. Whenever Docker requests an identifier, it is more than likely referring to this helpful reference title to distinguish it from the active component. Once the container stops, the associated resources for our simple container example will be released back to the host machine. Now that you know how to build and invoke an image, we can look at how to increase our productivity by introducing two developer tools: **Google Cloud Build** and **Container Registry**.

Populating Container Registry

In the previous section, we provided a high-level introduction to Docker and containers. In this section, we will expand on this discussion by looking at Google developer tools and how these increase developer productivity.

Before we continue, let's outline our assumptions for this section since there are going to be some dependencies. First and foremost, your environment should already have been set up to use the GCloud SDK and should be pointing to a valid project on Google Cloud. Also, the Docker application should be installed and capable of building images.

The following diagram shows a typical development environment:

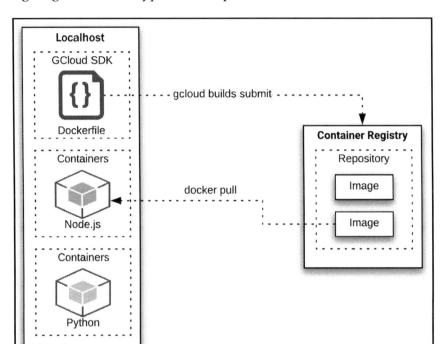

As you can see, rather than using a local repository, we have defined a remote repository based on **Google Container Registry (GCR)**. The remote registry replaces the use of Docker Hub for Google-based projects and gives us access to a multi-regional repository. In this example, we will use a simple manifest to build a small image and populate the Google Cloud Repository. Let's get started:

1. Create a Dockerfile manifest file:

```
FROM alpine
ENTRYPOINT [ "echo" ]
CMD [ "Hello Container Registry Repo!" ]
```

From here, we can initiate a local build to test the manifest file using the default Dockerfile, which is available in the build directory.

2. Build the Docker image:

```
docker build -t hello-docker:1.1 .
```

The first difference in this process is populating the repository based on the build output. The manual path to achieve this is by tagging the image with the identifier for the repository endpoint. We need to apply a `tag` to indicate that the created artifact resides in GCR. We do this by appending the `gcr.io/[PROJECT_ID]` label. This will tell the GCloud SDK to use the US repository and a particular Google Cloud project.

3. Tag the Docker image:

```
docker tag hello-docker:1.1 gcr.io/[PROJECT_ID]/hello-docker:1.1
```

Now that the image has been labeled correctly, we can push the image to the remote repository on Google Cloud.

4. Push the image to GCR:

```
docker push gcr.io/[PROJECT_ID]/hello-docker:1.1
```

At this point, the locally held image will be pushed to GCR and hence be available remotely. Remote repository image access requires a `pull` command to be used if we wish to retrieve it on the localhost. It is essential to note that authenticated access uses IAM to control access (even if you make the repository public).

5. Pull the image from GCR:

```
docker pull gcr.io/[PROJECT_ID]/hello-docker:1.1
```

Looking at the preceding example, it is clear that this process is incredibly similar to building and using the Docker Hub repository. Images that are stored locally will require storage, which means where disk space is tight, remotely hosting your images is a worthwhile endeavor. As we learned earlier, Docker images are very flexible and the convenience of remote repositories provides for more flexible deployment strategies.

Looking at remote repositories and how to populate Container Registry has taught us that it involves some additional steps. Fortunately, Google has created a versatile tool named Cloud Build that helps to remove some of that effort.

Using Cloud Build

To enhance the build process, tools such as Cloud Build can help us to build more sophisticated scripts for the creation of images. Cloud Build is a developer tool that doesn't get much fanfare, but it is beneficial for things such as offloading and automating mundane tasks such as building images. In terms of image creation, the images that are built will reside in Google Container Registry and be maintained within a project-bound repository. Information that's stored in these repositories can be declared public or private on an individual basis, which establishes a simple but effective way to manage the images that are generated by the build process.

Cloud Build is incredibly straightforward to integrate into your development workflow. The package is described as a language-independent manifest that is used to script the desired automation flow. Some key features of Cloud Build to consider are as follows:

- Native Docker support
- Supports multiple repositories (for example, Cloud Source Repositories, Bitbucket, and GitHub)
- Custom pipeline workflow
- Customized package support (for example, Docker, Maven, and Gradle)
- Local or cloud-based builds
- Package vulnerability scanning

Now, we are going to use some of these tools to build our images and add them to a remote repository hosted on Google Cloud. To start, we will update our example manifest once more and amend the message's output via the command parameter. Let's get started:

1. Create the Docker manifest file:

   ```
   FROM alpine
   ENTRYPOINT [ "echo" ]
   CMD [ "Hello Cloud Build!" ]
   ```

   When using Cloud Build, we no longer directly call Docker from the command line. Instead, to build the artifact, it uses the GCloud SDK command to create an image on the remote repository. The default Dockerfile needs to be present locally and should be used as the basis for image creation.

2. Initiate the build process based on the Docker manifest file:

   ```
   gcloud builds submit --tag gcr.io/[PROJECT_ID]/hello-docker:1.2 .
   ```

An additional option that starts to show the value of Cloud Build is that we can also create a file that will be responsible for automating the build process. Creating a `cloudbuild.yaml` file allows the developer to specify a series of steps to perform as part of the build process. The arguments for this process include a rich set of functionality that goes beyond Docker. It is highly recommended to investigate this at your leisure. In the following example, we're essentially replicating the `docker` command to build our image and tell it to hold the output in the Cloud Repository. The `images` line denotes the label associated with the build artifact. On completion, a new version (that is, `hello-docker:1.3`) is created and available on Container Registry.

3. Create the Cloud Build manifest file:

```
steps:
- name: 'gcr.io/cloud-builders/docker'
  args: [ 'build', '-t', 'gcr.io/$PROJECT_ID/hello-docker:1.3', '.'
]
images:
- 'gcr.io/$PROJECT_ID/hello-docker:1.3'
```

To build the preceding file using Cloud Build, we need to run the following from the command line.

4. Build the image with Cloud Build and submit the image to Google Container Registry:

```
gcloud builds submit --config cloudbuild.yaml
```

In the preceding example, we outlined a simple way to incorporate a Docker manifest into Cloud Build. There are a variety of ways in which you can enhance this model so that you can include more sophisticated options that can be combined. For now, that's all we need to cover in terms of establishing a Docker workflow. Having enhanced our general understanding of Docker and some of the development tools associated with Google Cloud, we will turn our attention to Cloud Run.

Introducing Cloud Run

Cloud Run (and Cloud Run for Anthos) is a container-based serverless technology. A distinct advantage here is that containerization is a widely adopted approach. Being able to package your application as a container and then subsequently migrate it to a fully managed serverless environment without any additional work is a desirable proposition.

When working with any technology, it is always good to have an understanding of the constituent parts. In this respect, Google Cloud has chosen to base its technology on several open source technologies that the community can contribute to. Underestimating the ability to move between cloud providers occurs frequently. When developing an application, an important consideration is how that product/service technology can be adapted and the support it will receive.

Beyond the fundamental proposition of running containers in the cloud, Cloud Run provides a fully managed, serverless execution environment. Similar to both App Engine and Cloud Functions, Google have predominantly done all of the heavy lifting in terms of infrastructure management. I say this mostly due to the inclusion of Cloud Run for Anthos, which requires the addition of a Kubernetes (Google Kubernetes Engine) cluster.

Building full-stack serverless applications is a reality right now, and the tools and patterns that allow you to take advantage are within your grasp. Integrating with other services and platforms should not require significant code rewrites. Similarly, moving between different products and cloud providers should not present an issue when they're based on standard components and compatible architectural platforms.

Before we continue our discussion of Cloud Run, we'll turn our attention to some key features that are used to enable this flexible serverless environment.

gVisor

The gVisor open source project provides a sandboxed runtime environment for containers. In this environment, the containers that are created are run against a userspace kernel in which compatibility exists through the use of the **Open Container Initiative** (**OCI**) runtime specification. Intercepting application system calls provides a layer of isolation so that interaction can occur with the controlled host. The central tenet of this approach is to limit the system call surface area to minimize the attack radius. For a container environment, being able to exploit kernel space provides access to the host machines. To reduce the possibility of that eventuality, gVisor seeks to restrict this access and limit untrusted userspace code. As shown in the following diagram, a sandboxing technique is used with gVisor to provide a virtualized environment for application execution:

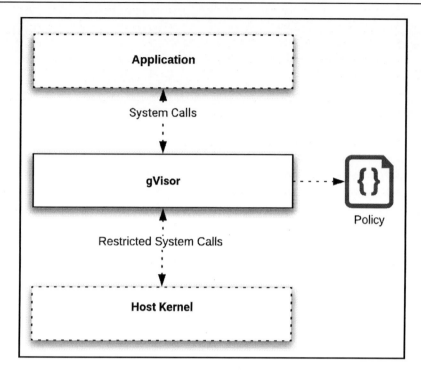

As we can see, the system calls from the application get passed to gVisor, and it is here that it's determined whether they're permissible or not. Restricting the system calls via gVisor means permission is only given to verified access at the **Host Kernel** level. An approach such as this is described as defense in depth, meaning multiple layers are used to provide increased isolation from the host.

Establishing an environment such as this allows us to run untrusted containers. In this instance, gVisor limits the possible interactions with the host kernel through the use of an independent operating system kernel. The beauty of OCI makes this type of integration possible and establishes an elegant way to interchange solutions such as Docker and gVisor seamlessly.

Knative

To begin our discussion, we'll delve into what Knative provides and then follow this up with an overview of the components within the project. Knative delivers APIs for close integration on the Kubernetes platform for both developers and operators. I would highly encourage further reading in this area to achieve greater insight than what would be possible given the brief synopsis provided in this book.

Knative offers a multifaceted solution for the Kubernetes platform by providing a series of components. These components are responsible for many standard aspects of working with a platform, such as deployment, routing, and scaling. As you might expect with something associated with Kubernetes, the components offer compatibility across both frameworks and application tiers, making it relatively simple to incorporate into any design:

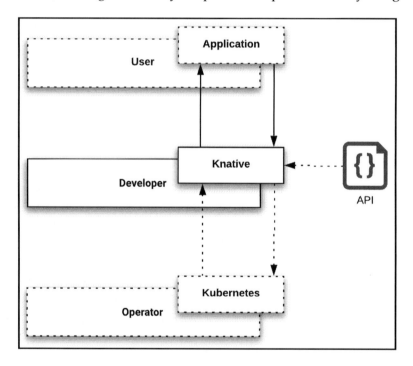

In the preceding diagram, we can see that different persona are involved in a Kubernetes workflow. Operators are typically responsible for infrastructure maintenance. Developers focus on creating application workloads that reside on the platform and interact with the API. It is at this level that Knative allows developers to deliver greater efficiency for their applications.

Discussions of Knative typically describe it as middleware since it sits between the Kubernetes platform and your application. Earlier in this chapter, we looked at microservice design patterns; Knative is essentially a fully realized expression of this approach for serverless workloads. In this relationship, two primary components are essential to the discussion, that is, Knative Serving and Knative Events:

- Serving relates to access to the **Custom Resource Definitions (CRDs)** that control workload interaction with the underlying Kubernetes cluster. The supporting compute resource for this service will be capable of scaling to zero. Note that, on Kubernetes, this relates to the resource, not the cluster. Interaction with the platform API provides us with an opportunity to enact more granular control. In this respect, being able to control elements such as service, route, configuration, and revision is possible using Knative serving. Each element is used to provide specific management of the desired state and communication via the rules put in place.

Knative Serving is capable of abstracting services such as ingress between different environments and cloud providers. By doing this, the interaction between application developers and Kubernetes becomes significantly more straightforward.

- Events follow the notion of producers and consumers in which responsibility is required for shared activities. Enabling the late binding of generated artifacts allows us to incorporate a loosely coupled service that is capable of interacting with other services. The list of event artifacts uses an event registry, thereby allowing a consumer to be triggered without the need to reference other objects. In this respect, the event consumer must be addressable; that is, they must be capable of receiving and acknowledging messages.

While on the subject of Knative, I will briefly mention Istio, which is a service mesh that provides policy enforcement and traffic management, among other things. So, what is a service mesh? A service mesh represents a network of microservices typically deployed on Kubernetes. Istio provides several sophisticated features, including metrics that support the overall management of the mesh network. For serverless workloads that are deployed on Cloud Run for Anthos, Knative, together with Istio, provides an extension to the Kubernetes platform to enable more granular control of the microservice architecture being implemented.

This brief overview of the lower-level components should have provided you with some additional context about the underlying Cloud Run architecture. In the next section, we'll return to the topic of Cloud Run and Cloud Run on Anthos to perform a brief comparison of the products.

Cloud Run versus Cloud Run for Anthos

Fundamentally, Cloud Run is a serverless platform for stateless workloads. For this solution, there is no requirement for infrastructure management. Alternatively, you may have an existing Kubernetes cluster. In this scenario, all of your workloads run from this environment. Additionally, you may need features such as namespacing, control over pod colocation, or additional telemetry. In this case, Cloud Run on Anthos provides a more considered choice. In both instances, the workloads to be deployed remain the same, so as a developer, the associated effort does not increase, despite the apparent differences in terms of deployment platform.

To understand what we mean in terms of Cloud Run/Cloud Run for Anthos, let's start with a diagram. This will help us to observe the technology stack of each so that we can understand the workflow:

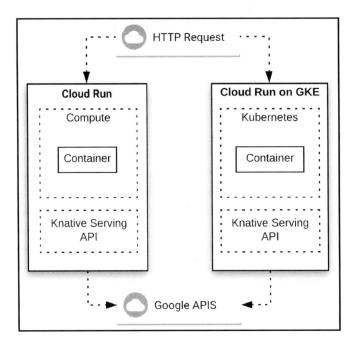

In the preceding diagram, it is clear that there is a lot of commonality between the two forms of Cloud Run. At the forefront of communication is a gateway that's used to consume HTTP traffic. Here, we can route traffic to the underlying product.

At the start of our diagram, we can discern that HTTP traffic is routed to our environment. Traffic to Google environments typically routes through the **Google Front End (GFE)**. For Cloud Run for Anthos traffic, there is additional routing configuration based on a Google Cloud Load Balancer that's active at the network layer (and potentially an Istio gateway).

From the perspective of the container, we can see a crucial difference at this level. The management of the artifact has explicit dependencies, based on which the platform takes precedent. This is a central difference between the compute platform that's used to run the objects. On Kubernetes, the deployment process uses **Google Kubernetes Engine (GKE)**. As we discussed earlier, the container artifact that's deployed uses the OCI to deliver the runtime and image specification. To access the broader services of Google, the Knative Serving API is used to communicate with Google APIs.

We already know that Knative is used to deliver both a portable and extensible API across different runtime environments in support of the development of serverless applications. Utilizing the Knative Serving API to provide portability and access to backend Google APIs is inherent with Cloud Run. Don't underestimate the power of portability, whether you are already reaping the benefits of Kubernetes or still undecided; having a core component to manage the transition seamlessly is a welcome addition. We touched on these high-level aspects of Knative earlier in this chapter; however, incorporating this capability makes for a great platform that we can use to extend applications to take advantage of orchestrated workloads.

Now that we have an understanding of the underlying architecture, we know that there are many moving parts that provide this serverless architecture on Google Cloud. In the next couple of chapters, we will turn our attention to the specifics of Cloud Run and Cloud Run for Anthos.

Summary

In this chapter, we discussed Cloud Run at a high level and introduced the constituent components that make all of this a reality. Just like Google's other serverless products, Cloud Run scales to zero, except here, the deployment artifact is now a container. Utilizing a container artifact provides additional benefits as Cloud Run can be deployed with Kubernetes or without it. In addition, any language runtime can be used, making for a very flexible product.

Familiarity with container environments (for example, Docker) is a real advantage here, but Cloud Run removes much of the complexity of deploying code. Once the container has been successfully built, it can be deployed. Support for serverless request/response messages is inherent in Cloud Run, so there is always a simple and consistent method for developing components. For those of you who weren't previously familiar with containers, hopefully, you now know enough to be able to utilize them.

Over the course of this chapter, we provided a common grounding for working with Cloud Run and containers. Whether or not you believe that containers are the future, they are an important topic to grasp. Now that we have gone through the basics of Cloud Run, we can move on to more interesting projects. In the next chapter, we will continue to investigate this serverless product and build some example projects.

Questions

1. Describe some differences between a monolith and a microservice application.
2. What function does the GFE perform?
3. Name two synchronous event processing patterns.
4. When using Docker, what is the `ENTRYPOINT` keyword used for?
5. What Docker command is used to build an image?
6. Can you name the product that Google Cloud uses for image management?
7. What purpose does Cloud Build fulfill?
8. Why is the Knative API an important component of Cloud Run?
9. What is OCI and what is it used for?
10. Can you name some different operating systems that support containers?

Further reading

- **Migrating monolithic application microservices on GKE**: `https://cloud.google.com/solutions/migrating-a-monolithic-app-to-microservices-gke`
- **Knative**: `https://cloud.google.com/knative/`
- **gVisor**: `https://gvisor.dev/`
- **Istio**: `https://istio.io/docs/concepts/`
- **Google Infrastructure Security Design Overview**: `https://cloud.google.com/security/infrastructure/design/`
- **Google Load Balancing**: `https://cloud.google.com/load-balancing/`
- **Quickstart for Docker**: `https://cloud.google.com/cloud-build/docs/quickstart-docker`

8
Developing with Cloud Run

In this chapter, we'll look into the feature set of Cloud Run. As we saw in `Chapter 7`, *Introducing Cloud Run*, Cloud Run allows stateless containers to be provisioned and run on serverless infrastructure based on Google Cloud. In this chapter, we will focus on working with Cloud Run and how to use some of the available developer tools to develop serverless applications.

Cloud Run is part of a wider ecosystem that provides us with the means to build web services at a wide scale. Interestingly, it can also exist within the Kubernetes ecosystem without changes needing to be made to the artifact configuration. If you have worked with Docker or Cloud Functions previously, much of the environment that supports Cloud Run will be familiar to you. At the time of writing, Cloud Run has just become generally available; however, some of the Google Cloud console components are still in alpha or beta stages and therefore are subject to change.

The following topics will be covered in this chapter:

- Exploring the Cloud Run dashboard
- Developing with Cloud Run
- Building a **Representation State Transfer (REST)** API
- Developer productivity

Technical requirements

To complete the exercises in this chapter, you will need a Google Cloud Project or Qwiklabs account.

You can find the code files for this chapter in this book's GitHub repository, under the `ch08` subdirectory, at `https://github.com/PacktPublishing/Hands-on-Serverless-Computing-with-Google-Cloud/tree/master/ch08`.

While you are going through the code snippets in the book, you will notice that, in a few instances, a few lines from the code/output have been removed and replaced with ellipses (. . .). The use of ellipses is only to show relevant code/output. The complete code is available on GitHub at the link mentioned previously.

Exploring the Cloud Run dashboard

The Cloud Run interface on Google Cloud has several options available. These options relate to the build process and include information such as build triggers and historical views of prior builds. Starting with the Cloud Run dashboard, this menu option relies on the builds that are triggered within the project. At the time of writing, the page is currently undergoing testing, so expect further changes as the product matures:

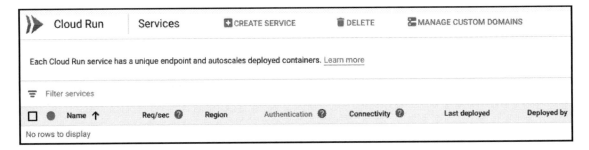

If you are not familiar with Cloud Build triggers, we will cover them in more detail later in this chapter. For now, all you need to know is that they are a way to automatically initiate a build and will be key when you use Cloud Run.

Developing with Cloud Run

At its most basic, Cloud Run allows container-based HTTP endpoints to be spun up and run in the cloud. In the previous chapter, we learned about the basics of how to create containers and build a simple application that was compatible with that environment. Understanding containers allows us to take whatever runtime language we want and make an artifact around our use case. At this point, we will take the opportunity to build our first Cloud Run application so that we can become familiar with both the environment and the product.

In this first exercise, we will call upon some existing code and revisit the static website example (refer `Chapter 6`, *Cloud Functions Labs*. Here, we will explore how we can potentially package an existing application. Remember that, in this example, the application is based on Node.js and incorporates peer dependencies. Let's get started:

1. To commence the project, we will need to retrieve the code from the GitHub repository using following command:

   ```
   git clone
   https://github.com/PacktPublishing/Hands-on-Serverless-Computing-wi
   th-Google-Cloud-Platform.git
   cd ch08
   ```

   The source code for the web application, which was initially built as a Cloud Functions application, will now transition to Cloud Run. First, we will take a look at the compatibility between the two products. It is important to note that we don't need to change the application as this was previously built using the Functions Framework.

2. We have already seen that creating a container requires the creation of a Dockerfile manifest. This example application runs on Node.js; thus, we can take a shortcut and use a preexisting manifest template that is compatible with this framework. Taking this approach means that we don't have to work out which packages are required and can quickly integrate them into our application requirements:

   ```
   FROM node:12-slim
   LABEL MAINTAINER Rich Rose

   # Create a work directory
   WORKDIR /usr/src/app

   # Add packages
   COPY package.json package*.json ./
   RUN npm install --only=production

   # Bundle app source
   COPY . .

   # Export application PORT
   EXPOSE 8080
   ```

3. To establish compatibility with our web application, we need to update the manifest so that it is aware of the application configuration we desire. We will only need to make minimal changes in order to achieve compatibility with our application:

```
FROM node:12-slim
LABEL MAINTAINER Rich Rose

# Create a work directory
WORKDIR /usr/src/app

# Add packages
COPY package.json package*.json ./
RUN npm install --only=production

# Bundle app source
COPY . .

# Export application PORT
EXPOSE 8080

# Create start command
CMD ["npm", "start"]
```

First, we needed to install the peer dependencies (for example, `functions-framework` and `pug`).

4. To install the peer dependencies, run the following command:

```
npm install @google-cloud/functions-framework
npm install pug
```

Doing so means we have these packages available within the image we created. Also, we correctly invoked the application by using the `npm start` command. Other than those changes, the manifest remains a pretty standard Node manifest. These changes are required to mirror the changes we might make when running via the command line.

In the preceding example, one thing to point out is the port that's being specified is `8080`; this is the default network port associated with Cloud Run applications. At the time of writing, I understand that further work is being done to support the use of alternative ports. Once this feature is available, it seems practical that it would be possible to specify the port requirements at the point of deployment. Therefore, the inclusion of this line provides a potential benefit.

5. To build the image, we will be using Cloud Build rather than Docker. We are doing this because we will be utilizing the Google ecosystem to manage our artifacts. Feel free to continue to use Docker to build; you will need to tag and upload your image for the Google Container Registry to do so. As a refresher, Cloud Build allows us to securely perform continuous integration on Google Cloud. This means that the build process can take place either locally or in the cloud. Cloud Build uses the GCloud SDK to initiate builds and post the resulting artifact to the Container Registry. Building our image can be done with the following line, in which we build a Docker image and tag the resource:

```
gcloud builds submit --tag gcr.io/[PROJECT-ID]/hello-cloudrun:1.0
```

Once the build has been successfully concluded, we will be able to see the output of the preceding command in the Container Registry. Holding assets in the repository enables a wide range of sharing options, both internally and externally, in relation to the project.

6. Now that the container image exists, it is automatically added to the image repository. The next step is to deploy the code. This is as simple as referencing the artifact that we stored in our repository earlier. Note that to access the image that's been saved, you need to use the full tag that's been given to the object:

```
gcloud run deploy hello-cloudrun --image gcr.io/$PROJECT_ID//hello-
cloudrun:1.0 --platform managed --region us-central1 --allow-
unauthenticated
```

Once the application has been successfully deployed, it responds in much the same way as a Cloud Functions deployment. The critical thing to note is how little work was required to transition from a Cloud Function to Cloud Run, using a Dockerfile manifest. In this instance, the manifest is straightforward and doesn't require much additional consideration to get it running. At this point, when returning to the Cloud Run console, we can not only see the deployed application but some ancillary information. Let's take a moment to explore this new information.

In this section, we had a brief tour of the Cloud Run interface and looked at the purpose of each of its components. Then, we built a simple container to render information on the screen. By doing this, we can develop our knowledge and skills by creating more compelling examples.

When working with containers and, more specifically, Cloud Run, it is essential to be able to incorporate existing applications. Creating a use case that is both informative and genuinely educational is a hard task, so massive props to the Google Cloud Run team for the PDF example. If you have not seen this example before, I would highly recommend viewing the Next 19 serverless sessions as these perfectly illustrate the ease and power of Cloud Run (reference link):

```
https://www.youtube.com/playlist?list=PLIivdWyY5sqLYz6HIadOZHE9PsKX-0CF8
```

To remove the existing service use the following command:

```
gcloud run services delete hello-cloudrun --platform
managed --region us-central1
```

In the next section, we are going to adapt the example we looked at in this section in order to incorporate additional processing capability. Hopefully, this will highlight both the power and flexibility of the Google Cloud environment.

Building a Representation State Transfer (REST) API

Providing an extensible API presents us with an opportunity to integrate other software into our application. We have already looked at how the building blocks have been put together in terms of developing serverless applications. With Cloud Run, we can expand this knowledge and build extensible interfaces that can expose access to selected parts of an application. If you come from a GNU/Linux background, this will be abundantly clear and something you may take for granted. For others, it can be a moment of clarity where an application allows you to do more than expected. There are times in which we might not even know that an implementation supports an interface that's being used for a task.

For this example, we will build a basic API that uses REST to demonstrate how Cloud Run can be used to meet this requirement. If you have not come across the term REST API, this typically refers to stateless operations, the most common of which are GET and POST. The API uses these operations to retrieve and send information using web resources.

Our first example will build a fundamental REST API that's built on Cloud Run to provide access to backend data. It will have the following components:

- **A basic API**: Used to retrieve retail data.
- **A list of goods available**: The API will be provided with a code and retrieve the associated object information.

From the preceding examples, it should be clear that the API provides us with a simple mechanism that we can use to retrieve information related to the data object. If we were to expand the data object, we would still be able to access this data, without any changes needing to be made to the API—that is, the power of abstracting information access away from the data so that it can be enhanced independently:

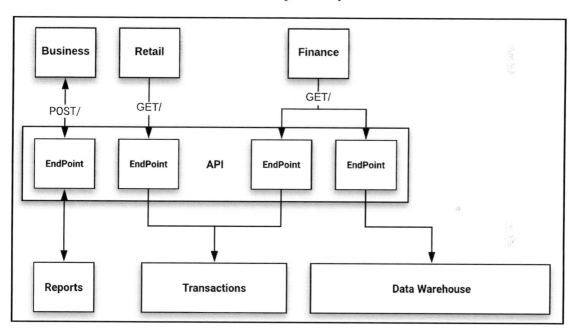

From the preceding diagram, we can see that a number of API calls have been defined that will call the various endpoints. Each of the API endpoints has a specific job; for example, retrieving management reports, handling transactional information, and storing information in the data warehouse. Here, we can see that the **Business Endpoint** uses a post API call, which indicates that information is posted to the endpoint (perhaps a set of filter information) for further processing. Both the **Retail** and **Finance** endpoint calls use GET to pull back information for **Transactions** and **Data Warehouse**.

The following are some general rules that help define good practices when building compelling REST APIs. The key principles we want to introduce are as follows:

- Base URL
- API consistency
- Error handling
- API versioning

To understand the theory and general rules behind this a bit more, we will explore the aforementioned key principles. This will assist us when we design an API later in this chapter.

Base URL

We want the base URL to have significance to the name query. A good starting point is to consider what the base URL is meant to represent and how this can be modeled to be representative of the underlying data.

Requirements

At this juncture in the development cycle, it seems rather sensible to have the means to access all of the data collection. It would also seem helpful to be able to isolate an element within that collection using the same API call.

If we consider these requirements, the need for an intuitive base URL capable of meeting our requirements should become more apparent. In the following diagram, we can see how this API would work with the help of two queries:

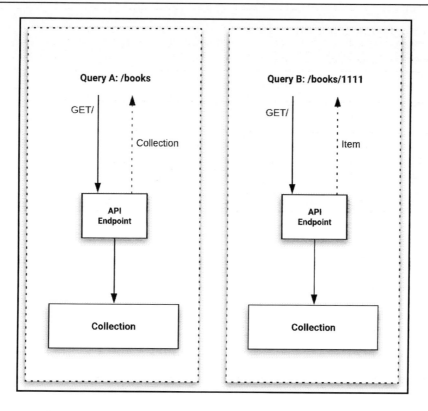

Here, the queries do the following:

- Query A will be capable of gathering all the books stored in the collection.
- Query B will be capable of gathering a specific item from within the collection.

The preceding diagram illustrates a situation in which the base URL encompasses two use cases for data access:

- /[collective noun]: Access to a collection; for example, retrieve all books
- /[collective noun]/[element]: Access to an element within the collection; for example, retrieve the books labeled 1234

Using a collective noun to categorize the base URL allows us to access the full collection and individual items. Now, we have to simplify the base URL; our next consideration is how to achieve greater API consistency. In the next subsection, we will explore how to implement this using Cloud Run.

Implementing a base URL

Our first task is to implement a base URL. Fortunately, in our case, the job is relatively simple; however, it also illustrates the point we are trying to make. Let's get started:

1. Within the ch08 folder create a new directory called baseURL and move to it:

   ```
   npm init --yes
   npm install express
   ```

2. Edit the generated package.json file and add the following line to the script section:

   ```
   . . .
   "start", "node index.js",
   . . .
   ```

3. Create a new file named index.js and add the following code:

   ```
   const express = require('express');
   const app = express();
   const port = process.env.PORT || 8080;

   app.listen(port, () => {
     console.log('Pet Theory REST API listening on port', port);
   });
   app.get('/books', async (req, res) => {
     res.json({status: 'running'});
   });
   ```

4. Create a new file named Dockerfile and add the following content:

   ```
   FROM node:12-slim
   WORKDIR /usr/src/app
   COPY package.json package*.json ./
   RUN npm install --only=production
   COPY . .
   CMD [ "npm", "start" ]
   ```

Working in Cloud Shell provides a number of features that are easy to take for granted. One particular thing is the current project identifier. To get the value of this at the command line, do the following:

```
gcloud config get-value project
```

Even better, you can assign it to an environment variable by doing the following:

```
PROJECT_ID=$(gcloud config get-value project)
```

5. Build an image based on the application (note that $PROJECT_ID is an environment variable that's been set to my Google Project Identifier):

   gcloud builds submit --tag gcr.io/$PROJECT_ID/base-url

6. Deploy the image to Cloud Run. Take note of the SERVICE_URL that's returned from this command:

   gcloud run deploy base-url --image gcr.io/$PROJECT_ID/base-url --platform managed --region us-central1 --allow-unauthenticated

7. Once the app has been deployed, we can test our API from the Cloud Shell using the following command:

   curl [SERVICE_URL]/books

From the preceding code, we can see that to implement a base URL, we need to choose something that complements our API. In this instance, the collective noun books also made for a good base URL.

When considering how to develop a URL, it is worth considering the use case for the API and applying some logic in terms of determining how the schema can be sensibly applied. Now that we have defined our base URL, we can look at how to develop a consistent interface for the API.

API consistency

The aim of API consistency is to simplify access to exposed information:

Resource	POST	GET	PUT	DELETE
/books	Create a new book	List books	Batch update	Delete the book collection
/books/1111	Invalid	Show a book	Invalid	Delete a book

In our example, the collections and elements can be made accessible through the use of HTTP verbs, as shown in the preceding table.

Requirements

From the preceding information, note how the API is used in relation to the HTTP verb. For example, we know the following to be true:

- POST events are used for sending data.
- GET events are used for listing (querying) data.
- PUT events are used for batch updates.
- DELETE events are used for removing items.

How would we use these capabilities in conjunction with our book API? As shown in the preceding table, the API being presented provides a consistent interface for expected outcomes. However, what would an implementation of this look like? We will look at this in the next subsection.

Implementing API consistency

Consistency is something all API developers strive for. To achieve this, we need to consider how the API will be used. In our example, we will update the API to provide a GET request for all the books, as well as a single book. Let's get started:

1. Edit the index.js file.
2. Add the HTTP GET ID:

```
app.get ('/books/:id', async(req, res) => {
  res.json({status: 'GET ID'});
});
```

3. Add the HTTP POST:

```
app.post ('/books', async(req, res) => {
  res.json({status: 'POST'});
});
```

4. Add the HTTP DELETE:

```
app.delete ('/books', async(req, res) => {
  res.json({status: 'DELETE'});
});
```

5. Add the HTTP DELETE ID:

```
app.delete ('/books/:id', async(req, res) => {
  res.json({status: 'DELETE ID'});
});
```

6. Add the HTTP PUT:

```
app.put ('/books/:id', async(req, res) => {
  res.json({status: 'PUT'});
});
```

7. Update the build image by running the following command:

```
gcloud builds submit --tag gcr.io/$PROJECT_ID/base-url
```

8. Redeploy the image to Cloud Run using the following command:

```
gcloud beta run deploy base-url --image gcr.io/$PROJECT_ID/base-url
--platform managed --region us-central1 --allow-unauthenticated
```

Now, we can use the `curl` command to test the enhancements that were made to the API:

HTTP verb	Test /books endpoint	Test result	Test /books/:id	Test result
GET	`curl [SERVICE_URL]/books`	`{"status":"GET"}`	`curl [SERVICE_URL]/books/1111`	`{"status":"GET ID"}`
POST	`curl --data "author=atwood" [SERVICE_URL]/books`	`{"status":"POST"}`	N/A	N/A
PUT	N/A	N/A	`curl -X PUT --data "author=atwood" [SERVICE_URL]/books`	`{"status":"PUT"}`
DELETE	`curl -X [SERVICE_URL]/books/1111`	`{"status":"DELETE"}`	`curl -X [SERVICE_URL]/books/1111`	`{"status":"DELETE ID"}`

From these changes, we can see that the API calls are now consistent in that a call to get an individual book or collection of books utilizes the same interface type. The commonality between interface calls provides continuity between calls so that the API developer is assured of the meaning of the call being made.

Now that we know what makes up an API, let's move on to handling errors.

Error handling

Handling error situations in code can be quite a complex affair. There's a wealth of HTTP status codes, but that doesn't mean an API should use all of them. In many respects, it can be clearer if a subset is used instead to indicate an error has occurred.

Requirements

At a high level, there are three specific outcomes that most definitely need to be mapped, as follows:

- 200: The application is working as expected. Everything is OK.
- 400: The application is not working as expected. A client error has occurred; that is, bad client data.
- 500: The API is not working as expected. A server error has occurred; that is, a bad server process.

This list can be expanded to include a more detailed analysis, but the preceding messages provide a good baseline for any further API development.

Error handling

It is important to have a consistent and clear understanding of the types of errors that are being managed by the API. In our example, we'll adopt the three outcomes we mapped previously. Let's get started:

1. Amend each API call to incorporate the return of a success status call, as follows:

```
res.status(200).json("{status: 'PUT'}");
...
res.status(200).json("{status: 'GET'}");
...
```

2. Add a client- and server-side error response state (note that we don't have any
   server-side resources, so this code is just being used as an example):

```
app.use (function(req, res) {
  if (some_server_side_test_fails)
    res.status(500).send("Server Error");
  else
      res.status(404).send("Page not found");
});
```

By making the preceding code changes, we can see that the status of an API call is more
clearly defined when an appropriate status code is returned. Being able to implement a
clear interface together with a consistent response allows developers to have confidence in
the use of the code that's provided. The final part of this section will cover how to approach
versioning.

API versioning

A good rule of thumb is to always include a version number in the signature of the REST
API to be released. Applying a version number to an API can be useful for managing
defects and maintaining backward compatibility. There are a number of strategies that we
can follow to include versioning within the URL; however, a good place to start is through
the use of an ordinal number to signify the interface, as shown in the following example:

```
/v1/books
```

In the preceding example, we relate the API to v1, which means we can clearly see which
version is being applied for the query. If we introduce a v2 API, again, it is clear to a user of
the API which version is in play without needing additional support. Version changes will
often be made to maintain backward compatibility or signify changes to the underlying
API. Presenting developers with an opportunity to update their code without breaking
existing integrations will be imperative to anyone using the API.

Requirements

We want an API that enables multiple revisions of the API to coexist, like so:

```
(v1/books or /v2/books/1111)
```

If we need to integrate alternative versions of an API, this is one approach that works well.

Express versioning with routing

Of course, we should also include versioning as part of our API. Here, we need to update the code to reflect that the code is based on v1 of the book's API by utilizing an awesome feature of express called **routing**. Let's get started:

1. Copy `index.js` to `bookapi_v1.js`.
2. Edit the `index.js` file and add the following declaration:

   ```
   const apiBooks_v1 = require("./bookapi_v1.js");
   ```

3. Remove all `app.put`, `app.get`, `app.delete`, and `app.post` functions. Your code base should look like this:

   ```
   const express = require('express');
   const app = express();
   const port = process.env.PORT || 8080;
   const apiBooks_v1 = require("./bookapi_v1.js");

   app.listen(port, () => {
     console.log('Pet Theory REST API listening on port', port);
   });

   app.use (function(req, res) {
     if (some_server_side_test_fails)
       res.status(500).send("Server Error");
     else
         res.status(404).send("Page not found");
   });
   ```

Next, we need to update our code so that it references our new book version. Follow these steps to do so:

1. Edit `bookapi_v1.js`.
2. Remove all `app.listen` and `app.use` functions, as well as the `const` port definition.
3. The file should now look like this:

   ```
   const express = require ('express');

   app.put () {...}

   app.delete() {...}
   ...
   app.get(){...}
   ```

4. Add a definition for the express `Router` after the `express` variable:

```
const bookapi_v1 = express.Router();
```

5. Rename all `app.` to `bookapi_v1`.
6. Add the following reference to the bottom of the file:

```
module.exports = bookapi_v1
```

Rebuild the image and deploy it. You will notice that you need to append the version to the URL; for example, `[SERVICE_URL]/v1/books`. Now that the API has been integrated into the query, it is much easier to ascertain which version is being called. As an API matures, it will likely incorporate additional features or replace existing ones. These changes may not always be backward compatible, meaning that API developers need to be made aware of any incompatibilities. Versioning is a good strategy if you wish to manage expectations and gain access to feature sets as the API is developed.

At this point, you should have a really good understanding of the type of things to consider when creating your own API. In the next section, we will look at developing an application using Cloud Run.

Developer productivity

In our second example, we will investigate the development tools that accompany the Cloud Run environment. Creating a PDF is something most of us now take for granted, and it is one of the easiest ways to share documentation. Many businesses utilize a service that sends out invoices or similar information to their customer base.

Similar to Cloud Functions, becoming familiar with the environment and establishing a development workflow can increase your levels of productivity. In this section, we will also take a look at how to integrate other developer tools such as Cloud Run, Cloud Build, Source Repositories, and Container Registry, as these can be hugely beneficial when developing on Google Cloud.

Before we begin looking at the example, let's take a moment to explore a typical development workflow. For many developers, their workflow resembles something like the following:

- Code is held in a repository; for example, GitHub, Bitbucket, or Source Repository
- A build process is initiated

Cloud Source Repository

The Cloud Source Repository is useful if you want to have a private repository for your code. However, it can also be used to mirror public repositories so that code assets are available within your project. Once the repository has been mirrored on Google Cloud, any commits that are pushed will be automatically synced to the Cloud Source Repository. This is important because it means you can continue to use your original repository and not be concerned about any maintenance tasks that ensure the repositories are kept in sync.

Cloud Build

Building source code is a dull activity. Whether it's a small or large component, the process is nothing more than a repetitive loop. Cloud Build, however, can take over this process and free up some of your time. While the main examples focus on building Dockerfile manifests, Cloud Build can actually build many other things (for example commands, `git`, `go`, `gcloud`, `gradle`, `kubectl`, and `npm`). Even better, it can be extended to build other things through the use of open source builders. Community builders are available for Helm, Flutter, and Android, and the list continues to grow.

Build events are triggered by changes that are made in the repository, at which point a predefined series of processes commence. In the Cloud Build history page (also in its alpha stage), access to prior builds is available. The page incorporates a range of fields with representative data, such as Build, Source, Commit, Time/Date created, and the duration of the build. Additional information totaling 13 fields is available, as well as a filter that can be applied to build a report.

The **Triggers** page is where the magic happens; if you have used Cloud Build previously, this page will be very familiar to you. While currently in its beta stage, the page specifies two views for active and inactive repositories, respectively. Active repositories have triggers associated with them, while inactive artifact repositories do not. A typical trigger would be **Push to any branch**, meaning that every addition of new code to a branch within the specified repository will mean the generation of an event. This event is associated with a build process, which enables a wide variety of predefined and custom processing to occur. We will cover more on triggers later in this chapter.

Finally, there is the **Settings** page, which is where service account management details are available. In order to use Cloud Build, you will need the service account to be bound to the permissions within the project. In most instances, the need for additional service account permissions for further access requires IAM. Bear in mind that in addition to screen, the majority of roles can be managed directly from the IAM section of the Google Cloud Console. Previously, we examined some of the core fundamentals of working with containers on Google Cloud. To baseline our shared understanding of this, in the next section, we will start with a simple introduction to Cloud Run and see how we can incorporate this knowledge into further examples.

The continuous integration example

In the following example, we will create an instance in which we will build a development workflow that utilizes a repository and shows how simple it is to create such a workflow in Cloud Build. Let's imagine that some code exists in a repository and that we have a predefined trigger associated with it. Each time code is committed to the repository, a signal will be sent to Cloud Build to initiate the event related to the mirrored repository. In the preceding examples, we saw that a variety of languages are supported. In our case, we will initiate an action that's been defined within the Cloud Build environment that will replace having to start a build process from the local development machine manually. To invoke the automated build, we will have to push code to the repository, as would typically be the case.

Our application is a simple one; the emphasis in this example will be on the tools rather than the code. In the `ch08` directory, change the current folder to be `node-ci`:

```
cd node-ci
```

In the directory, notice that there is a `cloudbuild.yaml` file. It is this file that ensures the build steps are performed. The contents of the file are outlined as follows:

```
steps:
- name: 'gcr.io/cloud-builders/npm'
  args: ['install']
- name: 'gcr.io/cloud-builders/npm'
  args: ['audit','fix']
- name: 'gcr.io/cloud-builders/docker'
  args: ['build', '-t', 'gcr.io/$PROJECT_ID/node-ci:0.1', '.']
images:
- 'gcr.io/$PROJECT_ID/node-ci:0.1'
timeout: "600s"
```

In the preceding example we omit tests as we haven't defined any. However if you want these to be included add the following line:

```
- name: 'gcr.io/cloud-builders/npm'
  args: ['test']
```

Note that three steps are defined in this file, all of which assist with our build process:

1. **Npm package installation**: Installs the dependency packages
2. **Npm audit fix**: Performs a check to see whether the packages can be automatically fixed
3. **Docker build**: Builds an image based on the node application using a Dockerfile

The final line represents a timeout setting for the `cloudbuild.yaml` file and the build max duration. At the time of writing, this is set to 10 minutes. If we were to run the preceding commands, it would output a new build image based on the code given. We can manually invoke the builder from the command line, as follows:

```
gcloud builds submit --config cloudbuild.yaml .
```

However, we don't want to run a `build` command manually; it should be run automatically when we push the code to the repository.

To ensure the repository responds in the way we want it to, we need to add the Google Cloud Build action. Back in the Google Cloud console, find the **Cloud Build** option. From the resulting menu, choose the **Triggers** option:

If you haven't created a trigger before, the screen will look similar to this graphic (if you have existing triggers already configured they will be present in this screen).

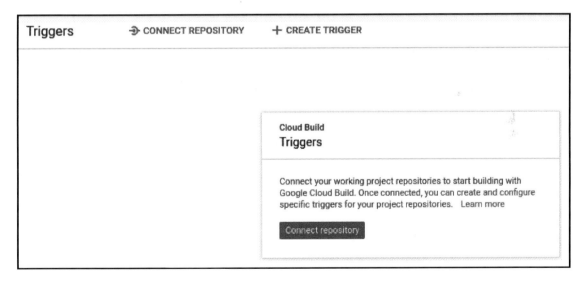

Creating a trigger makes a link between a source repository and Cloud Build. The following graphic illustrates the information required to create a new trigger. The setup for the application is highly customisable, but let's take a base case for our example. First, we need to enable Google Cloud Build in our repository. In this example, note that the source repository being used is GitHub.

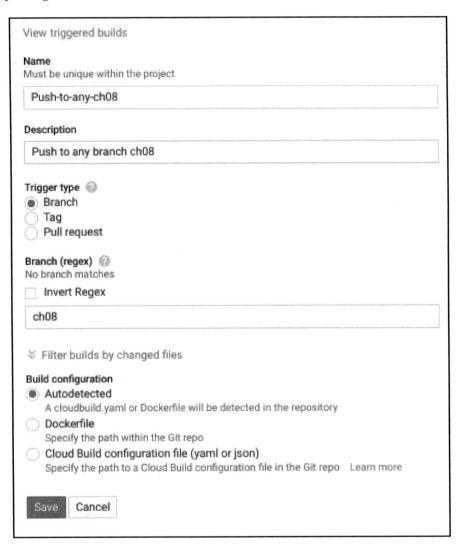

When you add the application, you will be asked for permission to access the repository, as well as which repositories should be granted access. It is important to remember that not all the repositories need to be made available to the application:

●	Build	Source	Commit	Created	Duration
✓	3e282efd	Google Cloud Storage	-	11/7/19, 7:56 PM	31 sec
✓	fdf8fb09	Google Cloud Storage	-	11/7/19, 7:51 PM	25 sec
✓	1a8fd573	Google Cloud Storage	-	11/7/19, 7:48 PM	25 sec
✓	032e6cd4	Google Cloud Storage	-	11/7/19, 7:29 PM	25 sec
✓	045e7749	Google Cloud Storage	-	11/7/19, 7:12 PM	24 sec
✓	8df8e515	Google Cloud Storage	-	11/7/19, 7:08 PM	23 sec
✓	ac5362b4	Google Cloud Storage	-	11/7/19, 7:04 PM	31 sec
✓	8bb60f7b	Google Cloud Storage	-	11/7/19, 7:00 PM	25 sec
✓	5dafbe41	Google Cloud Storage	-	11/7/19, 6:56 PM	24 sec
✓	595e6bc1	Google Cloud Storage	-	11/7/19, 6:39 PM	26 sec
✓	920b4d65	Google Cloud Storage	-	11/7/19, 6:35 PM	30 sec
✓	925cb5b4	Google Cloud Storage	-	11/7/19, 6:33 PM	28 sec
✓	6ff19561	Google Cloud Storage	-	11/7/19, 6:27 PM	24 sec
✓	697ef9e4	Google Cloud Storage	-	11/7/19, 5:12 PM	23 sec

Now that we have granted access, in the Google Cloud, we can use Cloud Build (alpha) to create a new trigger event based on the repository we have just configured. Use the connect repository option and set up the application so that whenever a branch is updated, the trigger will be invoked. The default settings are based on any branch within a repository being updated, but this can be amended to a tag or pull request. In addition, the build configuration can also be changed from implementing the auto-detect feature to using either a Dockerfile or Cloud Build configuration file (YAML or JSON).

Once you have set this up, update the code in order to push a change. You will see the backend code being triggered automatically. Congratulations! You have just become more productive by being able to automatically create an artifact by pushing code. In the next chapter, we will entertain a more intricate example of this workflow with multiple services.

Summary

In this chapter, we looked into the critical aspects of Cloud Run and worked through some everyday use cases. During this process, we observed many essential concepts, such as how to incorporate Cloud Build and Container Registry developer tooling into our workflow. For those of you who were unfamiliar with these tools, hopefully, you now know enough to use them in your day-to-day tasks. Building on our introduction of containerized environments (for example, Docker), we learned how Cloud Run removes much of the complexity of deploying consistent and isolated code. Once the container has been built successfully, it can be deployed. As with Google's other serverless products, Cloud Run scales to zero.

Support for serverless request/response messages is inherent in Cloud Run, so there is a consistent and straightforward method for developing components. Besides, adding a new language runtime can be achieved without distraction or negating the flexibility of the service. By utilizing the container artifact, Cloud Run can easily be enhanced to incorporate Kubernetes.

In the next chapter, we will continue our Cloud Run journey and explore the key differences when working on the Kubernetes platform.

Questions

1. What is a base URL?
2. Why is API versioning important?
3. What verbs would you expect to be available with a REST API?
4. When is it appropriate to return an HTTP status code of 4xx?
5. What is the maximum duration setting for a Cloud Build?
6. Cloud Build can be used for Android (True or False).
7. Where are the errors for Cloud Build shown?

Further reading

- **CI/CD on Google Cloud**: `https://cloud.google.com/docs/ci-cd/`
- **Creating and managing build triggers**: `https://cloud.google.com/cloud-build/docs/running-builds/create-manage-triggers`
- **Creating GitHub app triggers**: `https://cloud.google.com/cloud-build/docs/create-github-app-triggers`
- **Google Cloud APIs**: `https://cloud.google.com/apis/docs/overview`
- **Google Cloud Podcast – HTTP/2, SPDY, and QUIC with Ilya Grigorik**: `https://www.gcppodcast.com/post/episode-6-http2-spdy-and-quic-with-ilya-grigorik/`
- **Container Registry**: `https://cloud.google.com/container-registry/`
- **Serverless Sessions - Google Cloud Next '19**: `https://www.youtube.com/playlist?list=PLIivdWyY5sqLYz6HIadOZHE9PsKX-0CF8`

Developing with Cloud Run for Anthos

9

In this chapter, we will discover how to leverage more sophisticated tools and services to deliver production-level management of the environment. Kubernetes is a wide and intriguing subject that is beyond the scope of this book. However, knowing some of the background and key elements will make the transition to this platform easier.

As per earlier chapters, an introduction to Cloud Run and Kubernetes will cover the key aspects of the technology. In that respect, working through the first section should act as a primer on **Google Kubernetes Engine (GKE)** if you are unfamiliar with the topic. Working with Cloud Run for Anthos provides the ability to utilize many of the benefits of Kubernetes. This chapter will deliver sufficient information to get you started. If you are already familiar with GKE, then feel free to skip the initial section and move on to the specifics of Cloud Run for Anthos.

We will cover the following topics in this chapter:

- Setting up identity and policy management
- Working with environment monitoring
- Creating custom networking
- Establishing domains

Technical requirements

To complete the hands-on exercises in this chapter, you will require a Google Cloud project.

You can find the code files used in this chapter in the GitHub repository for the book under the `ch09` sub-directory, at `https://github.com/PacktPublishing/Hands-on-Serverless-Computing-with-Google-Cloud/tree/master/ch09`.

Identity and policy management

Understanding the identity and policy arrangement on Google Cloud is a major learning curve for most users. Identity Access Management is a major component and could easily be the focus of its own book. In short, IAM provides a policy on a project to provide the relevant permissions associated with roles.

On Google Cloud, administrative management operations are typically performed using a service account. Working with the Google Cloud catalog, the IAM roles are defined to address the needs of users across a wide variety of scenarios.

IAM objects

At a high level, Google Cloud uses a hierarchical structure made up of organizations, folders, projects, and resources to marshal access.

- The organization node is the root node for Google Cloud resources and containers all of the projects and resources.
- Folders are optional, used to group projects under an organization. A folder may contain both projects and other folders. IAM policies can be used to control access to the resources a folder contains.
- Google Cloud resources are always associated with a project. Google Cloud allows you to track resource and quota usage, enable billing, manage permissions and credentials, and enable services and APIs.

The hierarchy defined in the preceding list is combined with members (that is, **users** or **service accounts**) and roles to constrict project access to specific groups based on defined access permissions.

Members

Member accounts are important as they provide access to the organization. Think of member accounts as providing domain access, that is used to determine the actions that can be performed when using the services available in Google Cloud. There are two types to consider when working with member accounts:

- **Member roles**: Permissions given to members through the granting of roles. Roles define which permissions are granted. Google Cloud provides predefined roles, and also the ability to create custom roles.
- **Service accounts**: These allow us to control server-to-server interaction. Typically used to authenticate one service to another and control the application actions that a service can perform, service accounts on Google are referenced by an email address in the `gserviceaccount.com` domain.

Once a member account has been defined, the next step is to assign a role to the member. In effect, this is providing permissions to perform actions within the project.

Roles

On Google Cloud, roles provide a very flexible way to give access to resources. Access in this context is provided as a spectrum in which the range is coarse (in Google Cloud terms, primitive) to fine-grained (in Google Cloud terms, custom) depending on the use case. The three role types are outlined in the following list. In most instances, a mixture of these role types will be used to deliver the type of access required:

- **Primitive**: The least granular roles that existed before the introduction of Cloud IAM. Defined at the project level, these offer a coarse-grained level of access, for example, the **Owner**, **Editor**, and **Viewer roles**.
- **Predefined**: Predefined IAM roles are used to provide finer-grained access control than primitive roles. Each Google Cloud service incorporates predefined roles. These are used to map to a job function, for example, **Compute Network Admin**, **Security Reviewer**.
- **Custom**: Bespoke roles consisting of permissions and resources defined by the user.

Learning the preceding role types will make working with Google Cloud significantly easier, as each project defined will adhere to the structure we've outlined. In the next section, we will look at GKE and see how this can be used in conjunction with Cloud Run.

Overview of Google Kubernetes Engine

Hopefully, you have heard about Kubernetes and understand how important this platform is for the deployment of technical environments. As an introduction for those not familiar with Kubernetes, this section will give you an overview of the key parts.

Kubernetes is an orchestration platform for containers that enables scheduling and maintenance to be performed in an automated fashion by the system, rather than manually by a user.

During the last couple of chapters on Cloud Run, we have discussed the importance of containers. What we haven't spoken about yet is what to do to coordinate this management, once you start to use it, in a more production-friendly way (that is, consistent and reliable).

As you might imagine, containers and Kubernetes are complementary technologies that establish an environment in which applications can be run at scale. The platform itself can be run on a range of Linux servers, including **virtual machines** (**VMs**), cloud instances, and even on bare metal. As an open source project, the pace of development is astounding, as are the quality of contributions.

To use Kubernetes on Google Cloud, we use GKE. This provides a managed environment for Kubernetes. To access the environment, we use a command called `kubectl`, also known as Kubernetes control. Provisioning and maintaining a Kubernetes cluster is beyond the scope of this book, but we will refer to the underlying constructs as we deploy our artifacts to the GKE cluster.

Knowing the use case for a product can save effort in terms of building solutions. At this point, it is worth outlining the key differences between Cloud Run and Cloud on GKE (apart from the need for Kubernetes).

Differentiating Cloud Run from Cloud Run for Anthos

Cloud Run for Anthos provides many of the benefits of Cloud Run. In the following table, we illustrate some of the key differences that a user of the service should be aware of:

	Cloud Run	Cloud Run for Anthos
Billing	Pay per use	Provisioned cluster resource
Machine customization	Memory	Memory, CPU, GPU, networking
URL and SSL	Automatic HTTPS URL	Manual SSL certificates
Identity and Policy	Public, invoker IAM role, CICP	Public or internal

Despite the differences outlined in the preceding table, the services can actually be easily deployed without change via the simple deployment option. Development can be started on Cloud Run. Move to Cloud Run for Anthos where you need the platform resources associated with Kubernetes. There are also a number of features that are shared in common between the two:

- Autoscaling (GKE limited by the cluster in use) for any service deployed.
- Run HTTP-based apps and services easily over TCP port 8080.
- A simple developer experience based on containers using a manifest.
- Select any language, or any library that can be packaged within a container.
- Utilize custom domain names without the need to configure the environment.

Now that we have a general appreciation of GKE, we can move on to apply our knowledge and use Cloud Run for Anthos in the next section.

Using Cloud Run for Anthos

As mentioned earlier, working with Cloud Run for Anthos provides the ability to utilize many of the benefits of Kubernetes. In this section, we will explore some of these capabilities. Let's begin by creating (that is, provisioning) a cluster with access to Cloud Run a GKE environment.

Provisioning GKE

Cloud Run for Anthos requires a Kubernetes cluster. At a high level, Kubernetes provides a platform on which to manage (or *orchestrate*) containers. Outlining the value of Kubernetes is beyond the scope of this book, but it suffices to say it is something that is well worth the investment of time.

To deploy code to Cloud Run for Anthos, there is an assumption that there is a GKE cluster available. Cloud Run for Anthos requires some pre-existing infrastructure to be available prior to deployment taking place. In this section, we will spin up a cluster and then deploy our application to it to explore in what ways the process is different between Cloud Run for Anthos and Cloud Run.

The following example uses Cloud Shell to enter the command line and enable the services needed within a project.

1. To provision a cluster, the **Google Cloud Console** or **Cloud SDK (GCloud)** can be used. For this example, the Cloud SDK will be used so the underlying commands can be seen. Many of the features accessed in this section will reference beta/alpha, as, at the time of writing, this is their current state. As Cloud Run uses Google Container Registry and Cloud Build APIs, these services will need to be enabled within your project. Enabling the relevant `googleapis` can be done via the Console or using Cloud SDK:

   ```
   gcloud services enable container.googleapis.com
   containerregistry.googleapis.com cloudbuild.googleapis.com
   ```

2. Enabling Cloud Run on a cluster with beta status means the general format of the command may change once it moves to **general availability (GA)** status. If you are using Cloud Shell to run Cloud SDK commands, note this environment is automatically updated on a regular basis to incorporate the latest SDK changes. Other environments may need to be manually updated to ensure they have installed the correct components revisions. Here, we are going to store the cluster name and zone to be used, as this information is needed by both the cluster creation and `build` command:

   ```
   export CLUSTER_NAME="test-cluster"
   export ZONE="us-central1-a"
   ```

Note that it is often useful to set some local environment variables to store common parameters as a convenience measure. Ensuring the environment variables are formatted in uppercase text makes them stand out in your command-line scripts. To access the value of a variable, append the $ symbol in front of the variable name—for example, echo $CLUSTER_NAME will display the name associated with the cluster.

3. In the case of Cloud Run for Anthos, the element that is additionally required is the Cloud Run add-on. Our first use of the environment variable will be needed here. To reference this, we add the $ to the front of the variable, for example, $CLUSTER_NAME. To provision the cluster, we use the following command to initiate the environment on which to deploy Cloud Run:

```
gcloud beta container clusters create $CLUSTER_NAME \
--addons=HorizontalPodAutoscaling,HttpLoadBalancing,Istio,CloudRun \
--machine-type=n1-standard-2 \
--cluster-version=latest --zone=$ZONE \
--enable-stackdriver-kubernetes \
--scopes cloud-platform
```

Please be aware that there are restrictions on cluster names, so do check prior to creation that the details used conform. The following restrictions are applied; that is, they must be a match of regex (?:[a-z](?:[-a-z0-9]{0,38}[a-z0-9])?), meaning the following:

- Only alphanumerics and – allowed
- Start with a letter and end with an alphanumeric
- No longer than 40 characters

When the cluster is created, there are a number of parameters we need to supply to the command that will be familiar if you have used GKE previously. A standard cluster requires the following:

- Machine size—compute reference indicating the type of machine to be allocated per node
- Cluster version—signifies the version to be allocated to the Kubernetes cluster
- Zone—the zone in which the compute resource will be created
- Addons—ancillary commands providing additional functionality

During the provisioning process, in the GKE Cloud Console option, there is a more interactive version of the command line that shows what is being performed. However, there is no need to use this over the command other than curiosity.

4. Once the cluster provisioning process completes, it will denote the configuration created. As an option, we can also set the `gcloud` command defaults for the project at this stage:

```
gcloud config set run/cluster $CLUSTER_NAME
gcloud config set run/cluster_location $ZONE
```

5. To confirm the cluster has been successfully created, use the `kubectl` command to interact with GKE. Kubectl is the main way to interact directly with the cluster created. In order to check the nodes, we need to issue the following command:

```
kubectl get nodes
```

The output from the preceding command will display information such as the name, status, age, and version of the Kubernetes node deployed. In this context, a Kubernetes cluster is essentially our defined nodes working together as a unit.

In our GKE cluster, we now have the base platform on which to deploy Cloud Run. In the next section, we will take some time to explore how to deploy code to this environment. In addition, we will look at some workflow tips to aid development productivity.

Custom networking on GKE

When using Kubernetes on GKE, it's useful to understand that it will create a custom network. The key emphasis to note is that Kubernetes will utilize IP addressing to assist with communication across all of its resources (such as pods, nodes, and services, and so on).

Internal networking

The smallest element in a GKE cluster is called a **pod**. A pod is used to run containers and there can be just one or more, depending on the patterns used for a given application. Pods reside within the network namespace that is used to segregate access across the virtual network associated with Kubernetes.

Pods are scheduled to a node, and are able to communicate with any other pod, unless specifically restricted. Communication between pods is therefore taken as a given, even when they are removed and recreated dynamically. However, as pods are meant to be ephemeral, external access requires a separate mechanism called a service to provide a consistent point of access. Services use a label, which is basically a key-value pairing to a Kubernetes resource. Such a service retains a consistent IP address and port such that, externally, it can be used to access a grouping of pods as a logical unit.

External networking

For traffic outside of the cluster, the situation is managed in a different way. Kubernetes uses three distinct mechanisms to provide access to internal network resources.

NodePort and ClusterIP provide access using an HTTP load balancer. Ingress access to resources requires a service to be defined for the reasons mentioned previously. The communication then ensures traffic is directed to the logical group labeled for the service.

The main thing to note is that, as long as traffic remains within a cluster, communication between resources is enabled and supported. If external traffic is required, then a service and some form of load-balanced access should be made available.

Deploying Cloud Run for Anthos

Now that we have a cluster created, we can think about how to deploy an application. The main emphasis of this section is to cover the process to use in terms of deploying an application to the GKE cluster. Google has been very deliberate in terms of trying to keep the Cloud Run commands as similar as possible. As in the previous section, we will build a simple Node.js container and push this to GKE.

To demonstrate the capability of our new GKE cluster, we will deploy the `hello-node` Node.js application. Our `hello-node` application simply prints out a message to the screen, so there is no code complexity to worry about. In fact, we already have the code available in the repository, so let's clone that from the existing Cloud Shell environment:

1. Clone the GitHub repository:

```
git clone [github repo]/ch09/hello-node
```

Again, the `hello-node` application doesn't do anything amazing, it just outputs `Hello World!` on port `8080`. It is all packaged up (that is, into a `cloudbuild.yaml` file and a Dockerfile) and ready for use to push an image to the container repository.

2. To begin the Cloud Build process, run the following command:

```
gcloud builds submit --config cloudbuild.yaml
```

In the build process, we will be using Google Container Registry, rather than the Docker Registry. A registry is essentially a storage location for images that can be used to push and pull stored images. The benefit of using a registry is that it provides a centralized storage area in which to share your images.

 By default, the images stored in Container Registry are marked as private and require IAM permissions to access the content. Alternatively, images can also be marked as public, which means they can be shared outside of the project without requiring any additional authentication.

3. Once the build process has completed successfully, the image generated will be stored under the current Google Cloud project and given the tag specified in the `cloudbuild.yaml` file.

The important thing to observe here is the tag associated with the image, as this is how the artifact will be referenced when pulling the image from the repository:

Take a look in the Google Cloud Container Registry to see the image built in the previous step. Selecting the image in the registry will display further details, including the all-important tag reference.

From Container Registry, we can see the image, together with the hostname and level of visibility (that is, private/public) applied. The hostname provides the region for which the image is associated, outlined as follows:

- `gcr.io`: Currently located in the United States, but the location may change
- `us.gcr.io`: United States
- `eu.gcr.io`: European Union
- `asia.gcr.io`: Asia

When building images, it is advantageous to use a location closest to the data to maximize overall performance. The reason for this is that, when pulling the image (that is, the retrieval process), you want to minimize the distance between the registry source and destination host machine.

The visibility of an image is either private to the project or public (that is, accessible by everyone). By default, the images are set to private; however, the visibility can easily be changed if required.

At this point, as the image is present in the project registry, it will also be accessible to the cluster created earlier. Prior to deploying the image, let's take a moment to understand some of the terms used in the standard commands for deployment:

- `SERVICE`: Represents the name to be associated with the image to be deployed.
- `IMAGE`: An artifact available in Container Registry to be deployed as a service.
- `CLUSTER-NAME`: The name associated with the cluster created earlier; that is, `$CLUSTER_NAME`.
- `CLUSTER-LOCATION`: This is the zone allocated to the cluster; that is, `$ZONE`.

Take note that the `IMAGE` tag must exactly match what is available in Container Registry (including a version number, if applied). If you are unsure of the tag to use, visit the Cloud Console and select the image required to see the relevant tag detail.

The deployed container will be displayed with a service name, a revision (that is, a unique reference), and a URL for serving traffic. So far, we have created a placeholder for the service to be run. To make the container accessible as a named service, we need to deploy it. In the real world, the prior activities are likely going to be a one-off task and can be easily automated.

4. To deploy the artifact to the GKE cluster, we use the `gcloud run deploy` command in the following way:

```
gcloud run deploy [SERVICE] --image [IMAGE] --platform gke --
cluster [CLUSTER-NAME] --cluster-location [CLUSTER-LOCATION]
```

Now that the service has been deployed, there is a wealth of information suddenly available on the running of the application. There are two places of interest for information about the workloads running on GKE:

- The first is the Kubernetes Engine Workloads page, in which details of GKE deployments can be seen. If you are interested in the state of deployments or workloads sent to the cluster, this is a place to gather information. From here, it is possible to drill down into the various aspects of the deployment.
- The second is Stackdriver. In the next section, we will update the application to see the impact this has on the data displayed and how to track information when things go wrong.

Now that we have a base-level understanding of deployment, we can consider how to automate the process using the toolset available on Google Cloud.

Continuous deployment

As we have seen, there is a lot of work to get a Cloud Run for Anthos up and running in comparison with Cloud Run. What happens if we want to deploy another revision of the code? Do we need to go through the whole process once again? Well no: the deployment of the service is the only aspect that needs to be repeated. Taking some time to explore this in more detail will be interesting and will provide an understanding of what is happening when multiple revisions are available to the cluster:

1. Our previous image was version 0.1, so let's implement a small change (I added a +1 to the response string) and see the impact this has on the deployment process and rollout to the cluster:

```
const express = require('express');
const app = express();
```

```
const port = process.env.PORT || 8080;
app.get('/', (req, res) => res.send('Hello World! +1'));
app.listen(port, () => console.log(`Example app listening on port
${port}!`));
```

2. Next, update the stored image in Container Registry using the following command:

```
gcloud builds submit --config cloudbuild.yaml
```

3. Finally, we want to deploy the updated image in our cluster:

```
gcloud beta run deploy [SERVICE] --image [IMAGE] --platform gke --
cluster [CLUSTER-NAME] --cluster-location [CLUSTER-LOCATION]
```

The first this to do is confirm that the new service has been successfully deployed by looking at the command output. To get the status of a Cloud Run service, the Cloud console will always have an updated status in the workloads page and will show changes as they are initiated.

Unfortunately, it is a bit of a pain having to do these actions each time we want to deploy something. Never fear: there is a much more practical way of deploying our code that lets our trusty friends, the service account and Cloud Build, manage all the boring bits.

In the **Cloud Build** settings, amend the **Cloud Run service account (Cloud Run Admin)** and **Service Accounts (Service Account User)** to enabled. In the left-hand panel, select the **Triggers** option and connect to a valid repository.

 Note that, if a connection to GitHub has already been established, this will need to be done to successfully complete this setup.

Creating a push trigger can be set up for specific branches or for all pushes to the repository. Note the type of trigger will attempt to auto-detect the configuration file. In the case of the author, the `cloudbuild.yaml` file is renamed `cloudbuild.github`, so that it is patently obvious which environment file should be used.

Select the create button and the trigger will now be active for the selected repository.

4. Back with the source code, let's amend the source code once more with another simple change, so we have a visible way to discern the difference in deployed versions. Update the highlighted line so it reflects the change shown as follows:

```
const express = require('express')
const app = express()
const port = process.env.PORT || 8080;
app.get('/', (req, res) => res.send('Hello World! GitHub Build'))
app.listen(port, () => console.log(`Example app listening on port
${port}!`))
```

5. Finally, we will need to amend the `cloudbuild.github.yaml` file to refine our build process. The updated configuration file will look similar to that shown as follows:

```
steps:
  # Build the container image
- name: 'gcr.io/cloud-builders/docker'
  args: ['build', '-t', 'gcr.io/$PROJECT_ID/hello-node', '.']
  # push the container image to Container Registry
- name: 'gcr.io/cloud-builders/docker'
  args: ['push', 'gcr.io/$PROJECT_ID/hello-node']
  # Deploy container image to Cloud Run
- name: 'gcr.io/cloud-builders/gcloud'
  args: ['beta', 'run', 'deploy', 'hello-node', '--image',
'gcr.io/$PROJECT_ID/hello-node', '--platform', 'gke', '--cluster',
'test-cluster', '--cluster-location', 'us-central1-a']
images:
- 'gcr.io/$PROJECT_ID/hello-node'
timeout: "600s"
```

Taking a closer look at the build file outlined in the preceding code block, we can see the flexibility of Cloud Builds, as it allows commands to be directly initiated. A closer examination of the commands highlights the following activities:

- **Build the container image**: The `build` command is essentially a standard `docker build` command that tags the image with the appropriate naming convention.
- **Push the container image to Container Registry**: Once the `docker build` process is complete, the image built is then pushed to Google Container Registry with the specified tag. Again, the standard Docker command is used to send the image to the repository.
- **Deploy the container to Cloud Run**: The tagged image is deployed to the cluster.

A layout such as this provides a common build pattern for Docker-based environments.

6. To initiate a build, once again, we would need to initiate the build process from the command line:

```
gcloud builds submit --config cloudbuild.github
```

However, the preceding manual step is no longer necessary! The repository has now been linked directly to GitHub, so each time a branch change is detected, the build process will be automatically initiated. Working with Cloud Build can save a lot of effort for very little configuration, and is worth the investment in time to understand how it works.

Having successfully built a service, in the next section we take a quick look at domains and how these are applied on Google Cloud when using Cloud Run.

Applying a domain

Once a service has been deployed, Google Cloud provides a number of options to manage the associated domain name. In short, a domain name provides the ability to map a service IP address so that is accessible on the internet with a human-readable name. So, instead of accessing the IP 216.58.206.110, we can enter www.google.com into the browser—I will leave it to you to consider which is more memorable.

Registering a domain name has become increasingly easy over the years and many companies provide an opportunity to purchase your own part of the internet. Once you have a domain name, you can actually map this to your Cloud Run service.

If you do not wish to purchase a domain name, Google Cloud incorporates three external wildcard **domain name system (DNS)** test sites that can be associated with a deployed Cloud Run service, as follows:

DNS service	Information
nip.io	https://exentriquesolutions.com/
xip.io	https://basecamp.com/
sslip.io	https://github.com/sstephenson https://github.com/cunnie/sslip.io

Alternatively, if you already own a domain, this can also be set up and used instead of the default domain. When you are not running a live service, having your own domain will likely be of little concern. However, once your product moves to production, having a domain looks much more professional.

The default domain name used by Cloud Run for Anthos is actually `example.com`. When you change the domain, for example, to a test site, the service deployed will be registered against the selected name system, for example, `xip.io`. Changing the DNS setting requires the use of a config map to tell Kubernetes how the domain is to be configured:

> In the following section, we capture the output into environment variables. Doing this means we do not have to continually keep posting API requests to confirm values.

1. Get the service URL, currently using `default.com`, for example:

```
SERVICE_URL=$(gcloud beta run services describe [SERVICE-NAME] --
platform gke --cluster [CLUSTER-NAME] --cluster-location [ZONE] --
format "value(status.url)")
```

2. Get the external IP of the deployed service:

```
ISTIO_INGRESS=$(kubectl get svc istio-ingress -n gke-system -o json
| jq -r '.status.loadBalancer.ingress[0].ip')
```

3. Apply a patch to the config map using the Istio Ingress IP as the external IP:

```
kubectl patch configmap config-domain --namespace knative-serving -
-patch \
'{"data": {"example.com": null, "[EXTERNAL-IP].[DNS-SERVICE]":
""}}'
```

4. Update the service URL environment variable:

```
SERVICE_URL=$(gcloud beta run services describe [SERVICE-NAME] --
platform gke --cluster [CLUSTER-NAME] --cluster-location [ZONE] --
format "value(status.url)")
```

> The `gcloud sdk` and `kubectl` commands provide information in a number of formats, including JSON. Learning how to parse JSON is a very handy skill to acquire when learning to develop command-line scripts.

Congratulations! You have enabled a custom domain on your service. Now rather than displaying default.com, the service will be registered against the selected domain.

In the next section, we will cover the monitoring of an application and give some insights into the helpful information available.

Troubleshooting with Stackdriver

Earlier sections have discussed many of the key details of Cloud Run. So far, we have provisioned a cluster on GKE, deployed our application and utilized Cloud Build to make us more productive. At this point, we should probably also cover what to do when things go wrong.

Google Cloud provides a lot of environmental information, especially for compute-based resources such as GCE and GKE. For serverless workloads, fortunately, we can also take advantage of many of these key data points:

1. To start, let's continue with our hello-node application and introduce an error into the code. Access the source code for index.js and save the following erroneous entry to the code:

```
const express = require('express')
const app = express()
const port = process.env.PORT || 8080;
oops
app.get('/', (req, res) => res.send('Hello World! GitHub Build'))
app.listen(port, () => console.log(`Example app listening on port ${port}!`))
```

2. In the preceding code, we have intentionally added a code defect so that we can track this in Stackdriver. Once again we can run our cloudbuild.github to do all the hard work for us. However, this time the deployment task will fail! To see the details of the failure, we should go to the Cloud Run interface and investigate the existing services.

3. From the Cloud Run dashboard view, we have a green circle with a ticket mark present indicating the hello-node service has been successfully deployed and is operating within expected parameters. Contrast this with our latest deployment of the hello-node service that has encountered an error, as indicated by the red circle with an exclamation mark in the center. Furthermore, neither the **GKE Cluster** or **Namespace** detail is present, meaning the image has not been deployed to its end destination.

4. Select the application with the error to display further information on the **Services details** page, as follows:

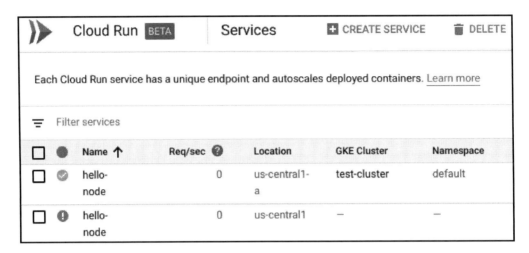

Before we get into how to explore further information about the error displayed, we should take a moment to highlight the Cloud Run **Service details** page and the information accessible from there.

Whenever you deploy a service, there is a tremendous amount of information exchange taking place, much of it in the background. One of the important aspects of working with Google Cloud is the centralized management of resource-related data. Much of the information relating to services or resources deployed within your project will be captured in Stackdriver. Thankfully, the engineers at Google have taken the most common elements exposed in Stackdriver and added them to a handy dashboard covering **METRICS, REVISION, LOGS, DETAILS**, and **YAML**, as follows:

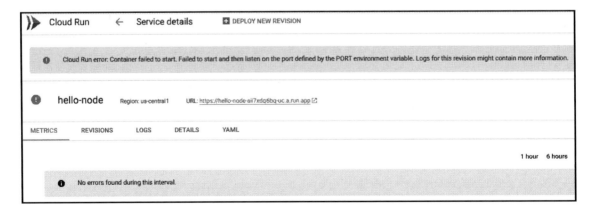

Let's explore these dashboard elements one by one:

- **METRICS**: The metrics screen provides a range of data that is commonly used by an application, for example, a request count. In addition, the information presented can also be filtered by time period (such as 1 hour, 6 hours, 7 days, or 30 days). From this screen, an application state can easily be viewed and issues relating to the service performance can begin to be investigated. So, if you have an issue relating to the performance of a service, for example, such as latency or bottlenecking, this is the screen where the attributes of an application can be viewed to get a sense of what is happening.
- **REVISIONS**: An overview of the revisions deployed, including environment variables and Cloud SQL connectivity.
- **LOGS**: Access the logged information for the service. The detail available is based on the system logs, so information captured by an application will be available here.
- **DETAILS**: From this page, the service connectivity and authentication information are shared.
- **YAML**: The last tab provides an overview of the YAML associated with the service being viewed.

Remember that, at the time of writing this book, the dashboard capability was still being revised, so expect changes of a subtle (and not-so-subtle) nature in the feature set.

Now we have outlined the relative capabilities of the dashboard, we can move on to resolving our service error.

Earlier, you will remember that we updated our application and introduced an error. We can see in the main dashboard of Cloud Run that our service was unsuccessful.

Over the course of the chapter we have started with a simple application, and then incorporated it into a continuous integration build process. Traditionally, we use logs to get insight into applications that are not operating within standard procedures. Given that we have handed over much of the build process to an automated process, it makes sense that the logs for each stage of this process are also available centrally:

1. Go to Stackdriver. The logs that would naturally be available locally to the developer are now present in a central repository.
2. In the Cloud Run dashboard, select the item indicating an error to once again go to the **Service details** page.

3. From here, select the **LOGS** tab and take a closer look at what information has been captured by the logging process.

 Note that each entry in Stackdriver is timestamped, and associated with this is some form of command that returned a status update.

Working through the content displayed on screen, we can see that our application is executed with the `index.js` command node. If you are unclear why, it is because this relates to the start command we entered into the `package.json` file.

Looking further down the list, we can see reference to `/usr/src/app/index.js:5`. This is telling us that something interesting occurred at the fifth line in `index.js`. In the following line, the logs indicate something curious: `oops` has been found in the source file. Well, that is clearly not meant to be there, so we have found our typo.

4. Now that we have explored the logs for valuable clues to correct our application defect, go back to the source code and remove the typo on line five of `index.js`.
5. Resubmit the changed code to a branch and see the code once again automatically update to take account of the changes made.
6. At this point, the code should be successfully working, based on the update made. Confirm the code is working by checking the text displayed is the same as that displayed in the current version of the source code.

Hopefully, the process on which to debug an application has been made clearer with this preceding example. By incorporating the development workflow earlier into the Cloud process, it makes the overall integration more complete. Being able to utilize built-in tools such as Stackdriver provides an easier path to increased productivity.

Deleting the cluster

To complete the chapter, the final activity to cover is deleting the cluster. Removing a cluster is not a common activity; in fact, the only reason it is included here is to show the process. As we now know, the cluster incorporates all the base-level functionality associated with Kubernetes. On GKE, our cluster is managed; that is, you don't need to concern yourself with low-level activities such as node creation, TLS certification creation, and so on.

With that said, in order to remove the cluster created previously, use the following command:

```
gcloud beta container clusters delete CLUSTER_NAME
```

 Just to be clear, at the time of writing, the `cluster delete` command is in beta, so there may be some potential changes going forward.

Once we embark on deleting the cluster, it removes all the associated workloads, that is, the deployed containers. To restart, a new cluster would need to be created in order to deploy Cloud Run for Anthos.

Summary

In this chapter, we introduced the high-level concept of Kubernetes and then looked at how Cloud Run for Anthos can be used. If your platform of choice is Kubernetes, Cloud Run for Anthos is the path to follow. As we have seen, the migration between non-Kubernetes and Kubernetes environments requires no additional configuration as the delivery artifact is based on a container.

Through this chapter, we have discovered a more productive way to incorporate Cloud Build into our developer workflow. Utilizing the developer tools provided by Google is a sensible way to minimize the repetitive aspects that are integral to the build and deploy process.

In the next chapter, we develop a couple of Cloud Run examples to illustrate some key features. Working through some example use cases will help to illustrate how to utilize Cloud Run in your own projects.

Questions

1. What type of machine customization is possible when using Cloud Run for Anthos?
2. Are SSL certificates automatic or manual when using Cloud Run for Anthos?
3. What platform flag is required when deploying to Cloud Run for Anthos?
4. What port is used for service access when using Cloud Run for Anthos?

5. Is a pre-provisioned cluster required for Cloud Run for Anthos? (True or False)
6. What addons are required for Cloud Run for Anthos?
7. Which command is used to manage a GKE cluster from the command line?
8. What is a pod?
9. How does GKE support external traffic?

Further reading

- **Istio**: `https://cloud.google.com/istio/`
- **Cloud Run Authentication**: `https://cloud.google.com/run/docs/authenticating/overview`
- **Google Kubernetes Engine**: `https://cloud.google.com/kubernetes-engine/`
- **Mapping Custom Domains**: `https://cloud.google.com/appengine/docs/standard/python/mapping-custom-domains`
- **Filtering and formatting fun with gcloud, Google Cloud's command-line interface**: `https://cloud.google.com/blog/products/gcp/filtering-and-formatting-fun-with`
- **JQ tutorial**: `https://stedolan.github.io/jq/tutorial/`

10
Cloud Run Labs

In this chapter, we will explore some use cases to see how Cloud Run can be deployed on **Google Kubernetes Engine (GKE)**. The most common use cases revolve around building web applications, performing deployments, and the need for **continuous integration (CI)**.

The focus of this chapter is to illustrate the wide spectrum of use cases that are possible using Cloud Run. This chapter will also show how to perform many of the activities required to deploy your container when using this platform.

Over the course of this chapter, we will discuss the following topics:

- Building a container
- Deploying Cloud Run on GKE
- Creating a simple web application
- CI on GKE

Technical requirements

To complete the exercises in this chapter, you will require a Google Cloud Project or a Qwiklabs account.

You can find the code files of this chapter in the GitHub repository for this book in the `ch10` subdirectory at `https://github.com/PacktPublishing/Hands-on-Serverless-Computing-with-Google-Cloud/tree/master/ch10`.

 While you are going through the code snippets in this book, you will notice that, in a few instances, a few lines from the code/output have been removed and replaced with dots (. . .). Ellipses are used to only show relevant code/output. The complete code is available on GitHub at the link mentioned previously.

Building a container

Building a container for an application should be a familiar activity at this point in this book. For the most part, when building an image, we can normally rely on existing knowledge to determine how to incorporate a runtime language or package. From a personal perspective, I like to containerize applications as it provides a consistent and well-understood interface. The isolation from system updates and other changes impacting an application is a very common and annoying aspect of maintaining a computer.

At this point, the assumption is that building images is second nature and the next challenge relates to deploying the containers. What your container is actually meant to do will probably influence the complexity of the running container. For example, running a container with a graphical user interface (potentially) presents more issues than one using a command-line interface. Over the course of this chapter, we will walk through a couple of examples dedicated to indicating how this process can be performed.

Creating a service

We will be using Cloud Shell or a local development environment (Cloud SDK) to create the next example, which is a fun example to demonstrate how to build an application running in a container. In this example, we will develop a simple application called **announce** (based on the command-line utility **Boxes**) that will display a message on the command line.

 If you are not familiar with Boxes, it draws ASCII art around text. To begin, we want to create an application that can call the Boxes application to output some arbitrary text.

To commence the example, let's initialize the environment ready to build our application.

1. Initialize the npm package:

   ```
   npm init --yes
   ```

2. Edit the package.json to add a start command:

   ```
   ...
   "scripts": {
   "start": "node index.js",
   "test": "echo \"Error: no test specified\" && exit 1"
   },
   ...
   ```

3. Install the npm packages:

   ```
   npm install express
   npm install util
   npm install child-process
   ```

4. Create and edit a file named index.js:

   ```
   const {promisify} = require('util');
   const exec = promisify(require('child_process').exec);
   const express = require('express');
   const app = express();
   const port = process.env.PORT || 8080;

   app.listen(port, () => {
     console.log('Listening on port', port);
   });
   ```

5. Add the main functionality to the index.js file:

   ```
   app.get('/', async (req, res) => {
     try {
       let message = req.query.message;
       console.log ('Message: ' + message);
       const cmd='echo ' + message + ' | boxes -d boy';
       const {stdout, stderr} = await exec(cmd);
       if (stderr) {
         throw stderr;
       }
       res.status(200).send("<pre>" + stdout + "</pre>");
     }
   ```

```
  catch (ex) {
    console.log(`${ex}`);
    res.status(500);
  }
});
```

You can check your application at this stage by just running `npm start` from the command line. It won't do anything spectacular, but it will give you the chance to correct any issues in terms of code not working as expected. Assuming you don't have `boxes` installed locally, the output would be similar to the following:

```
Message: undefined
Error: Command failed: echo undefined | boxes -d boy
```

Don't worry—this is expected and will be corrected with the creation of our application image.

6. Create a Dockerfile:

```
FROM node:12-slim
LABEL MAINTAINER Rich Rose
RUN apt-get update -y && apt-get install -y boxes && apt-get clean
WORKDIR /usr/src/app
COPY package*.json ./
RUN npm install --only=production
COPY . .
CMD [ "npm", "start" ]
```

7. Build the image:

gcloud builds submit --tag gcr.io/$GOOGLE_CLOUD_PROJECT/announce-service:1.0

Once the build process is invoked, an output similar to the following will be displayed:

```
Step 6/8 : RUN npm install --only=production                                    [6/1932]
 ---> Running in c3c7fb515deb
npm WARN 01-boxes@1.0.0 No description
npm WARN 01-boxes@1.0.0 No repository field.

added 70 packages from 47 contributors and audited 168 packages in 2.688s

10 packages are looking for funding
  run `npm fund` for details

found 0 vulnerabilities
Removing intermediate container c3c7fb515deb
 ---> 29007d00fe27
Step 7/8 : COPY . .
 ---> 4e4b27ae0517
Step 8/8 : CMD [ "npm", "start" ]
 ---> Running in 482fd9875fbf
Removing intermediate container 482fd9875fbf
 ---> af18f8027d0b
Successfully built af18f8027d0b
Successfully tagged gcr.io/roselabs-212512/annouce-service:1.0
PUSH
Pushing gcr.io/roselabs-212512/annouce-service:1.0
The push refers to repository [gcr.io/roselabs-212512/annouce-service]
0883f871f6a7: Preparing
9cf3696cbee7: Preparing
34da121bd32f: Preparing
f5ac4b6ca0a7: Preparing
5c6905a058c3: Preparing
13f3b2f86aa9: Preparing
8d2b54d2b4c8: Preparing
be6f968c509e: Preparing
4a7eecae00c6: Preparing
e0db3ba0aaea: Preparing
13f3b2f86aa9: Waiting
8d2b54d2b4c8: Waiting
be6f968c509e: Waiting
4a7eecae00c6: Waiting
e0db3ba0aaea: Waiting
34da121bd32f: Pushed
13f3b2f86aa9: Layer already exists
f5ac4b6ca0a7: Pushed
8d2b54d2b4c8: Layer already exists
be6f968c509e: Layer already exists
4a7eecae00c6: Layer already exists
e0db3ba0aaea: Layer already exists
5c6905a058c3: Pushed
0883f871f6a7: Pushed
9cf3696cbee7: Pushed
1.0: digest: sha256:27dbb23ed4f15098094a2f127f3b72a666d19a3fb8bbfe122127bf4d0345286f size: 2415
DONE
--------------------------------------------------------------------------------------------

ID                                      CREATE_TIME            DURATION  SOURCE                                                    IMAGE
S                                                              STATUS
78d8ad57-fc32-4964-8ac6-f25e13c1bc3e    2020-02-06T10:17:56+00:00   33S      gs://roselabs-212512_cloudbuild/source/1581013073.9
2-e82fc415d5fa4a9f97442b238993f72f.tgz  gcr.io/roselabs-212512/annouce-service:1.0  SUCCESS
```

Pushing the image to the Container Registry means we have more control over how and where our image can be accessed. Now that the image has been built, we can perform an initial test of the container by deploying it locally.

Testing the announce service

Having a container deployed to Container Registry is only part of the work to be performed. Next, we need to run the container from the image stored. Cloud Run containers run on port 8080, so we should enable port mapping for images pulled from the repository:

1. Run the container from the command line:

```
docker run -d -p 8080:8080 gcr.io/$GOOGLE_CLOUD_PROJECT/announce-
service:1.0
```

2. Test the output from the application:

```
curl 127.0.0.1:8080
```

3. Test sending a message to the application:

```
curl 127.0.0.1:8080/?message=cloud+run+on+anthos
```

4. Stop the Docker container running on the local machine:

```
docker stop $(docker ps -aq)
```

Congratulations, you have now deployed and tested the application to generate box ASCII art from a container. In the next section, we will deploy the application to **Google Kubernetes Engine** (**GKE**) and access the service from a cluster.

Deploying Cloud Run on GKE

Now that we know how to create an image of an application, how does that translate to running an image on GKE? Fortunately, we already know how to deploy a container on Cloud Run, which means we know most of what is required for deployment on GKE.

From an external perspective, we interact with the Cloud Run service URL. Internally, when running on GKE, there is actually a lot more going on in the background. However, we will focus on how to replicate our application when running as a service.

Provisioning a GKE cluster

Before we can deploy our application onto Cloud Run on GKE, we need to create a
GKE cluster. So, let's begin:

1. In this example we use the standard cluster definition. So, create a GKE cluster
   called `hos-cluster-1`:

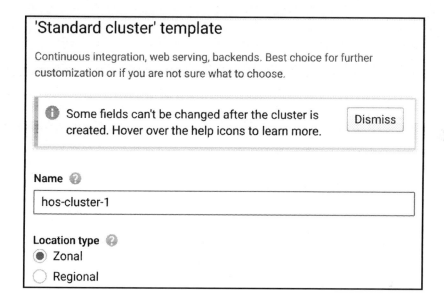

It's important to select the **Enable Cloud Run for Anthos** option.

The following screenshot indicates that Cloud Run for Anthos has been enabled for the cluster. By default, monitoring is enabled on the cluster to be created:

Enable Cloud Run for Anthos

To enable Cloud Run for Anthos, the following modifications will be made on the cluster configuration:

- Stackdriver Kubernetes Engine Monitoring will be enabled
- Machine type will be set to 2 vCPUs for default-pool

Learn more 🗗

CANCEL   CONTINUE

We can also use the command line to create a cluster and perform tasks on Google Cloud. In this instance, creating a cluster requires quite a long command, so I normally stick to doing this activity through the Cloud Console.

The Kubernetes cluster to be created is standard apart from the checkbox located right at the bottom of the cluster configuration screen. For Cloud Run to be enabled within the cluster, this box needs to be checked.

2. Once the cluster has been successfully provisioned, configure kubectl to connect to the cluster:

```
gcloud container clusters get-credentials hos-cluster-1 --zone us-central1-a --project $GOOGLE_CLOUD_PROJECT
```

3. Deploy the service to the `hos-cluster-1` Kubernetes cluster. Note that we now specify GKE as the platform as well as the cluster and cluster location:

```
gcloud run deploy announce-service \
--platform gke \
--cluster hos-cluster-1 \
--cluster-location us-central1-a \
--image gcr.io/$GOOGLE_CLOUD_PROJECT/announce-service
```

4. Make an environment variable called `ANNOUNCE_URL` to store the URL of the deployed service:

```
ANNOUNCE_URL=$(gcloud beta run services describe announce-service -
-platform gke --cluster hos-cluster-1 --cluster-location us-
central1-a --format "value(status.url)")
```

External access to the Cloud Run service is provided via Istio, which is deployed to another namespace. The deployed namespaces are displayed in the Cloud Console. However, if you were to do `kubectl get service` from the command line in the default namespace, there would be no reference to Istio. To access the Istio gateway service from the command line, we need to indicate that we would like to use the `gke-system` namespace.

Testing the GKE service

We have a service deployed, but we need to know how to access it. Cloud Run on GKE utilizes an Istio Ingress to enable external access to the GKE cluster:

1. To show the details on the Istio Ingress (which is a `loadBalancer` created in the `gke-system` namespace), use the following command:

```
kubectl get svc istio-ingress -n gke-system
```

2. Assign the `loadBalancer.ingress` address to the `ISTIO_INGRESS` environment variable:

```
ISTIO_INGRESS=$(kubectl get svc istio-ingress -n gke-system -o json
| jq -r '.status.loadBalancer.ingress[0].ip')
```

In the following screenshot, we can see the result of the cluster. The information we need is labeled `istio-ingress`:

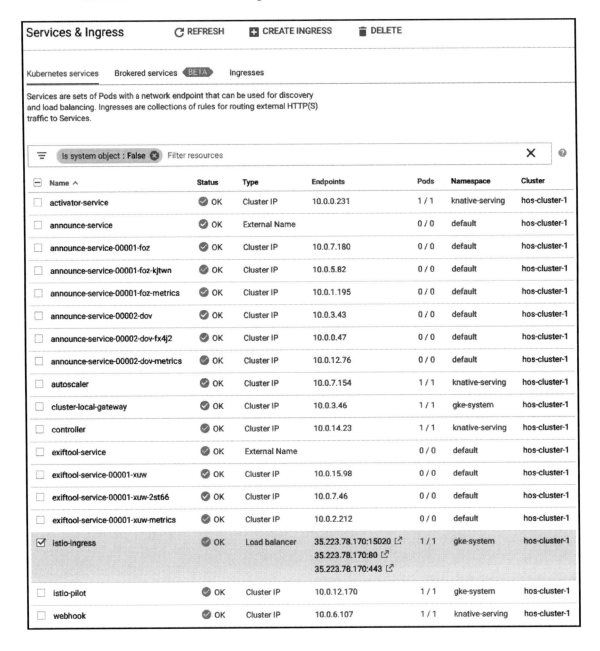

Information returned from the kubectl command can be filtered to only display the field required. For example, in this instance, we only require the IP address. If we would like to filter the output to return specific information, we can use JQ to filter on the information desired.

JQ is a lightweight command-line tool built to process JSON objects. Using this tool, you can manipulate JSON objects in a similar fashion to using sed or awk. You can find more information on this amazing tool at https://stedolan.github.io/jq/.

3. The application running in the cluster can be tested by visiting the Cloud Run service page or by using curl on the external IP associated with istio-ingress displayed in the Cloud Run console. For example, in my case, it is announce-service.default.35.223.78.170.xip.io:

```
curl -v http://announce-service.default.[EXTERNAL_IP].xip.io
```

The namespace default can be seen in the service details screen for Cloud Run, as follows:

For the deployed service, you may have noticed that the domain associated with our service is registered as xip.io. The default used by Cloud Run on GKE is actually example.com. So, how did this address become assigned to the deployed service? When testing, it is possible to change from the default domain to an alternative. Google currently provides three wildcard DNS test sites that can be set up to be used with Cloud Run services:

- nip.io
- xip.io
- sslip.io

The sites declared above represent a simple and effective way to register a temporary domain for the purposes of testing.

Applying a custom domain

Alternatively, if you own a domain, this can also be set up instead of the default domain. Changing to use one of the free DNS sites requires doing the following:

1. Set the cluster to use a custom domain by patching the `configmap` for the cluster:

```
kubectl patch configmap config-domain --namespace knative-serving --patch \
  '{"data": {"example.com": null, "[EXTERNAL-IP].xip.io": ""}}'
```

   To determine the external IP of a Cloud Run service on GKE, remember that this is referring to the external IP of the Istio Ingress. Once the DNS has been updated, you will see that the address of the deployed service will use the new DNS reference.

   In addition to an alternative domain, there might also be a need to incorporate HTTPS for the cluster in use. For most situations, it is advisable to utilize a service such as Let's Encrypt on your cluster. Note that when using a Google service, HTTPS may be required, so it is important to know how to apply this to your environment so that the authentication methods work as expected.

   The console output includes a reference to **service and ingress**. The deployed service URL will be available in the Cloud Run console. The externally available IP is only available to the Istio Ingress of the load balancer type. Note that the internal address range, that is, `10.0.x.x`, is not accessible to the `curl` command.

2. Access the service URL and store it in an environment variable:

```
SERVICE-URL=$(gcloud beta run services describe password-service --platform gke --cluster hos-cluster-1 --cluster-location us-central1-a --format "value(status.url)")
```

3. List the information for the `istio-ingress` associated with the `gke-system` namespace:

```
kubectl get svc istio-ingress -n gke-system
```

4. Get the external IP associated with the `istio-ingress` endpoint:

```
ISTIO_INGRESS=$(kubectl get svc istio-ingress -n gke-system -o json
| jq '.status.loadBalancer.ingress[0].ip')
```

5. Use the external IP of the Istio Ingress to patch the endpoint for testing:

```
kubectl patch configmap config-domain --namespace knative-serving -
-patch \
'{"data": {"example.com": null, "[EXTERNAL_IP].xip.io": ""}}'
```

6. Next, we need to generate a digital SSL certificate. We can do this by using the `Certbot` utility. Certbot automates certificate generation using **Let's Encrypt** as its backend. Download the Certbot (`https://certbot.eff.org/`) application and use it to generate a digital SSL certificate:

```
wget https://dl.eff.org/certbot-auto
chmod a+x ./certbot-auto
./certbot-auto --help
```

7. Add the SSL certificate to the domain to provide SSL access for the domain:

```
./certbot-auto certonly --manual --preferred-challenges dns -d
'*.default.[EXTERNAL_IP].xip.io'
```

Congratulations! We have successfully built and deployed a simple service on Cloud Run on GKE. However, to use it, we need to add some additional components. In the next section, we will expand on this example to illustrate how application components are integrated.

Creating a simple web application

Now that we know how to build and deploy a container on Cloud Run on GKE, the next step is to explore how to link this together with other services to create an application. With our application deployed on GKE, we now need to configure Cloud Storage and Cloud Pub/Sub.

For our example, we are going to build a form to call our announce service:

1. Create a new directory called `simple-form`:

```
mkdir simple-form && cd $_
```

2. Initialize the environment:

```
npm init --yes
```

3. Edit the `package.json` file and add the `start` command:

```
...
"scripts": {
"start": "node index.js",
"test": "echo \"Error: no test specified\" && exit 1"
},
...
```

4. Install the `npm` packages (`pug` and `express`):

```
npm install pug
npm install express
```

In the following code, we will call our `announce-service:1.0`. Replace the service URL endpoint with the address that was generated on Google Cloud for your Cloud Run deployment.

To get a list of services that have been deployed, use the following command:

```
gcloud run services list --platform managed
```

In the following table, the commands that were used to deploy has been listed for reference. Take note of the platform command as this determines the target system:

Platform	Command
Cloud Run	`gcloud run deploy SERVICE --platform managed --region REGION`
Cloud Run for Anthos (Google Cloud)	`gcloud run deploy SERVICE --platform gke --cluster CLUSTER-NAME` `        --cluster-location CLUSTER-LOCATION`
Cloud Run for Anthos (VMware)	`gcloud run deploy SERVICE --platform kubernetes --kubeconfig KUBECONFIG-FILE`

5. Create an `index.js` file and add the following content to it:

```
const express = require('express');
const pug = require('pug');
const app = express();
const port = process.env.PORT || 8080;

app.get("/", function(req, res) {
  const pugTemplate = pug.compileFile('./views/index.pug');
  res.status(200).send(pugTemplate({
    service_url: 'http://do.com'}));
});

app.listen(port, () => {
  console.log('Listening on port', port);
});
```

6. Create a new directory for a pug view:

```
mkdir views && cd $_
```

7. Create an `index.pug` file in the `views` directory and add the following style content:

```
html
head
style.

  input[type=text], select {
    width: 100%;
    padding: 12px 20px;
    margin: 8px 0;
    display: inline-block;
  }

  input[type=submit] {
    width: 20%;
    padding: 14px 20px;
    border-radius: 4px;
  }
```

8. Add the form controls to the `index.pug` file (replace ANNOUNCE_URL with the URL for the `announce-service` URL identified earlier in the project):

```
body
  div.header Cloud Run for Anthos:
  p
  div.card
```

```
    p.
    Add the text you want to see displayed in the boxes
application.
    form(action="[ANNOUNCE_URL]/?message" method="get"
target="_blank")
       label Message to display: <input type="text"
name="message"><br>
       p
       input(type='submit', value='Submit')
```

9. Run the application to test and see that the form calls the service and displays the message:

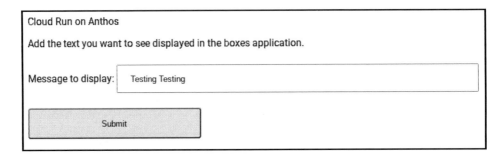

On entering a message and pressing the **Submit** button, the form will call the announce-service and display the message that was entered, as shown in the following screenshot:

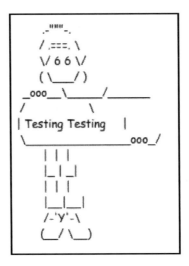

Congratulations! At this point, when a message is entered, it will invoke the service associated with the ANNOUNCE_URL. As the service URL is exposed, we can easily integrate other applications or services using web forms or other straightforward applications built around the service.

Now that we have looked at the general interface associated with deploying a web application, let's turn our focus to CI. In the next section, we will look at how to automate the build process.

CI on GKE

As we have already seen, getting Cloud Run on GKE up and running takes a lot of work in comparison to Cloud Run. Besides that, we also need to iterate against the development cycle to ensure the build, testing, and deployment processes are performed consistently.

Fortunately, there is a mechanism available to help out with the development life cycle. Cloud Build is used to automate development tasks and can easily be extended to automate many of the tasks associated with developing code. Making the transition to working with containers provides many benefits, but does add the additional layer of effort necessary to ensure the images reflect the latest changes. A typical life cycle may look something like the following:

1. Amend the code.
2. Build the code.
3. Test the code.
4. Push the code to version control.

Additionally, there may be different environments, tools, and processes to contend with outside of the typical stage gates associated with a developer pipeline. However, by using Cloud Build, we can easily create a CI pipeline that can initiate a build function based on committing code.

Defining a pipeline uses three parts:

- Service account permissions
- Build triggers
- Cloud Build file

To get started with Cloud Build, there are some additional permissions that need to be granted to the **Cloud Run service account (Cloud Run Admin)**, and **Service Accounts (Service Account User)** need to be set to enabled:

1. The permission state can be viewed in the Cloud Build interface:

Settings

Service account permissions

Cloud Build executes builds with the permissions granted to the Cloud Build service account tied to the project. You can grant additional roles to the service account to allow Cloud Build to interact with other GCP services.

Service account email: 1063197016786@cloudbuild.gserviceaccount.com

GCP Service	Role ❓	Status
Cloud Functions	Cloud Functions Developer	DISABLED ▾
Cloud Run	Cloud Run Admin	ENABLED ▾
App Engine	App Engine Admin	DISABLED ▾
Kubernetes Engine	Kubernetes Engine Developer	DISABLED ▾
Compute Engine	Compute Instance Admin (v1)	DISABLED ▾
Firebase	Firebase Admin	DISABLED ▾
Cloud KMS	Cloud KMS CryptoKey Decrypter	DISABLED ▾
Service Accounts	Service Account User	ENABLED ▾

Roles not listed here can be managed in the IAM section

2. Triggers a signal when a build should be initiated:

← **Edit trigger** ■ DISABLE 🗑 DELETE

Source: **Cloud Build GitHub App**   Repository: https://github.com/rosera/cloud-build-cd ⬀

View triggered builds

Name
Must be unique within the project

> Push-to-any-branch

Description

> Push to any branch

Trigger type ❓
◉ Branch
○ Tag
○ Pull request

Branch (regex) ❓
Matches 2 branches: master, wip

☐ Invert Regex

> .*

⌄ Filter builds by changed files

Build configuration
○ Autodetected
  A cloudbuild.yaml or Dockerfile will be detected in the repository
○ Dockerfile
  Specify the path within the Git repo
◉ Cloud Build configuration file (yaml or json)
  Specify the path to a Cloud Build configuration file in the Git repo   Learn more

Cloud Build configuration file location ❓

> / cloudbuild.github

Substitution variables (Optional)
Substitutions allow to re-use a cloudbuild.yaml file with different variable values   Learn more

> ＋ Add item

[Save] Cancel

Creating a push trigger can be set up for specific branches or for all pushes to the repository. Note the type of trigger will attempt to auto-detect the configuration file.

3. The build process steps are defined in a `cloudbuild.yaml` file:

```
steps:
# Build the container image
- name: 'gcr.io/cloud-builders/docker'
args: ['build', '-t', 'gcr.io/$PROJECT_ID/hello-node', '.']
# push the container image to Container Registry
- name: 'gcr.io/cloud-builders/docker'
args: ['push', 'gcr.io/$PROJECT_ID/hello-node']
# Deploy container image to Cloud Run
- name: 'gcr.io/cloud-builders/gcloud'
args: ['beta', 'run', 'deploy', 'hello-node', '--image',
'gcr.io/$PROJECT_ID/hello-node', '--platform', 'managed', '--
region', 'us-central1', '--quiet']
images:
- 'gcr.io/$PROJECT_ID/hello-node'
timeout: "600s"
```

Clearly, working with Cloud Build can save a lot of effort in exchange for very little configuration. The dividend from using these types of development tools also has a high payoff for Google Cloud because the tool can be adapted to run a wide spectrum of packages. Indeed, the community for Cloud Build projects is quite significant and includes many different runtime languages beyond the scope of this book. Suffice to say it is well worth investing the time to understand how it works. A fully working example of how to incorporate Cloud Build for this type of CI pipeline is provided in `Chapter 12`, *Consuming Third-Party Data via a REST API*.

Summary

Over the course of this chapter, we have highlighted the initial elements of migrating to Cloud Run on GKE. Containers are fundamental to working with Kubernetes and provide a solid foundation on which to build both experience and expertise. To gain experience with the platform, we deployed a simple web application that illustrated many of the common elements that will need to be mastered as part of developing with Cloud Run on GKE.

The additional complexity of managing a Kubernetes environment should not dissuade you from using this platform. While serverless does provide many benefits already alluded to in this book, having a self-healing platform supporting critical infrastructure should provide additional comfort. Having the ability to seamlessly transition between Cloud Run and Cloud Run for Anthos ensures that, whenever it is needed, the choice exists and is accessible.

This chapter concludes our brief introduction to Cloud Run and GKE. In the next couple of chapters, we'll change pace once again. We'll introduce two case studies to illustrate the power of serverless and expand on some of the techniques we've acquired over the previous chapters.

Questions

1. What is a key advantage of using Container Registry over another registry?
2. When is it useful to use an environment variable such as `$GOOGLE_CLOUD_PROJECT`?
3. What trigger types are supported by Cloud Build?
4. What domain is used for the Cloud Build service account?
5. What build configurations types are supported by Cloud Build?
6. Who provides the Certbot SSL certificates used in this chapter's example?

Further reading

- **Cloud SDK**: `https://cloud.google.com/sdk`
- **Creating and Using SSL Certificates**: `https://cloud.google.com/load-balancing/docs/ssl-certificates`
- **Certbot**: `https://certbot.eff.org/instructions`
- **Let's Encrypt**: `https://letsencrypt.org/`

Section 4: Building a Serverless Workload

4

In this section, you will develop a serverless workload designed around a fictitious business named **Pet Theory**. These chapters demonstrate several techniques, as well as the most common use cases for serverless workloads.

The first example illustrates how to incorporate an open source application and extend its use to producing PDF documents. In this example, you will learn how to integrate multiple components to build a serverless application.

The second example provides more of a challenge to you. In this use case, you will create and integrate multiple services through the use of a scalable architecture. Developer productivity will increase through the use of a CI pipeline and Cloud Build triggers that automatically build and deploy components.

This section comprises the following chapters:

- Chapter 11, *Building a PDF Conversion Service*
- Chapter 12, *Consuming Third-Party Data via a REST API*

11
Building a PDF Conversion Service

In the previous chapters, we have discussed the relative merits of working with serverless computing on Google Cloud. Over the course of this chapter and the next, we will look at a case study to explore how a solution might be deployed. Working through the examples will illustrate how to use many of the techniques we've previously discussed.

In order to do this, we will use an example case study based on Pet Theory, a hypothetical veterinary practice that is making the transition to using serverless technology on Google Cloud.

Over the course of this chapter, we will discuss the following topics:

- Designing a document service
- Developing a document service
- Developing a Cloud Run service
- Securing service access
- Testing the document access

Technical requirements

To complete the exercises in this chapter, you will require a Google Cloud project or a Qwiklabs account.

You can find the code files of this chapter in the GitHub repository for this book, under the `ch11` **subdirectory**, at `https://github.com/PacktPublishing/Hands-on-Serverless-Computing-with-Google-Cloud/tree/master/ch11`.

While you are going through the code snippets in this book, you will notice that, in a few instances, a few lines from the codes/outputs have been removed and replaced with ellipses (. . .). The use of ellipses is only to show relevant code/output. The complete code is available on GitHub at the link mentioned previously.

Pet Theory case study overview

For our case study, we will be exploring the Pet Theory veterinary practice. In this scenario, the business is looking to transition to serverless technology and provide some practical methods to incorporate Google Cloud and its products within the business.

The full Pet Theory case study incorporates a number of different scenarios that demonstrate how to resolve typical real-world issues with serverless technology. To view the complete scenario, visit the Qwiklabs site and search for *Serverless Workshop: Pet Theory Quest* (`https://www.qwiklabs.com/quests/98`) to see the associated labs.

Over the course of this chapter and the next, we will be working through two lab examples that illustrate the power and flexibility of serverless technologies. In the first example in this chapter, we will look at how Pet Theory deals with moving to a unified document process based on the automatic conversion of documents. To begin our review, we will outline what the proposed architecture is attempting to achieve and the component roles and requirements involved.

Designing a document service

Pet Theory has an issue with its existing process for document management. Currently, they use multiple document formats within the business and want to rationalize this to use a single unified approach. After some consultation, they decided to transition to **Portable Document Format (PDF)** so that they could continue to use rich media when sending information electronically to their clients and suppliers.

In terms of requirements, the Pet Theory team have decided they need a system capable of the following:

Requirement	Component
Storing document information	Storage
Handling processing requests	Processing
Securing service access	Security
Processing document conversions	Service

Now we have the high-level requirements for the application, we should add to our understanding by describing each requirement.

Storing document information

From the preceding information, we know that storage is a key component in our architecture, as the documents will need to be stored somewhere. We also know that Google Cloud has a number of products that would suit this type of requirement.

Typically, the obvious choice for storage is to use a disk or shared filesystem to persist the data to be processed. However, in this instance, this type of storage may not be the best option for the situation presented. The general remit is to minimize the maintenance of the infrastructure required, and creating a traditional database on managed infrastructure would not meet this requirement.

Thinking about what we have learned regarding Google Cloud Storage, we know that short-term object storage can be used for transient information. We also know that Cloud Storage provides an event framework that supports interaction with serverless computing. On that basis, Cloud Storage seems like a good candidate that is capable of meeting our storage requirement.

Handling processing requests

Processing requests can be handled in a number of ways. In this example, we are going to build a solution that can scale on demand. To that end, we want to decouple the storage requirement from the processing component, meaning we need to add some middleware capable of efficiently handling the information.

In our application, we have already decided to utilize Cloud Storage and therefore we will need a mechanism to asynchronously communicate this service with the backend processing to be performed. The application needs to work autonomously as much as possible to minimize both user interaction and the potential for errors.

Adding Cloud Pub/Sub to the application enables the application to define a consistent and scalable messaging service. The service can consume information from Cloud Storage and propagate this information to the component performing the backend processing. At this point, you may be thinking that Cloud Tasks would be a good alternative for this solution. However, the use case for Cloud Tasks states that it is better suited to a scenario where control of execution timing (that is, rate-limiting) is required. In our scenario, we do not need that level of control over execution. We have a need for general data ingestion and distribution for which the Cloud Pub/Sub product is better suited.

When using Cloud Pub/Sub, we will need to provide information relating to a topic that provides the information to be transported. In our application, this will contain information relating to the file that's uploaded to the Cloud Storage bucket. To consume information relating to a topic, we will also create a subscription that will receive an event notification based on a new message being added to the topic.

Securing service access

As part of our requirements, we also need to implement security permissions for service access to ensure that only authorized accounts can invoke the new service. Our assumption with this service is that we can use an account to manage the necessary permissions. Over the course of the chapters relating to Cloud Functions and Cloud Run, we have seen how valuable these service accounts are for non-interactive solutions. To achieve this requirement, we can use service accounts that will be allocated the necessary permissions associated with the appropriate roles.

Processing document conversations

In order to select a service capable of performing the document conversion, take a moment to recap the relative merits of the serverless options available on Google Cloud:

Product	Scenario	Typical use case
App Engine	Serverless HTTP applications	Web applications
Cloud Functions	Serverless functions and events	Event-driven functions
Cloud Run	Serverless HTTP containers	Fully managed HTTP request-response containers

In addition to the original requirements, the Pet Theory team want to be able to do the following:

- Process information in a scalable manner
- Leverage existing code/application where practical
- Minimize application maintenance
- Utilize in-house knowledge and skills as much as possible

A team member has identified that the LibreOffice application can handle the conversion of documents to PDF. Packaging this application as a Docker image will allow the team to easily reuse and standardize the integration within their project.

From the preceding paragraphs, it seems that Cloud Run is a good fit for the current requirements. As we have learned, Cloud Run supports stateless HTTP and custom libraries. Furthermore, the established integration with services such as Cloud Pub/Sub means this is perfect for our proposed solution. Once the initial build has been tested and verified, the solution can be further enhanced by utilizing Google Developer tools such as Cloud Build to achieve continuous integration.

Awesome job! We have walked through a high-level analysis of requirements, broken it down into components, and now have the essence of a solution. To confirm our understanding, the following diagram covers the solution we have designed:

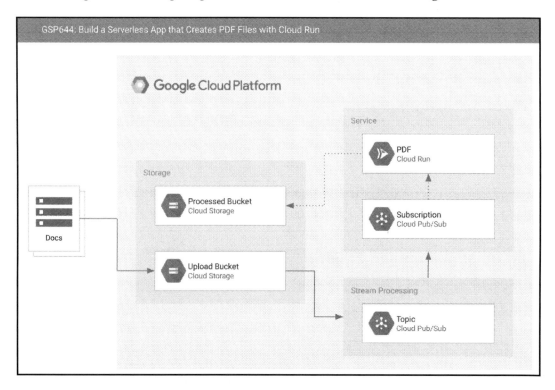

In this diagram, we have defined three distinct stages to be run on Google Cloud that represent the components we previously defined in order to manage our document processing. Our architecture can be described by the following steps:

1. A source document uploads to system storage (that is, a Cloud Storage bucket).
2. A life cycle event is triggered and generates a new payload for the Pub/Sub topic.
3. A Pub/Sub subscription polls for new data notifications.
4. A Cloud Run service processes the uploaded content and creates a PDF.

Note that in the preceding diagram, the main boxes are general abstractions to indicate service isolation. For our simple service, this should help clarify each stage of processing and the responsible component. In addition, we can also see that the majority of processing does not require the creation of code to handle storage event notifications and the message queue data objects. Our efforts are largely focused on the creation of the service for which we have sensibly opted for a preexisting application to handle the PDF conversion.

Based on this discussion, we now have a general understanding of the PDF creation process for documents that are submitted to our service. In the next section, we will start to look at the practical elements of developing the PDF service in order to fulfill the requirements.

Developing a document service

In the previous section, we outlined an architecture for our serverless application. During this analysis phase, we worked out the high-level components required and then theorized on the type of activities required. Creating a document service requires the creation of a Cloud Run service to consume information from a Cloud Pub/Sub subscription. As we have chosen to minimize the code development process, our productivity has been significantly increased. Code for complex notifications and message queues has been deferred to existing mechanisms managed by Google Cloud. Instead, we will concentrate on building only the specific element needed for our requirements, for example, PDF conversion.

> In your Google Cloud project, open Cloud Shell and make sure a clone of the lab repository for Chap11 is available.

Storing document information

To get the project started, we need to create the storage for the application. In the following diagram, we can see that the solution uses two storage buckets. The first bucket stores document uploads while the second stores the output, that is, the processed PDF file:

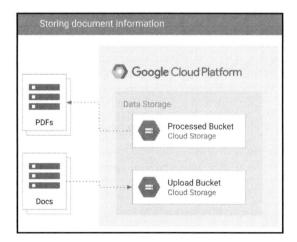

Creating storage buckets on Google Cloud is straightforward, and at this point should be a familiar activity, whether it's performed from the console or Cloud Shell. For this example, we will use Cloud Shell to complete the task:

1. Create a multi-region storage bucket for uploaded files:

```
gsutil mb gs://$GOOGLE_CLOUD_PROJECT-upload
```

2. Create a multi-region storage bucket for processed files:

```
gsutil mb gs://$GOOGLE_CLOUD_PROJECT-processed
```

Google Cloud Storage provides the ability to enable a notification event linked to Pub/Sub. The event notification system is extremely powerful and will be used to raise a new message for each document that's deposited in the upload bucket.

Take a look at the following architecture diagram, which shows that we automatically receive a notification when data is added to the upload bucket. Linking Cloud Storage and Cloud Pub/Sub together in this way provides a sensible usage pattern that can be used in other projects to indicate the availability of data:

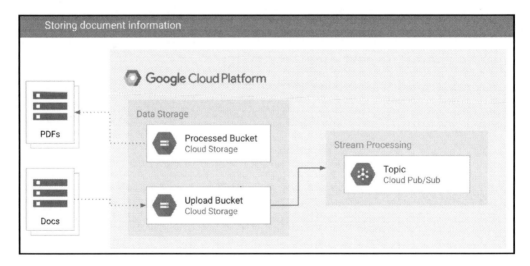

Now, whenever a file is deposited in the upload bucket, a new Pub/Sub topic message will be queued, indicating that new content has been made available.

To set up the notification mechanism on the existing bucket, we use the `gsutil` command. The command will need to know what notification is to be triggered and also that a new topic is to be created for the upload bucket.

3. Create a Pub/Sub topic notification called `new-doc` when a file is added to the upload bucket:

```
gsutil notification create -t new-doc -f json -e OBJECT_FINALIZE
gs://$GOOGLE_CLOUD_PROJECT-upload
```

In the preceding command, we use the `OBJECT_FINALIZE` command, which indicates a new object being presented to a Google Cloud Storage bucket. Take note that the information generated uses the JSON format to pass information to the `new-doc` topic.

 We will only receive a notification about the file that's been uploaded after deploying the PDF service (as there is no active subscription for this new topic).

Great work! We now have the data storage and stream processing services up and running. Next, we will see how to build a PDF service using Cloud Run.

Developing a Cloud Run service

Building a service can be both daunting and challenging. In this section, we will walk through an example of how to build a service based on an existing application. In this instance, we will be using LibreOffice to create a PDF.

One thing to mention about this example is how an external application can easily be integrated to build a simple service. Applications (specifically Linux) encompass a lot of versatility, which means they typically offer a great way to extend and incorporate these within a solution. For example, Inkscape can be used to convert SVG into PNG, while Calibre can convert EPUB into PDF. The bottom line, before going down the route of developing an application, is to investigate what is possible using already-existing applications.

Going back to the creation of our service, to build our application, we will encapsulate LibreOffice in a Docker image. The information for the service is provided through a Cloud Pub/Sub subscription that encapsulates the Cloud Storage notification event.

Our application will be built using Node.js and will demonstrate how to access the message queue information. Although the code base is relatively short, it demonstrates how to integrate external applications with Cloud Run. Remember when exploring alternative applications that Cloud Run applications are meant to be stateless, as well as utilize HTTP.

The document service receives HTTP through the subscription interface to Cloud Pub/Sub, which means this provides a straightforward mechanism to exchange data between products. Additionally, state information is not required for the request-response life cycle associated with the data exchange. Processing the file with LibreOffice will, however, use the /tmp directory allocated to Cloud Run to temporarily hold information on the output file.

To enable Cloud Run to perform document conversions, we are going to consume notification messages derived from Cloud Storage, as follows:

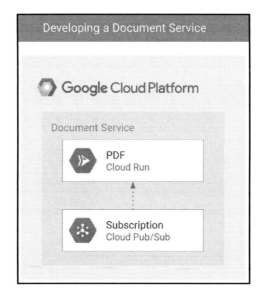

Building the Cloud Run service incorporates a Node.js application to process the information, as well as the creation of a Docker container. As in previous examples, we start with the package.json file and install packages to enable access to additional resources (for example, Cloud Storage and Express.js).

Developing the service

First, we need to populate our configuration files with the correct information:

1. Amend the package.json file to add a start script, as follows:

```
...
"scripts": {
 "start": "node index.js",
```

```
"test": "echo \"Error: no test specified\" && exit 1"
},
...
```

2. Add the packages used by the conversion process:

```
npm install express
npm install body-parser
npm install child_process
npm install @google-cloud/storage
```

3. Edit the `index.js` file to add the required references and additional code. Add the following package requirements to the top of the code file:

```
const {promisify} = require('util');
const {Storage} = require('@google-cloud/storage');
const exec = promisify(require('child_process').exec);
const storage = new Storage();
```

4. Replace the existing `app.post` function with the code outlined, as follows:

```
app.post('/', async (req, res) => {
try {
const file = decodeBase64Json(req.body.message.data);
await downloadFile(file.bucket, file.name);
const pdfFileName = await convertFile(file.name);
await uploadFile(process.env.PDF_BUCKET, pdfFileName);
await deleteFile(file.bucket, file.name);
}
catch (ex) {
console.log(`Error: ${ex}`);
}
res.set('Content-Type', 'text/plain');
res.send('\n\nOK\n\n');
})
```

5. Add the `downloadFile` function:

```
async function downloadFile(bucketName, fileName) {
const options = {destination: `/tmp/${fileName}`};
await storage.bucket(bucketName).file(fileName).download(options);
}
```

The next function is where the magic happens in our program. From the following code snippet, we can see that LibreOffice is called in a headless state (that is, with no graphical interface) to generate a PDF. The resultant file is stored in the /tmp directory for postprocessing.

6. Add the convertFile function:

```
async function convertFile(fileName) {
  const cmd = 'libreoffice --headless --convert-to pdf --outdir /tmp
' +
  `"/tmp/${fileName}"`;
  console.log(cmd);
  const { stdout, stderr } = await exec(cmd);
  if (stderr) {
  throw stderr;
  }
  console.log(stdout);
  pdfFileName = fileName.replace(/\.\w+$/, '.pdf');
  return pdfFileName;
}
```

7. Add the deleteFile function:

```
async function deleteFile(bucketName, fileName) {
  await storage.bucket(bucketName).file(fileName).delete();
}
```

8. Add the uploadFile function:

```
async function uploadFile(bucketName, fileName) {
  await storage.bucket(bucketName).upload(`/tmp/${fileName}`);
}
```

Nice work! We now have an application capable of generating a PDF from an object passed to it. The next step is to create a Docker image that will run the application when the container is run.

Deploying the service

To create a Dockerfile manifest for the application, follow these steps:

1. Add the definition to install the libreoffice package to the Dockerfile:

```
FROM node:12
RUN apt-get update -y \
```

```
       && apt-get install -y libreoffice \
       && apt-get clean
    WORKDIR /usr/src/app
    COPY package.json package*.json ./
    RUN npm install --only=production
    COPY . .
    CMD [ "npm", "start" ]
```

2. From the command line, build the service, create an image from the manifest, and store it in `gcr.io`:

```
gcloud builds submit \
  --tag gcr.io/$GOOGLE_CLOUD_PROJECT/pdf-converter
```

3. Once the build process has successfully completed, deploy the service:

```
gcloud beta run deploy pdf-converter \
  --image gcr.io/$GOOGLE_CLOUD_PROJECT/pdf-converter \
  --platform managed \
  --region us-central1 \
  --memory=2Gi \
  --no-allow-unauthenticated \
  --set-env-vars PDF_BUCKET=$GOOGLE_CLOUD_PROJECT-processed
```

The preceding properties for Cloud Run provide an overview of the key attributes associated with a typical deployment. We have increased the memory allocated for Cloud Run as the conversion process is memory intensive.

4. Create a new environment variable to hold the SERVICE_URL parameters:

```
SERVICE_URL=$(gcloud beta run services describe pdf-converter --
platform managed --region us-central1 --format "value(status.url)")
```

We now have an image built and stored in Google Cloud. The image is maintained in the Container Registry and the artifact can be deployed with additional properties to specify additional memory and the region in which it will be run. Notably, when the instance is run, we need to specify an environment variable that names the bucket that data will be output to.

As the final step for this build and deployment section, we capture the service URL assigned to the deployed Cloud Run instance. Capturing the service URL enables the user to access the service via an environment variable. We will use this environment variable later on in this exercise.

Congratulations – there now exists a service on Google Cloud capable of automatically creating a PDF based on an uploaded file.

Securing service access

With the service enabled successfully, we will turn our attention to securing access. To achieve this, we will be creating a new service account with the specific task of managing the invocation of the new service.

Thinking back to the original design, the service is actually invoked by Cloud Pub/Sub rather than a user. As we have chained together a series of events, we can take advantage of this to minimize the external sources that are able to initiate our new service. The following steps illustrate how to create a service account tasked with the invocation of a new Cloud Run PDF service instance.

Creating a service account

To create a service account, follow these simple steps:

1. Create a new service account:

   ```
   gcloud iam service-accounts create pubsub-cloud-run-invoker --
   display-name "PubSub Cloud Run Invoker"
   ```

2. Give the service account permission to invoke Cloud Run:

   ```
   gcloud beta run services add-iam-policy-binding pdf-converter --
   member=serviceAccount:pubsub-cloud-run-
   invoker@$GOOGLE_CLOUD_PROJECT.iam.gserviceaccount.com --
   role=roles/run.invoker --region us-central1
   ```

3. Create an environment variable to hold the PROJECT_ID:

   ```
   PROJECT_NUMBER=$(gcloud config get-value project)
   ```

4. Allow the project to create Cloud Pub/Sub authentication tokens:

   ```
   gcloud projects add-iam-policy-binding $GOOGLE_CLOUD_PROJECT --
   member=serviceAccount:service-$PROJECT_NUMBER@gcp-sa-
   pubsub.iam.gserviceaccount.com --
   role=roles/iam.serviceAccountTokenCreator
   ```

Congratulations – using a service account to manage resources follows best practice guidelines laid out by Google Cloud. Following these simple steps ensures that the identity and access permissions are limited to only the service account requiring access.

Now that we have a backend service constrained to a service account invocation, we can set up the message queue to process requests.

Handling processing requests

The final development task is to add a subscription to the solution. The subscription is used to consume information from the selected topic on Cloud Pub/Sub. A simple mechanism such as this allows information to be channeled between different services with minimal effort.

In the following diagram, we bind the push endpoint for Pub/Sub to the SERVICE_URL and tie the invocation of the function to the service account we created earlier. Fortunately, initiating a processing request like this is straightforward on Google Cloud:

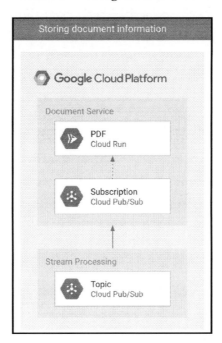

To initiate a subscription on an existing Cloud Pub/Sub topic, do the following:

1. Create a new Pub/Sub subscription bound to the SERVICE_URL:

    ```
    gcloud beta pubsub subscriptions create pdf-conv-sub --topic new-
    doc --push-endpoint=$SERVICE_URL --push-auth-service-
    account=pubsub-cloud-run-
    invoker@$GOOGLE_CLOUD_PROJECT.iam.gserviceaccount.com
    ```

2. Now that a subscription has been declared, the information that's passed to the `new-doc` topic will be automatically pushed to the subscriber by Cloud Pub/Sub:

```
{
  "message": {
    "attributes": {
      "key": "value"
    },
    "data": "V2VsY29tZSB0byBHb29nbGUgQ2xvdWQgU2VydmVybGVzcwo=",
    "messageId": "123456789012"
  },
  "subscription":
"projects/[PROJECT_ID]/subscriptions/[SUBSCRIPTION_ID]"
}
```

The message object indicates both a subscription and message. A subscription key/value pair defines the project and subscription ID to be used in the message queue. Additionally, a message object that details the key/value pairs for the attributes, data, and message ID allocated to the data to be sent.

3. In the preceding example, once the message/data has been successfully retrieved, the endpoint will use base64 to decode the message passed.

Both the `PROJECT_ID` and `SUBSCRIPTION_ID` values need to be valid for the Google Cloud project being used.

In case you are wondering, the data value displayed in the preceding example is a base64-encoded message. To encode a message, use the base64 application; for example, `echo "Welcome to Google Cloud Serverless" | base64`.

To decode a message, add `-d` to the application command line; for example, `echo "V2VsY29tZSB0byBHb29nbGUgQ2xvdWQgU2VydmVybGVzcwo=" | base64 -d`

The HTTPS request will be passed to the predefined endpoint and acknowledged on receipt. If the object passed is not acknowledged as successful, a retry mechanism will be employed, indicating the message needs to be resent. The retry process will be marshaled by a default acknowledgment deadline, which means the endpoint needs to respond before this timeout is in effect.

When working with Cloud Pub/Sub, it is useful to note that Google Cloud serverless systems (that is, App Engine, Cloud Functions, and Cloud Run) use the push mechanism. As flow control is automatically established, the client only needs to indicate success/failure on message processing.

Congratulations—the create-a-PDF service has now been designed and developed using Google Cloud serverless technologies. That concludes the development phase, and we can now progress to testing our new service.

Testing the document service

Once the service has been successfully configured, we can commence testing the service. Before we begin that activity, let's take a moment to view the service architecture that has been built:

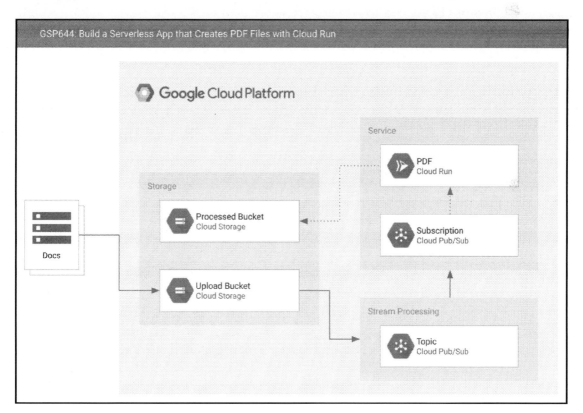

Despite the simplicity of our service, the constituent components remove much of the complexity associated with processing information. The use of Cloud Storage negates the need to work with a database and provides an effective event notification system for content changes that are made to the storage.

Once the data has been uploaded, the event notification generates a new Cloud Pub/Sub message containing relevant information on the file uploaded. Again, we are not required to do any processing to achieve this result. The **Topic/Subscription** mechanism provides all the message-processing capability required.

Finally, the message that a new file has been uploaded reaches our PDF backend service. This is the point at which we see the inclusion of the image we built earlier. When Cloud Run executes, it receives the payload from Cloud Pub/Sub before seamlessly processing the information.

Why was it worth recounting what we did? Well, it should indicate how little we actually need to test in terms of the end-to-end process we've defined. Basically, we need to confirm the following:

- That the Storage Service uses a managed activity
- That the Stream Processing Service uses a managed activity
- That the PDF Service is based on our code

So, how and what would we test with the PDF service?

Basic testing of the service can be performed by checking the service is online and by adding documents to the specified upload bucket.

To test the PDF service is active, we will use the cURL program to retrieve an authorization token:

1. Initially, test that the service has been deployed successfully:

    ```
    curl -X POST -H "Authorization: Bearer $(gcloud auth print-
    identity-token)" $SERVICE_URL
    ```

    Now that we know the service is online, we can begin to test the service. Remember, we have added a Pub/Sub notification event to our upload storage. Once data is added, the message queue will be updated and send a request to the service to transform the data file.

2. Test the conversion process by uploading some public Qwiklabs example files:

    ```
    gsutil -m cp gs://spls/gsp644/* gs://$GOOGLE_CLOUD_PROJECT-upload
    ```

3. To confirm the files have been processed, check the processed Cloud Storage bucket:

| Upload files | Upload folder | Create folder | Manage holds | Delete |

Q Filter by prefix...

Buckets / qwiklabs-gcp-b264c74144701c24-processed

	Name	Size	Type	Storage class
☐	cat-and-mouse.pdf	1.7 MB	application/pdf	Standard
☐	file-sample_100kB.pdf	125.36 KB	application/pdf	Standard
☐	file-sample_1MB.pdf	1.06 MB	application/pdf	Standard
☐	file-sample_500kB.pdf	611.97 KB	application/pdf	Standard
☐	file_example_XLSX_50.pdf	37.01 KB	application/pdf	Standard
☐	file_example_XLS_10.pdf	32.24 KB	application/pdf	Standard
☐	file_example_XLS_100.pdf	43.16 KB	application/pdf	Standard
☐	file_example_XLS_50.pdf	37.05 KB	application/pdf	Standard

In the preceding screenshot, you will note that the original files have now been transformed into PDFs. Take a moment to also check the original upload folder on Cloud Storage and notice that the upload folder is now empty. What happened to all those files that were uploaded? Well, the application includes a hygiene element that also helpfully removes the files once they've successfully processed. Therefore, the upload folder only contains files that have not been converted.

There was a lot of work involved in this scenario; however, none of the techniques presented should be unfamiliar now that you've worked through the various chapters in this book. Congratulations on successfully creating the PDF service – learning how to build the components services will enable more complex systems to be developed over time.

Summary

In this chapter, we detailed the process for fulfilling project requirements with Google Cloud serverless technologies. As part of this process, we broke down the initial customer requirements and matched those to pre-existing Google Cloud products. Taking this approach significantly shortened our development cycle and minimized the level of testing required.

Working with serverless architectures on Google Cloud presents a number of opportunities to build some exciting applications. As we have seen in this chapter, the design and development process can be extremely rewarding. In most instances, working with the system to minimize both the code developed and the complexity of the application is time well spent. Our application example clearly demonstrates how using existing packages can significantly increase overall productivity and deliver on customer requirements. Hopefully, this chapter has ignited your imagination and provided the inspiration needed to build the next great application.

In the next chapter, we will introduce a more advanced example in which multiple services are run at the same time.

Questions

1. What command is used to access Google Cloud Storage from the command line?
2. When would Stackdriver Logging be the most useful?
3. What is the purpose of a Docker manifest file?
4. Where does Cloud Build store the images it creates?
5. The `curl` command can test GET and POST requests? (True or False)
6. Why would you use the `gsutil` command with the `-m` parameter?
7. What type of permission is required to call a service?

Further reading

- **Connecting to Cloud Storage Buckets**: `https://cloud.google.com/compute/docs/disks/gcs-buckets`
- **Stackerdriver Logging**: `https://cloud.google.com/logging/docs/view/logs_index`
- **Qwiklabs Serverless Workshop**: `qwiklabs.com/quests/98`

12
Consuming Third-Party Data via a REST API

Previously, in Chapter 11, *Building a PDF Conversion Service*, we learned how to create a PDF service using Cloud Run. In this final chapter, we will turn the complexity up a gear in order to build a more complex example based on the Pet Theory case study. The requirement is to implement a serverless solution on Google Cloud using multiple services.

Through this chapter, your knowledge of serverless workloads and the experience required for real-world enterprise products will be challenged. By the end of it, a real-world application will be created that demonstrates the key aspects of serverless workloads on the Google Cloud.

Over the course of this chapter, we will discuss the following topics:

- An overview of the Pet Theory case study
- Designing a lab report solution
- Developing the lab solution
- Email SMS communication
- The continuous integration workflow
- Testing a lab service

Technical requirements

To complete the exercises in this chapter, you will require a Google Cloud project or a Qwiklabs account.

You can find all the code files for this chapter in the GitHub repository for this book, under the ch12 subdirectory, at https://github.com/PacktPublishing/Hands-on-Serverless-Computing-with-Google-Cloud/tree/master/ch12.

While you are going through the code snippets in this book, you will notice that, in a few instances, a few lines from the code/output have been removed and replaced with dots (. . .). The use of ellipses is only to show relevant code/output. The complete code is available on GitHub at the previously mentioned link.

An overview of the Pet Theory case study

As per the previous chapter, our case study is based on the Pet Theory veterinary practice. The full Pet Theory case study incorporates a number of different scenarios that demonstrate how you can resolve typical real-world issues with serverless technology. To view the complete scenario, visit the Qwiklabs website and reference the Pet Theory Quest in order to see the associated labs.

In this exercise, the Pet Theory management team has expressed their concern regarding the level of manual effort that is required to process lab reports. Currently, clinical reports sent from third-party labs are received electronically and are then manually processed by the internal admin team. The process of managing the report is effectively to download the information and add it to a report that is then communicated to the pet owner via email or SMS. Since the veterinary practice has become more and more successful, the number of reports associated with this process has become unmanageable.

To resolve the issue relating to processing lab reports, it has been proposed that a proof of concept should be built. The initial revision should demonstrate how to automate processing the lab reports that are received and also the distribution of report information.

To begin our review, we will outline, at a high level, what the proposed architecture should achieve and the associated component roles and requirements.

Designing a lab report solution

In this scenario, the Pet Theory team is keen to explore how they can use serverless technologies to automate the receiving and processing of lab results. Lab reports are currently received electronically and then have to be manually sent to clients. As per previous examples, the emphasis of the activities to be performed is to demonstrate how to replace existing tasks with minimum development effort. In addition to this, the components used should be loosely coupled so that further enhancements are straightforward to implement and do not require significant rework.

In terms of the requirements stated, the Pet Theory team has decided they need a system capable of the following:

Requirement	Service
Report collation	Reporting
Message handling	Message
Email communication	Email
SMS communication	SMS
Test data capture	Test

Let's add to our understanding by describing each requirement.

Report collation

Lab reports are sent directly to the Pet Theory web endpoint using an HTTP(S) POST command. The information received utilizes the JSON format and the external application has already agreed on the content for the message communicated.

Both Cloud Run and Cloud Functions provide the ability to consume web endpoints. Apart from consuming messages, a reporting service also needs to be capable of propagating the message to downstream services.

Message handling

Pet Theory has experienced a similar requirement for the lab, which was discussed in Chapter 11, *Building a PDF Conversion Service*. In that example, the sender and receiver used asynchronous messaging via Cloud Pub/Sub to achieve their aim.

In this situation, lab reports are to be delivered to email and SMS services for further processing.

Email communication

The email service represents a new requirement and delivers the ability to communicate with clients using an existing email solution. Information is to be passed to this component via a Cloud Pub/Sub subscription.

SMS communication

Similar to email communication, the SMS component offers an alternative way to communicate with clients when receiving test results.

Now that we have a shared understanding of the key components of the architecture, the elements necessary for building the solution should be clearer. From an overview perspective, our solution architecture can be described with the following steps:

1. A JSON formatted lab report is submitted to the Pet Theory HTTP(S) endpoint.
2. A report service consumes the JSON message.
3. The lab information in the JSON message is published to a Cloud Pub/Sub topic.
4. A subscription notification is received by the email service.
5. A subscription notification is received by the SMS service.

In addition, we can see that the following components are required:

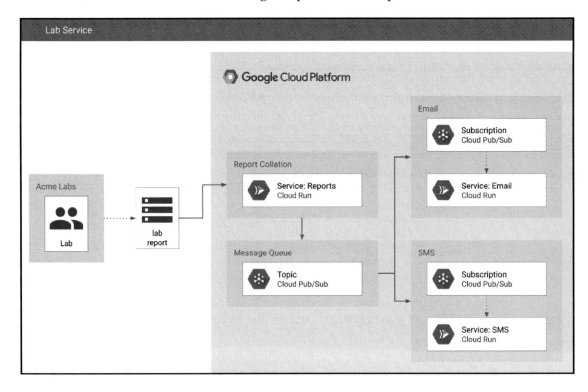

It is important to note that there are many other ways to resolve the requirements outlined here.

In the preceding diagram, we have defined a number of components to meet our initial requirements. Remember that Pet Theory is a small organization, so it will not want to incur development costs unnecessarily.

In this example, we are going to implement multiple services, each of which will perform a specific task. As such, later in this exercise, we will look at how to test the individual components by enhancing them to write a status update within a document.

Based on what we've just covered, we now have a general understanding of the lab report solution for processing reports submitted to our service. In the next section, we will start to look at the practical elements of developing the solution in order to fulfill the requirements.

Developing the lab solution

Several advanced topics will be covered in this chapter; so, having worked through the examples presented in prior chapters is highly recommended. Over the course of the previous chapters, knowledge of Google Cloud and its serverless product portfolio has been presented in order to guide you on this journey.

 Using your Google Cloud account, open the Cloud Shell and make sure that a clone of the lab repository for Chap12 is accessible.

Unlike the earlier chapters, some activities will not be covered in detail. Instead, this chapter is devoted to bringing together a skeleton solution that illustrates how to construct an application to meet requirements. If you get stuck or need help, don't forget that you can consult the solution directory.

Linking to Google Docs

In addition to using a centralized service such as Stackdriver, we can also introduce alternative tooling. In this section, we will be demonstrating how to integrate Google Docs (specifically, Google Sheets).

When you create a spreadsheet on Google Sheets, by default, only the creator has permission to read and write to the sheet. To allow the Cloud Run application access to the sheet, we need to provide it with access permissions. As you might have guessed, for this task, we will use a service account.

From Cloud Shell, we need to retrieve the name of the service account for our project:

```
gcloud iam service-accounts list --filter="Compute Engine default service
account" --format='value(EMAIL)'
```

Now, we can use that information to link to Google Docs:

1. Create a new spreadsheet in Google Sheets (that is, `https://docs.google.com/spreadsheets`).
2. Click on the default spreadsheet name of `Untitled spreadsheet`.
3. Rename the spreadsheet to `Lab Results Status`.
4. Click on the **Share** button and enter the service account email address we retrieved previously.

Great! We now have a spreadsheet available that is linked to our service account project. To link our new spreadsheet with our services, we need to use the `SHEET-ID` variable. The `SHEET-ID` variable is a unique identifier for your document and is accessible by accessing the URL of the Google Sheet, as per the following example URL:

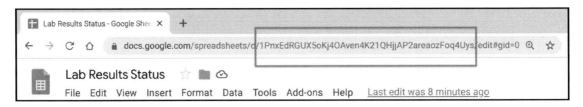

From the preceding graphic, we can see the `SHEET-ID` has been clearly marked. Now, we need to incorporate that identifier into our application code.

Perform the following steps to access the spreadsheet using Cloud Run:

1. Access the URL for the spreadsheet we created.
2. Copy the string that starts after `spreadsheets/d/` and ends before `/edit`, as shown in the preceding screenshot.

3. Now, go back to Cloud Shell and edit the file named `pet theory/lab05/common/sheet.js`.

4. Replace the `SHEET-ID` variable with the value copied from the URL.

Excellent! Now, the spreadsheet can be accessed using our Cloud Run application.

Report collation

From our prior discussion on the Lab Service architecture, we know that the initial service to be created relates to report collation. If we focus on the requirements for this stage of processing, we can see that we need to consume a JSON file that's received from external sources:

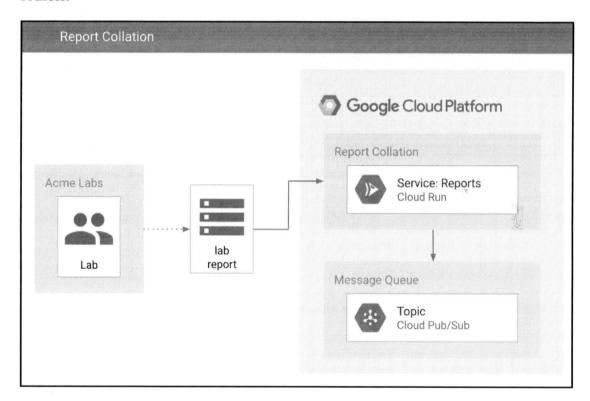

At this point in this exercise, let's take the opportunity to create a Cloud Pub/Sub topic, as follows:

1. Run the following command:

```
gcloud pubsub topics create new-lab-report
```

   The Cloud Pub/Sub topic will be used to communicate lab reports between the report collation service and backend email/SMS services.

2. Install the npm packages dependencies for the lab report:

```
npm install express
npm install body-parser
npm install @google-cloud/pubsub
npm install googleapis
```

3. Amend the package.json file to incorporate a start command:

```
"scripts": {
 "start": "node index.js",
  "test": "echo \"Error: no test specified\" && exit 1"
},
```

4. Create an index.js file with the following content:

```
const sheet = require('./common/sheet.js');
const {PubSub} = require('@google-cloud/pubsub');
const pubsub = new PubSub();
const express = require('express');
const app = express();
const bodyParser = require('body-parser');
app.use(bodyParser.json());
const port = process.env.PORT || 8080;

app.listen(port, () => {
  console.log('Listening on port', port);
});
```

5. Append the following content to index.js:

```
app.post('/', async (req, res) => {
  try {
    await sheet.reset();
    const labReport = req.body;
    await publishPubSubMessage(labReport);
    res.status(204).send();
  }
```

```
    catch (ex) {
      console.log(ex);
      res.status(500).send(ex);
    }
  })
```

6. Finally, in `index.js`, add the following function, and then close the file for editing:

```
async function publishPubSubMessage(labReport) {
  const buffer = Buffer.from(JSON.stringify(labReport));
  await pubsub.topic('new-lab-report').publish(buffer);
}
```

7. Copy across the `common` directory that includes the Google API's code:

```
cp -R ../pet-theory/lab05/common/ .
```

Take a moment to look at the `index.js` source code, taking note of the following elements:

- The `request.body` property represents the lab report to be processed.
- The schema associated with the lab report is not required at this point.
- The data from the lab report is added to a Cloud Pub/Sub topic named `new-lab-report`.
- Once the topic has been published, the service returns an HTTP status code of 204 (that is, successful but no data to return).
- If an error occurs, an HTTP status code of 500 (a server error) is returned.

Besides the Node.js source code for the report service, we also require a Dockerfile to be created in the same directory.

8. Create a Dockerfile, as follows:

```
FROM node:12
WORKDIR /usr/src/app
COPY package.json package*.json ./
RUN npm install --only=production
COPY . .
CMD [ "npm", "start" ]
```

The content of this manifest should, at this stage, be familiar and require no further explanation. We will deploy the manifest later in this exercise when we discuss component deployment.

Congratulations! The code definition for a report service capable of consuming external lab reports is available and ready to be deployed. A Cloud Pub/Sub has been provisioned and made ready to accept information that's received from external third parties.

Next, we will take a closer look at the email and SMS services and review the instructions associated with their implementation.

Email/SMS communication

For the sake of brevity in our proof of concept, the email and SMS services will utilize a similar code base to demonstrate how background services can be designed within Google Cloud. While these components are meant to provide isolated services, in our example, we will use common code to demonstrate their functionality. In a real-world situation, the communication component presents an opportunity for a common code base to be replicated/extended for different solutions (for example, email, bots, SMSes, pagers, and more).

The Cloud Pub/Sub topic we previously created pushes the data to be consumed by the communication components. In this instance, the lab report data object represents a JSON file that is used to communicate lab results:

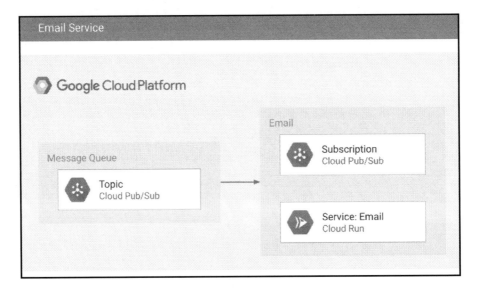

It is worth pointing out that we have not actually referenced the data passed in the lab report, nor do we know the content schema being used. Instead, we treat it as a black box and, therefore, don't have any data validation to be performed on the content. Taking this step reduces the level of testing to be performed later on in the development cycle.

In the context of Cloud Run message processing, this means the following processes are observed when using Cloud Pub/Sub:

- Cloud Pub/Sub maintains its responsibility for pushing messages.
- The subscriber is responsible for consuming the messages.
- A service is aligned with the subscriber to accept the message payload.

Once again, we are using techniques that should now be familiar, as these same design patterns are common when using Cloud Pub/Sub to interact between resources.

Email

From the `email-service` directory, we need to perform a couple of activities. If you are unsure of the exact command, refer to the *Designing a lab report solution* section earlier in this chapter:

1. Amend the `package.json` file to include a node start `index.js` statement.
2. Add package dependencies for `express`, `body-parser`, and `googleapis`.
3. Create an `index.js` file and populate it with the following code:

```
const sheet = require('./common/sheet.js');
const util = require('./common/util.js');
const express = require('express');
const app = express();
const bodyParser = require('body-parser');
app.use(bodyParser.json());

const port = process.env.PORT || 8080;
  app.listen(port, () => {
  console.log('Listening on port', port);
});
```

4. Add the `index.js` file and populate it with this additional code:

```
app.post('/', async (req, res) => {
  const labReport = util.decodeBase64Json(req.body.message.data);
  try {
    await sheet.update('email', labReport.id, 'Trying');
    const status = await util.attemptFlakeyOperation();
    await sheet.update('email', labReport.id, status);
    res.status(204).send();
  }
  catch (ex) {
    await sheet.update('email', labReport.id, ex);
    res.status(500).send();
  }
})
```

5. Copy across the `common` directory that includes the Google API's code:

```
cp -R ../pet-theory/lab05/common/ .
```

Once more, take a moment to observe the `index.js` source code, taking note of the following key elements:

- The `request.body` property translates the Cloud Pub/Sub message using `decodeBase64`.
- Data processing uses a `console.log` statement.
- The service returns an HTTP status code of `204` (that is, successful but no data to return).
- If an error occurs, an HTTP status code of `500` (that is, an unsuccessful server error occurred) is returned.

We also need a Dockerfile manifest that will be used later to build the image for the Node.js application.

6. Create a Dockerfile for a `Node.js` application.

Great! Let's move on.

SMS

From the SMS service directory, we need to perform the same steps. If you are unsure of the exact command, reference to the Developing the *Lab solution* section earlier in this chapter:

1. Amend the `package.json` file to include a node start `index.js` statement.
2. Add package dependencies for `express`, `body-parser`, and `googleapis`.
3. Create an `index.js` file and populate it with the following code:

```
const sheet = require('./common/sheet.js');
const util = require('./common/util.js');
const express = require('express');
const app = express();
const bodyParser = require('body-parser');
app.use(bodyParser.json());

const port = process.env.PORT || 8080;
  app.listen(port, () => {
  console.log('Listening on port', port);
});
```

4. Add the `index.js` file and populate it with this additional code:

```
app.post('/', async (req, res) => {
  const labReport = util.decodeBase64Json(req.body.message.data);
  try {
    await sheet.update('sms', labReport.id, 'Trying');
    const status = await util.attemptFlakeyOperation();
    await sheet.update('sms', labReport.id, status);
    res.status(204).send();
  }
  catch (ex) {
    await sheet.update('sms', labReport.id, ex);
    res.status(500).send();
  }
})
```

5. Copy across the `common` directory that includes the Google API's code:

```
cp -R ../pet-theory/lab05/common/ .
```

Add a Dockerfile manifest that will be used later to build the image for the Node.js application.

6. Create a Dockerfile for a `Node.js` application.

Congratulations! The email and SMS services are now available and ready to be deployed. Now that we have looked at the general code base, we can move on to thinking about how to efficiently build the multiple components needed for this solution.

The continuous integration workflow

While building components, using a manual approach may seem like a good technique due to its implementation simplicity. In this chapter, we will automate this process. The reason for this is that there are multiple code bases that need to be built and deployed, which, if done manually, can result in unnecessary errors in the process.

Instead of a manual build, we turn our focus to a development tool to take care of this repetitive build and deploy process. In our project, we intend to use Cloud Build to manage the build workflow on Google Cloud. To use Cloud Build, it is worth understanding the actual process to be automated, since the configuration required will often be an approximation of the manual steps to be followed.

When working in this project, our developer workflow can be defined using the following steps:

1. A developer commits their code using `git`.
2. Code commits are notified to Source Repositories.
3. Cloud Build triggers when a matching pattern is found.
4. If the build process fails, the developer is required to rectify the code (go to *step 1*).
5. If the build process succeeds, the image is added to the Container Registry.
6. A **Quality Assurance (QA)** team member can then access the new image.

As you can see, there are multiple steps involved in this process, and an error could potentially occur during any one of these stages. Introducing automation in this process can help to remediate any errors through consistency and also make the overall maintenance of the project more straightforward.

The defined steps provide a common approach to ensure building software can be achieved in an iterative manner. Using a development tool such as Cloud Build ensures that the build process remains both consistent and flexible and that the process is managed through an external build file. The build file can easily be shared between team members and means updates and build profiles can be managed under version control.

Developers are part of a continual feedback workflow based on their code commits, meaning they control code submissions and can also react directly to any issues. The initiation of the build process, based on a code commit, will feedback on the success or failure of the relevant component submitted.

Take a look at the following diagram to see how this process could work in practice:

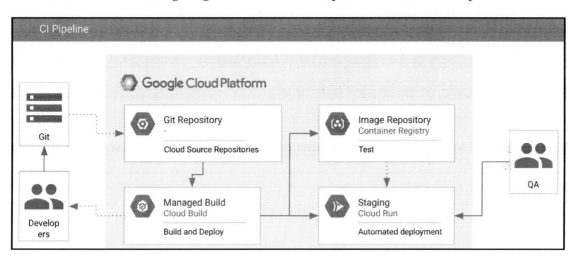

Once the code component has been successfully built, it will be stored in the Container Registry. From here, the QA team members have access to the latest verified image and are able to test each of the images independently, without needing to refer to the development team. In this way, alternative versions such as dev, staging, and prod could be deployed and tested as different stage gates.

Configuring Lab Service CI

To understand how this process will be used in our example, we can create a configuration for Pet Theory based on a basic Cloud Build script.

You can refer to the *Further reading* section at the end of this chapter for more information regarding account permissions.

To get started, go back to the `lab-service` directory. This is where we will create a basic Cloud Build configuration:

1. Create and edit a new `cloudbuild.yaml` file for `lab-service`:

```yaml
steps:
# Build the container image
- name: 'gcr.io/cloud-builders/docker'
args: ['build', '-t', 'gcr.io/$PROJECT_ID/lab-service', 'lab-
service/.']
# Push the container image to Container Registry
- name: 'gcr.io/cloud-builders/docker'
args: ['push', 'gcr.io/$PROJECT_ID/lab-service']
# Deploy the image to Cloud Run
- name: 'gcr.io/cloud-builders/gcloud'
args: ['beta', 'run', 'deploy', 'lab-service', '--image',
'gcr.io/$PROJECT_ID/lab-service', '--region', 'us-central1', '--
platform', 'managed', '--no-allow
-unauthenticated']
images:
- 'gcr.io/$PROJECT_ID/lab-service'
timeout: "600s"
```

    Next, we are going to set up Google Source Repositories for our project. We need to create a temporary repository in order to host our code and demonstrate some additional features of Google Cloud.

2. Create a Cloud Source Repositories configuration:

```
gcloud source repos create pet-theory-test
```

3. Clone the newly created repository, noting you will need to supply your project identity as a parameter:

```
gcloud source repos clone pet-theory-test --project=[PROJECT_ID]
```

4. Copy across the subdirectories (that is, `email-service`, `sms-service`, `lab-service`, and `common`) to the new Google Source repository directory. Your new `pet-theory-test` directory should look like this:

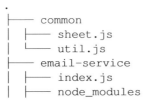

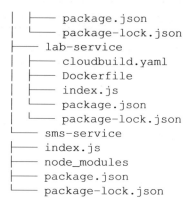

```
|   |—— package.json
|   └── package-lock.json
|—— lab-service
|   |—— cloudbuild.yaml
|   |—— Dockerfile
|   |—— index.js
|   └── package.json
|   └── package-lock.json
└── sms-service
|—— index.js
|—— node_modules
|—— package.json
└── package-lock.json
```

5. Check the status of the `git` directory to ensure you have the common `email-service`, `lab-service`, and `sms-service` subdirectories as untracked files:

   `git status`

6. Add the amended files to `git`:

   `git add .`

7. Set up the email credentials using your email address:

   `git config --global user.email "EMAIL"`

8. Set up the name credentials using your username:

   `git config --global user name "MY NAME"`

9. Add a commit message to the repository:

   `git commit -m "Initial commit - Pet Theory CH12"`

10. Commit the code for the repository directly to the master branch:

    `git push origin master`

11. Check the Cloud Source Repositories in the console to ensure the code is now available.

Congratulations! Knowing how to use Cloud Source Repositories can save time when hosting code in Google Cloud. In general, being able to use a Git-based solution provides some assurance over the safety of code.

Triggering Cloud Build

So, now that we have our code in Cloud Source Repositories, how do we get it to automatically build using the Google Cloud developer tools? To automatically build code on commit, we can use our old friend Cloud Build. For this example, we will use our `lab-service` directory to demonstrate the build process:

> For this example, make sure that you are in the `pet-theory-test/lab-service` directory. The initial steps in Cloud Build requires the selection of a repository.

1. From the Cloud Console, access Cloud Build (located under the **Developer Tools** options).
2. Select the **Triggers** menu option and the **Create Trigger** option.
3. Set up the trigger using the following information:

Field	Value
Name	`trigger-lab-service`
Description	`Push to the lab branch`
Trigger type	`Branch`
Branch (regex)	`^([lL]ab)/\w+`
Cloudbuild configuration	`lab-service/cloudbuild.yaml`
Substitution variables	`N/A`

4. Select the **Create Trigger** button at the bottom of the screen to enable the trigger.

> The regex branch in the Cloud Build trigger table is a common way of filtering which content should be built. In many instances, developers will want to only build a specific branch, and using regex helps to isolate particular branches.

To test the trigger has been successfully set up, commit a code change to the `lab-service` trigger. Follow these steps:

1. Add a comment to the `cloudbuild.yaml` file:

    ```
    steps:
    # comment
    # Build the container image
    - name: 'gcr.io/cloud-builders/docker'
    args: ['build', '-t', 'gcr.io/$PROJECT_ID/lab-service', 'lab-
    service/.']
    # Push the container image to Container Registry
    - name: 'gcr.io/cloud-builders/docker'
    args: ['push', 'gcr.io/$PROJECT_ID/lab-service']
    # Deploy the image to Cloud Run
    - name: 'gcr.io/cloud-builders/gcloud'
    args: ['beta', 'run', 'deploy', 'lab-service', '--image',
    'gcr.io/$PROJECT_ID/lab-service', '--region', 'us-central1', '--
    platform', 'managed', '--no-allow
    -unauthenticated']
    images:
    - 'gcr.io/$PROJECT_ID/lab-service'
    timeout: "600s"
    ```

2. Add the updated file to `git`:

    ```
    git add cloudbuild.yaml
    ```

3. Add a commit message:

    ```
    git commit -m "Add updated cloudbuild.yaml"
    ```

4. Push the change to Cloud Source Repositories:

    ```
    git push origin lab/fix-1
    ```

In the final command, we use a special regex command to indicate that the change refers to the `lab-service` trigger. When we set up the trigger, we used a regular expression to only look at branches that were labelled with `lab`:

Build information

Status	✅ Build successful
Build id	239f9e3e-0b9a-4c52-aacc-1ff3083d4abc
Image	gcr.io/qwiklabs-gcp-00-06244e0ab4f5/lab-service
Trigger	Push to lab/fix-1 branch (Push to the lab branch - regex ^([lL]ab)/\w+)
Source	Cloud Source Repository pet-theory-test
Git commit	b517818cb3f2c8b9fced344decd883feea339915
Started	November 28, 2019 at 3:04:14 PM UTC
Duration	1 min 35 sec

Build steps   expand all

✅ gcr.io/cloud-builders/docker   46 sec ⌄
build -t gcr.io/qwiklabs-gcp-00-06244e0ab4f5/lab-service lab-service/.

✅ gcr.io/cloud-builders/docker   9 sec ⌄
push gcr.io/qwiklabs-gcp-00-06244e0ab4f5/lab-service

✅ gcr.io/cloud-builders/gcloud   24 sec ⌄
beta run deploy lab-service --image gcr.io/qwiklabs-gcp-00-06244e0ab4f5/lab-service --region us-central1 --platform managed --allow-unauthenticated

Once the code has been committed, checking the **Cloud Build History** will indicate a new build job has commenced. After each Git commit to a branch, our components will automatically trigger a build process. Now that we know that the build configuration works correctly, let's roll out the same changes to the email and SMS directories. We will ensure each build is maintained on a separate branch to minimize the potential for code merging.

Triggering email and SMS

As per the work we did with the `lab-service` trigger, we need to set up a Cloud Build trigger. However, this time, we can just duplicate the existing `lab-service` trigger:

> In this example, we used a single repository for services. However, in the real world, this approach would not be optimal. Instead, I would suggest that a repository for each service is used for better code isolation.

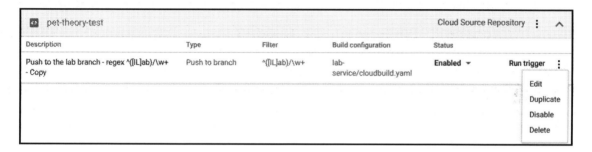

To set up the trigger perform the following steps:

1. From the **Cloud Console**, access **Cloud Build** (located under the **Developer Tools** options).
2. Select the three-dot menu item to open the pop-up menu and select **Duplicate.**
3. Select the three-dot menu (of the newly created trigger) item to open the pop-up menu and select **Edit**.
4. Set up the trigger with the following information:

Field	Value
Name	`trigger-email-service`
Description	`Push to the email branch`
Trigger type	`Branch`
Branch (regex)	`^([eE]mail)/\w+`
Cloudbuild configuration	`email-service/cloudbuild.yaml`
Substitution variables	N/A

5. Select the **Save** button at the bottom of the screen to enable the trigger.

6. Now, do exactly the same again; however, this time, create an SMS trigger using the following details:

Field	Value
Name	`trigger-sms-service`
Description	`Push to the sms branch`
Trigger type	`Branch`
Branch (regex)	`^([sS]ms)/\w+`
Cloudbuild configuration	`sms-service/cloudbuild.yaml`
Substitution variables	N/A

7. Select the **Save** button at the bottom of the screen to enable the trigger.

Having created three triggers, the Cloud Build screen should look similar to the following screenshot:

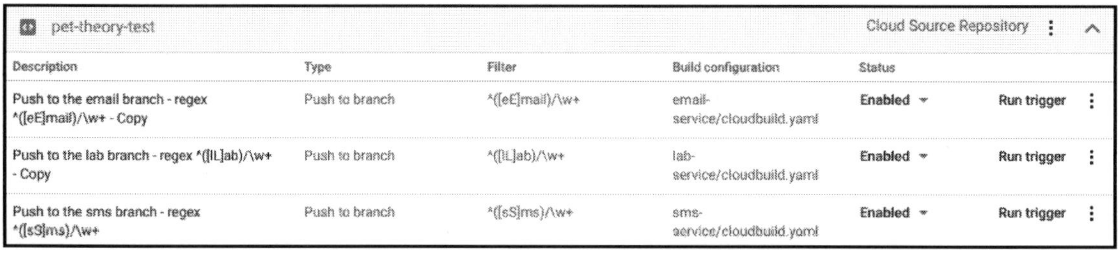

Each of these triggers operates in isolation using a different branch to signify work that's been performed on a specific service. Thanks to our regex filter, each branch will be checked and a new build job will be created when code is committed to the repository. To make this work, we need to add the `cloudbuild.yaml` file to the email and SMS directories to initiate the build process.

Let's create some configurations using `cloudbuild.yaml`:

1. In the `email-service` directory, create a new `cloudbuild.yaml` file containing the following:

```
steps:
# Build the container image
- name: 'gcr.io/cloud-builders/docker'
args: ['build', '-t', 'gcr.io/$PROJECT_ID/email-service', 'email-
service/.']
# Push the container image to Container Registry
```

```
- name: 'gcr.io/cloud-builders/docker'
args: ['push', 'gcr.io/$PROJECT_ID/email-service']
# Deploy the image to Cloud Run
- name: 'gcr.io/cloud-builders/gcloud'
args: ['beta', 'run', 'deploy', 'email-service', '--image',
'gcr.io/$PROJECT_ID/email-service', '--region', 'us-central1', '--
platform', 'managed', '--no-allow-unauthenticated']
images:
- 'gcr.io/$PROJECT_ID/email-service'
timeout: "600s"
```

If you do not remember how to perform any of these actions in Git, you can review the earlier examples on how to use Google Source Repositories. The commands are similar; we are just working on a different branch.

2. Create a new branch in `git` called `email/fix-1`.

3. Use `git` to add the updated `cloudbuild.yaml` file to the `email/fix-1` branch.

4. Add a commit message: `Initial revision - email/fix-1`.

5. Push the `email/fix-1` branch code to the repository.

6. In the `sms-service` directory, create a new `cloudbuild.yaml` file containing the following:

```
steps:
# Build the container image
- name: 'gcr.io/cloud-builders/docker'
args: ['build', '-t', 'gcr.io/$PROJECT_ID/sms-service', 'sms-
service/.']
# Push the container image to Container Registry
- name: 'gcr.io/cloud-builders/docker'
args: ['push', 'gcr.io/$PROJECT_ID/sms-service']
# Deploy the image to Cloud Run
- name: 'gcr.io/cloud-builders/gcloud'
args: ['beta', 'run', 'deploy', 'sms-service', '--image',
'gcr.io/$PROJECT_ID/sms-service', '--region', 'us-central1', '--
platform', 'managed', '--no-allow-unauthenticated']
images:
- 'gcr.io/$PROJECT_ID/sms-service'
timeout: "600s"
```

7. Create a new branch in `git` called `sms/fix-1`.
8. Use `git` to add the updated `cloudbuild.yaml` file to the `sms/fix-1` branch.
9. Add a commit message: `Initial revision – sms/fix-1`.
10. Push the `sms/fix-1` branch code to the repository.
11. Pushing the final piece of code automatically initiates Cloud Build and the associated three-stage script.

Congratulations! Using Cloud Build for build process automation increases developer productivity. Now that we have integrated a component-based build capability, we can move on and look at how to test the multiple components for this solution.

Testing a lab service

Technically, if you need to log information, the correct answer is typically Stackdriver as it is already integrated into Google Cloud. However, there are instances where you may need an alternative solution – such as in this scenario, in which a quick and easy method of checking the services is required.

In this test section, rather than utilizing *Logging* to a centralized system such as Stackdriver, we will be posting our data to a Google Sheet. An approach such as this can be a very handy technique to know, so it is worth incorporating it into our solution to demonstrate how this is achieved.

From a high level, the following process is applicable to the test service:

1. Write information to sheets
2. Application Audit
3. Vulnerability Fix

Take a look at the following diagram in order to understand the components involved in this solution:

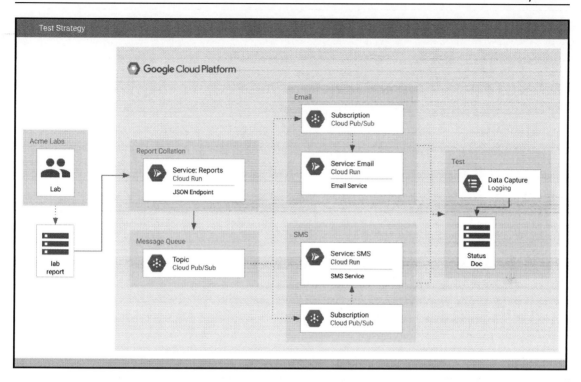

In the preceding diagram, we add a new service component to the existing code to log information into a Google spreadsheet. Being able to demonstrate the resilience of the solution is a handy feature in order to build into our proof of concept. The spreadsheet will be completed by the service; so, if it is working successfully, the output will be indicated in the spreadsheet. If the service is unavailable for some reason, then an alternative status message is written for the service that is unable to complete the task:

	A	B	C	D	
1		Report 12	Report 34	Report 56	
2	SMS	Trying		Trying	
3	Email				
4					
5					

The spreadsheet is dynamically linked to each of the services and writes a message to a spreadsheet cell when invoked by a service. The new component will provide a straightforward method to test each service in isolation and show whether a service component is operating to specification. As we now have a description of the service and properties, we can begin developing the code base to deliver against requirements.

Accessing the credentials

In this section, we'll begin by accessing the Compute Engine service account:

1. List the service accounts associated with the project:

```
gcloud iam service-accounts list
```

2. Copy the Compute Engine service account email address listed.
3. Open a new Google Sheets document.
4. Rename the sheet to `Lab Results Status`.
5. Click on the **Share** button and add the Compute Engine service account email with full edit rights.

Next, we need to set up the email Cloud Pub/Sub subscription.

Setting up the email Cloud Pub/Sub subscription

To set up the email Cloud Pub/Sub subscription, follow these simple steps:

1. Create a service account with invoking privileges:

```
gcloud iam service-accounts create pubsub-cloud-run-invoker --
display-name "PubSub Cloud Run Invoker"
```

2. Give the service account permissions to invoke the email service:

```
gcloud beta run services add-iam-policy-binding email-service --
member=serviceAccount:pubsub-cloud-run-
invoker@$GOOGLE_CLOUD_PROJECT.iam.gserviceaccount.com --
role=roles/run.invoker --region us-central1 --platform managed
```

3. Get the Google Cloud project number:

```
PROJECT_NUMBER=$(gcloud projects list --
format="value(projectNumber)" --
filter="projectId=$GOOGLE_CLOUD_PROJECT")
```

4. Create a role binding of `serviceAccountTokenCreator` using the `PROJECT_NUMBER` environment variable:

```
gcloud projects add-iam-policy-binding $GOOGLE_CLOUD_PROJECT --
member=serviceAccount:service-$PROJECT_NUMBER@gcp-sa-
pubsub.iam.gserviceaccount.com --
role=roles/iam.serviceAccountTokenCreator
```

5. Get the `EMAIL_URL` endpoint for the email service:

```
EMAIL_URL=$(gcloud beta run services describe email-service --
platform managed --region us-central1 --format
"value(status.address.url)")
```

6. Create the Cloud Pub/Sub subscription:

```
gcloud pubsub subscriptions create email-service-sub --topic new-
lab-report --push-endpoint=$EMAIL_URL --push-auth-service-
account=pubsub-cloud-run-
invoker@$GOOGLE_CLOUD_PROJECT.iam.gserviceaccount.com
```

Great work! We have now set up email subscriptions for Cloud Pub/Sub. Next, we need to repeat the process for SMS subscriptions.

Setting up the SMS Cloud Pub/Sub subscription

To set up the SMS Cloud Pub/Sub subscription, complete the following steps:

1. Create a role binding of `run.invoker`:

```
gcloud beta run services add-iam-policy-binding sms-service --
member=serviceAccount:pubsub-cloud-run-
invoker@$GOOGLE_CLOUD_PROJECT.iam.gserviceaccount.com --
role=roles/run.invoker --region us-central1 --platform managed
```

2. Get the `SMS_URL` endpoint for the `sms-service`:

```
SMS_URL=$(gcloud beta run services describe sms-service --platform
managed --region us-central1 --format "value(status.address.url)")
```

3. Create the Cloud Pub/Sub subscription:

```
gcloud pubsub subscriptions create sms-service-sub --topic new-lab-
report --push-endpoint=$SMS_URL --push-auth-service-account=pubsub-
cloud-run-invoker@$GOOGLE_CLOUD_PROJECT.iam.gserviceaccount.com
```

Fantastic! We have now set up both subscriptions for Cloud Pub/Sub. Next, we need to test our services.

Testing the service

Now, it's time to test the service. To do this, follow these steps:

1. Get the `LAB_URL` endpoint for the `lab-service`:

```
LAB_URL=$(gcloud beta run services describe lab-service --platform
managed --region us-central1 --format "value(status.address.url)")
```

2. Post some data to the lab report service:

```
curl -X POST \
-H "Content-Type: application/json" \
-d "{\"id\": 12}" \
$LAB_URL &
curl -X POST \
-H "Content-Type: application/json" \
-d "{\"id\": 34}" \
$LAB_URL &
curl -X POST \
-H "Content-Type: application/json" \
-d "{\"id\": 56}" \
$LAB_URL &
```

In the following screenshot, you can see the result of posting information to the lab service:

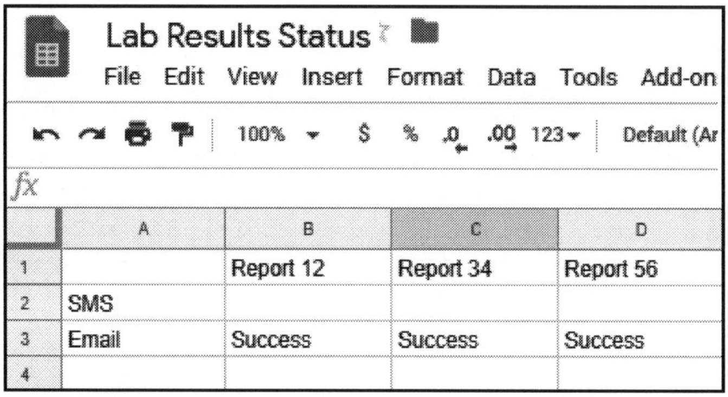

	A	B	C	D
1		Report 12	Report 34	Report 56
2	SMS			
3	Email	Success	Success	Success
4				

Congratulations! The application is now responding to external stimuli.

To test our service for resilience, we need to add an error that will mean the service will not be able to process information. For this example, we will use the email service to introduce an error.

3. Change to the `ch12/email-service` subdirectory and edit the `index.js` source code – add the erroneous `oops` line entry:

```
Add an error in the app.post function
...
app.post('/', async (req, res) => {
oops
const labReport = util.decodeBase64Json(req.body.message.data);
...
```

4. Entering the invalid code will ensure the service will not be able to complete successfully when invoked.
5. Commit the updated `email-service` code.
6. The code will be automatically built, pushed to the registry, and deployed.

Now, when the application is run, the email service will be unable to complete as the erroneous line entry, `oops`, stops the service from working correctly. Consequentially, no entries will be written in the spreadsheet. To validate this, check the Stackdriver logs to see that an error is shown relating to the defect entered.

Finally, correct the source file to remove the code defect to resume normal service and have the information successfully logged to the spreadsheet.

Congratulations! We have now successfully concluded testing the various components. We will now provide an overview of this chapter's contents.

Summary

Over the course of this final chapter, we built an application to consume external information based on JSON. To our credit, we used a scalable and resilient mechanism to handle messaging so that retries occur seamlessly. We also learned how to incorporate Google Sheets to output information. A new technique like this has many applications and will prove useful time and time again. To complete our application, we also looked at developer productivity so that we can use tools such as Cloud Build when building multiple components.

Throughout this chapter, you have learned how to integrate with Google APIs, initiate Cloud Pub/Sub, and consume JSON information from external services. Learning how to aggregate services is part and parcel of working with serverless on Google Cloud. For example, achieving scalable application messaging is simple when using Cloud Pub/Sub. Each of the patterns that's been used over the previous chapters can easily be enhanced for your own projects. Hopefully, you will be able to create the next big thing or encourage your colleagues to build even more awesome products on Google Cloud.

Questions

1. What products can be used for asynchronous messaging on Google Cloud?
2. Can you name some notifications supported by Google Cloud Storage?
3. Why are there beta commands for the GCloud SDK?
4. What is regex and why is it useful for creating triggers for branch names?
5. Cloud Source Repositories are project-based. (True or False)
6. If I wanted to invoke rate limiting on messages, I would use Cloud Tasks over Cloud Pub/Sub. (True or False)
7. Where would I be able to see HTTP latency associated with a Cloud Run application?

Further reading

- **Deploying builds**: https://cloud.google.com/cloud-build/docs/deploying-builds/deploy-cloud-run
- **Google Docs**: https://www.google.co.uk/docs/about/
- **Stackdriver**: https://cloud.google.com/stackdriver/
- **Cloud Run API**: https://cloud.google.com/run/docs/reference/rest/
- **Troubleshooting Cloud Run – fully managed**: https://cloud.google.com/run/docs/troubleshooting
- **Stackoverflow [google-cloud-run]**: https://stackoverflow.com/questions/tagged/google-cloud-run

Assessments

Chapter 1: Introducing App Engine

1. Push Queue and Pull Queue are the types of service dispatch that are supported by task queues.
2. The two levels of service supported by memcache are Shared Memcache and Dedicated Memcache.
3. Cloud Datastore is a managed schemaless (NoSQL) document database.
4. Language supported by GAE: Python, Go, Node, and PHP.
5. IP traffic, Cookie, and Random are the forms of traffic-splitting algorithms that are supported on GAE.
6. The purpose of GFE in relation to GAE is routing of Google App Engine traffic through an autoscaling infrastructure.
7. The three types of scaling supported by GAE are Automatic, Basic, and Manual.
8. Task queues mechanism is used to isolate long-lived workloads for efficiency purposes from the HTTP request/response life cycle.

Chapter 2: Developing with App Engine

1. False.
2. IP address, Cookie, or Random options are available with GAE.
3. Basic and Advanced are the filter logging options that are present for Stackdriver Logging.
4. False.
5. True.
6. The `gcloud app deploy` command.
7. The `appspot.com` domain.

Chapter 3: Introducing Lightweight Functions

1. True.
2. Deferred or delayed tasks are asynchronous tasks.
3. True.
4. True.
5. The `trigger-http` command.
6. Stackdriver Logging.
7. The `gcloud functions deploy NAME --runtime RUNTIME TRIGGER` command.
8. The exports function is the entrypoint - this indicates to Cloud Functions that the interface is public.

Chapter 4: Developing Cloud Functions

1. Cloud Functions run on port `8080`.
2. The topic trigger is used by Cloud Pub/Sub.
3. Go, Node, and Python are the runtime languages are supported by Google Cloud Functions.
4. The HTTP response code for success is 2xx.
5. The HTTP response code for a client-side error is 4xx.
6. The HTTP response code for a server-side error is 5xx.
7. The purpose of CORS is that it allows resources on the web page to be accessed from another domain.
8. HTTP headers – add `access-control-allow-origin` to the header name.

Chapter 5: Exploring Functions as a Service

1. Cloud Pub/Sub supports Push/Pull subscriptions.
2. Straight through processing, multiple publishers, multiple subscribers.
3. GET, DELETE, POST, and PUT verbs are associated with HTTP.
4. Use GET to have user data accessible in the URL.
5. The metadata property contains information relating to the Cloud Storage object.

6. An issue on the server.
7. Yes, Google Cloud supports OAuth v2.
8. No – the message will be queued for a retry.

Chapter 6: Cloud Functions Labs

1. A Cloud Function requires `cloudfunctions.invoker` permission to be invoked.
2. Google KMS provides storage of cryptographic keys.
3. The `allUsers` permission effectively means that public access is for everyone.
4. The `allAuthenticated` permission effectively means that public access is for authenticated users.
5. The `--max-instances` parameter.
6. The `gcloud functions add-iam-policy` command.
7. The `gcloud iam service-accounts create` command.
8. A bastion host is an isolated host, which is useful to restrict access via the network to in/out.

Chapter 7: Introducing Cloud Run

1. Differences between a monolith and a microservice application is that microservices are loosely coupled architecture, isolated, standard interface, easier to debug. Monoliths typically are tightly coupled, difficult to debug.
2. The GFE performs the routing of traffic function to the project resources.
3. Two synchronous event processing patterns: Request/Response, Sidewinder.
4. The `ENTRYPOINT` keyword used for command run upon execution of the container.
5. The `docker build -t NAME .` command.
6. Container Registry is the product that Google Cloud uses for image management.
7. Automation.
8. Knative (middleware) sits between the application and K8s.

9. Open Container Initiative – a standardized container interface.
10. Debian, Ubuntu, and Windows are some operating systems that support containers.

Chapter 8: Developing with Cloud Run

1. A base URL is the access endpoint for a service.
2. API versioning is important because it enables multiple versions to be deployed.
3. The GET, PUT, POST, and DELETE verbs are expected to be available with a REST API.
4. It is appropriate to return an HTTP status code of 4xx when data sent from the client is incorrect.
5. The maximum duration for Cloud Build is 600s.
6. True.
7. Cloud Build errors are show in the Cloud Build Dashboard (an overview) and History (a detailed view).

Chapter 9: Developing with Cloud Run for Anthos

1. The type of machine customization is possible when using Cloud Run for Anthos are OS, GPU, CPU.
2. SSL certificates are manual when using Cloud Run for Anthos.
3. The `--platform gke` platform flag is required when deploying to Cloud Run for Anthos.
4. Port `8080` is used for service access when using Cloud Run for Anthos.
5. True.
6. Cloud Run on Anthos is required for Cloud Run.
7. The `kubectl` command.
8. Pods are a unit of replication within Kubernetes.
9. GKE supports external traffic through Ingress.

Chapter 10: Cloud Run Labs

1. A key advantage of using Container Registry over another registry is Container Registry is within the Google network.
2. It is useful to use an environment variable such as $GOOGLE_CLOUD_PROJECT at the time of scripting at the command line.
3. Branch and Tag types are supported by Cloud Build.
4. The @cloudbuild.gserviceaccount.com command.
5. Dockerfile and Cloudbuild.yaml are supported by Cloud Build.
6. Let's Encrypt provides the Certbot SSL certificates.

Chapter 11: Building a PDF Conversion Service

1. The gsutil command.
2. Stackdriver Logging would be the most useful at the time of issue relating to logs.
3. The purpose of a Docker manifest file is the specification for the image to be built.
4. Cloud Build stores the images in the Container Registry when it creates.
5. True.
6. Use the gsutil command with the -m parameter for multi-region request on Cloud Storage.
7. The type of permission required to call a service is invoker.

Chapter 12: Consuming Third-Party Data via a REST API

1. The products that can be used for asynchronous messaging on Google Cloud is Cloud Pub/Sub.
2. Notifications supported by Google Cloud Storage are finalize, delete, archive, and metadataUpdate.

3. For testing of new services/products, there are beta commands for the GCloud SDK.

4. Regex is regular expressions/shorthand for specifying text.

5. True.

6. True.

7. Stackdriver Trace.

Other Books You May Enjoy

If you enjoyed this book, you may be interested in these other books by Packt:

Google Cloud Platform for Architects
Vitthal Srinivasan, Janani Ravi, Judy Raj

ISBN: 978-1-78883-430-8

- Set up GCP account and utilize GCP services using the cloud shell, web console, and client APIs
- Harness the power of App Engine, Compute Engine, Containers on the Kubernetes Engine, and Cloud Functions
- Pick the right managed service for your data needs, choosing intelligently between Datastore, BigTable, and BigQuery
- Migrate existing Hadoop, Spark, and Pig workloads with minimal disruption to your existing data infrastructure, by using Dataproc intelligently
- Derive insights about the health, performance, and availability of cloud-powered applications with the help of monitoring, logging, and diagnostic tools in Stackdriver

Google Cloud Platform for Developers
Ted Hunter, Steven Porter

ISBN: 978-1-78883-767-5

- Understand the various service offerings on GCP
- Deploy and run services on managed platforms such as App Engine and Container Engine
- Securely maintain application states with Cloud Storage, Datastore, and Bigtable
- Leverage StackDriver monitoring and debugging to minimize downtime and mitigate issues without impacting users
- Design and implement complex software solutions utilizing Google Cloud Integrate with best-in-class big data solutions such as Bigquery, Dataflow, and Pub/Sub

Leave a review - let other readers know what you think

Please share your thoughts on this book with others by leaving a review on the site that you bought it from. If you purchased the book from Amazon, please leave us an honest review on this book's Amazon page. This is vital so that other potential readers can see and use your unbiased opinion to make purchasing decisions, we can understand what our customers think about our products, and our authors can see your feedback on the title that they have worked with Packt to create. It will only take a few minutes of your time, but is valuable to other potential customers, our authors, and Packt. Thank you!

Index

A

announce application 220
announce service
  testing 224
API consistency
  about 182
  implementing 182, 183
  requisites 182
API versioning
  about 185
  express versioning, with routing 186, 187
  requisites 185
App Engine components
  about 16
  data storage 18
  defining 21
  GAE Flex 23
  GAE Standard 22
  memcache 17, 18
  runtime languages 22
  task queues 16
App Engine deployments
  troubleshooting 46
App Engine features
  about 23
  application versioning 24, 25
  diagnostics 27, 28
  logging 27, 28
  monitoring 27, 28
  traffic splitting 25, 26
App Engine framework 14, 16
App Engine
  auto-scaling, handling 20
application programming interface (API) 147
application
  building, on GAE 32

  deploying, on GAE 37, 38, 39, 40
  language runtime and environment, selecting 34
  region, selecting for 33
asynchronous event processing pattern 148

B

base URL
  about 178
  implementing 180, 181
  requisites 178, 179
Business endpoint 178

C

Cloud Build
  about 188, 189
  triggering 280, 281, 282
  using 160, 161
Cloud Datastore 19, 20
Cloud Function, elements
  about 133
  private function 134
  public function 134
  variable definition 133
Cloud Functions-based application
  Cloud Functions, using 62, 63, 65, 66
  developing 61
  HTML output, decoupling 72, 73, 74, 75
  migration, to Cloud Shell 67, 68
  RSS reader, extending 75, 76
  view, adding 68, 69, 71, 72
Cloud Functions
  about 60, 62, 80
  APIs 61
  authentication 90
  backend service 111, 114, 115
  exploring 108
  frontend service 110, 111

general architecture 108
Internet-of-Things (IoT) 61
processing, with backend services 81
processing, with real-time data 82
properties 88, 89
runtime triggering event, testing 94
source control 91
use cases, defining 81
workflow, exploring 88
Cloud Load Balancer 11
Cloud Pub/Sub trigger 103, 104, 106
Cloud Run for Anthos
  cluster, deleting 216
  continuous deployment 208, 210
  custom networking, on GKE 204
  deploying 205, 207, 208
  domain, applying 211, 213
  GKE, provisioning 202
  Stackdriver, used for troubleshooting 214, 216
  troubleshooting, with Stackdriver 213
  using 201
  versus Cloud Run 166, 167
Cloud Run service
  deploying 254, 255
  developing 251, 252, 253, 254
Cloud Run
  about 161
  dashboard, exploring 172
  deploying, on GKE 224
  developing 172, 174, 175
  gVisor 162, 163
  Knative 164, 165
  versus Cloud Run for Anthos 166, 167, 201
Cloud Scheduler
  about 56
  creating 57
  defining 58, 59
  key elements 57
Cloud SDK (GCloud) 202
Cloud Source Repository 188
Cloud SQL 20
Cloud Storage
  triggering 106, 107, 108
Cloud Tasks, versus Pub/Sub documentation
  reference link 56

Cloud Tasks
  about 55
  characteristics 55
Compute Engine service account 288
Container Registry
  populating 157, 159
containers
  announce service, testing 224
  building 220
  Cloud Build, using 160, 161
  Container Registry, populating 157, 159
  Docker, leveraging 151, 152, 153, 155, 156, 157
  service, creating 220, 221, 223
  working with 149, 150, 151
continuous integration (CI)
  example 189, 190, 192, 193
  on GKE 235, 236, 238
continuous integration workflow
  about 276, 277
  Cloud Build, triggering 280, 281, 282
  email, triggering 283, 284, 285
  Lab Service CI, configuring 277, 279
  SMS, triggering 283, 284, 285
Cross-Origin Resource Sharing (CORS)
  working with 98
custom domain
  applying 230, 231
custom networking, GKE
  about 204
  external networking 205
  internal networking 204
Custom Resource Definitions (CRDs) 165

D

data sources, in Stackdriver
  app logs 28
  request logs 28
  third-party logs 28
Data Warehouse 178
Denial of Service (DoS) 10
deployment
  strategies 41
developer productivity
  about 187

Cloud Build 188, 189
Cloud Source Repository 188
Continuous Integration, example 189, 190, 192, 193
Docker
leveraging 151, 152, 153, 155, 156, 157
document service development
about 249
document information, storing 249, 250, 251
document service, designing
about 245
document conversations, processing 247, 248
document information, storing 245
processing requests, handling 246
service access, securing 246
document service
designing 245
testing 259, 260, 261
domain name system (DNS) test sites
reference link 211

E

email Cloud Pub/Sub subscription
setting up 288
email communication 272, 273
email service directory 273, 274
email
triggering 283, 284, 285
enhanced signed URL
backend service 120, 121, 122
building 118
frontend service 119
error handling
about 184
implementing 184
requisites 184
express versioning
with routing 186, 187
Express.js 91

F

Finance endpoint 178
Functions as a Service (FaaS) 83
Functions Framework
application, deploying locally 84, 85, 86

application, deploying to cloud 86, 87
using 82, 83

G

general availability (GA) 202
GKE cluster
provisioning 225, 227
GKE service
testing 227, 228, 229
Go 93
Google APIs
exploring 108
Google App Engine (GAE)
about 10
application, building on 32
application, deploying on 37, 38, 39, 40
target audience 14
Google Cloud Console 202
Google Cloud Platform (GCP) 10
Google Cloud SDK (GCloud SDK)
working with 35, 36
Google Cloud Storage (GCS) 54
Google Cloud Storage events
exploring 115
frontend service 117
general architecture 116
storage service 117
Google Compute Engine (GCE) 13
Google Container Registry (GCR) 158
Google Front End (GFE) 10, 167
Google Kubernetes Engine (GKE)
about 167, 197, 224
Cloud Run, deploying 224
Cloud Run, versus Cloud Run for Anthos 201
continuous integration (CI) 235, 236, 238
custom networking 204
overview 200
provisioning 202, 203, 204
gRPC
reference link 12
gVisor 162, 163

H

HTTP endpoint application
Cloud Pub/Sub trigger 103, 104, 106

Cloud Storage, triggering 106, 107, 108
  developing 102, 103
HTTP protocol
  about 96
  GET method 96
  POST method 97
HTTP response codes
  unmasking 97

I

Identity Access Management (IAM) 80, 136
identity and policy management
  about 198
  IAM objects 198
  members 199
  roles 199
intellectual property (IP) 141
Internet Assigned Numbers Authority (IANA) 98
Internet-of-Things (IoT) 60

J

JavaScript Object Notation (JSON) 128

K

Key Management Service (KMS) 137
key principles, Representation State Transfer
    (REST) API
  API consistency 182
  API versioning 185
  base URL 178
  error handling 184
Knative 164, 165
Kubernetes control 200

L

lab report solution
  designing 264
  email communication 265
  message, handling 265
  report collation 265
  SMS communication 266, 267
Lab Service CI
  configuring 277, 279
lab service

credentials, accessing 288
  email Cloud Pub/Sub subscription, setting up
    288
  SMS Cloud Pub/Sub subscription, setting up 289
  testing 286, 288, 290, 291
lab solution
  developing 267
  linking, to Google Docs 267, 268
  report collation 269, 270, 272
Line of Business Applications (LOB) 14

M

Managed Instance Groups (MIGs) 13
member accounts
  member roles 199
  service accounts 199
Memcache 27
memcache service, for service layer
  dedicated memcache 17
  shared memcache 17
microservices
  asynchronous event processing pattern 148
  synchronous event processing pattern 149
  working with 146, 147, 148

N

Node.js 91

O

Online Transactional Processing (OLTP) 20
Open Container Initiative (OCI) 162
operational management tools
  about 54
  Cloud Scheduler 56
  Cloud Tasks 55, 56

P

Pet Theory case study
  overview 244, 264
pod 204
Portable Document Format (PDF) 245
Python 92

Q

Quality Assurance (QA) 276
Qwiklabs
  about 32
  URL 32

R

region
  selecting, for application 33
Representation State Transfer (REST) API
  building 176, 178
Retail endpoint 178
role types
  custom 199
  predefined 199
  primitive 199
routing 186
runtime languages
  Go 93
  Node.js 91
  Python 92
  working with 91

S

security in depth 11
serverless
  with GAE 10, 12, 13
service access
  processing requests, handling 257, 258, 259
  securing 256
service account security
  about 136
  credential storage, insecure 137
  economic limits 137
  execution flow, manipulating 138, 139, 140
  FunctionShield 141
service account
  creating 256
service
  creating 220, 221, 223
SMS Cloud Pub/Sub subscription
  setting up 289

SMS communication 272, 273
SMS service directory 275, 276
SMS
  triggering 283, 284, 285
Stackdriver Debug 48
Stackdriver Logging
  about 48
  advanced filter 48
  basic mode 47, 48
  modes 47
Stackdriver Monitoring 48
Stackdriver Trace 48
Stackdriver
  about 95, 267
  used, for troubleshooting 213, 214, 215, 216
static website
  building 126
  Cloud Function, analyzing 133, 135
  data source, creating 128, 129, 130
  environment, provisioning 126, 127, 128
  frontend, designing 131, 132
synchronous event processing pattern 149

T

Task Queues 27
traffic splitting
  about 25, 26, 43, 44
  cookie splitting 25
  IP traffic 25
  randomization algorithm 25
traffic
  migrating 45, 46
Transport Layer Security (TLS) 10

V

version
  creating, of application 41, 42
virtual machines (VMs) 200

W

web application
  creating 231, 233, 234, 235

Printed in Great Britain
by Amazon